Short-Term Trading in the New Stock Market

Short-Term Trading in the New Stock Market

TONI TURNER

St. Martin's Press ♏ New York

SHORT-TERM TRADING IN THE NEW STOCK MARKET. Copyright © 2005 by Toni Turner. Foreword copyright © by Price Headley. All rights reserved. Printed in the United States of America. No part of this book may be used or reproduced in any manner whatsoever without written permission except in the case of brief quotations embodied in critical articles or reviews. For information, address St. Martin's Press, 175 Fifth Avenue, New York, N.Y. 10010.

www.stmartins.com

Library of Congress Cataloging-in-Publication Data

Turner, Toni.
    Short-term trading in the new stock market / by Toni Turner.
        p. cm.
    Includes bibliographical references (p. 329).
    ISBN 0-312-32569-X
    EAN 978-0-312-32569-5
        1. Speculation.   2. Stocks.   3. Investment analysis.
    I. Title.
    HG6041.T873 2005
    332.63'22—dc22

                                                        2004065654

First Edition: July 2005

10   9   8   7   6   5   4   3   2   1

I dedicate this book to my husband, Mike.
You are truly "the wind beneath my wings."

CONTENTS

Chapter Three. Point 'Em Downhill!   33

Chapter Four. Spend Quality Time with Your Money   49

Chapter Twelve. Day Trading Stocks— Setups and Strategies   269

Chapter Thirteen. Introduction to E-Mini Index Futures and Cash Forex Markets   294

Chapter Fourteen. Your Journey Through Inner Space   326

A NOTE TO READERS

ACKNOWLEDGMENTS

Writing a book is truly a labor of love. And those who traveled this writing journey with me deserve a large portion of credit for this book's completion.

First, a big "thank-you" goes to my husband, Mike, who provided a bottomless well of patience and support. He endured cold dinners, dead houseplants, and vague answers. I couldn't have written this book without him!

More thanks go to my daughter, Adrienne. She is an ever-present treasure of encouragement, joy, and wisdom. Best of all, she keeps me laughing at myself.

I am thankful to family members, Missy, Jenny, John, Chuck, and Tammy. They cheered me on with their hugs, consideration, and support.

Much appreciation goes to George Witte, editor in chief at St. Martin's Press, who exuded the patience of a saint, and then molded and shaped this book into its final form. Tons of credit also goes to Daniela Rapp, another patient soul who helped engineer the outcome of this book.

Thanks go to Deidre Knight, my mega-agent, the best business ally and friend an author could have . . . plus thanks to Jud, her terrific husband, who also gave support.

Appreciation goes to David Kohn, my "writing shrink," who alternately goaded and inspired me.

Finally, my heartfelt thanks to the terrific people at Townsend Analytics, Ltd., and Terra Nova Trading, including MarrGwen Townsend, Mike Felix, Sarah Neis, Cindy Cromwell, Dan Diversy, Janice Kaylor, Marco Hildalgo, Mike Kurze, Matt Pecak, John Connelly, and Tim Gentry.

Again, thank you all, and God bless!

FOREWORD

What is it about a good book that you just can't put it down? Toni Turner certainly knows the answer, as her newest book is simply a pleasure to read. Toni covers trading in a way that closely ties your experiences as a trader with you as a person. I've always said that trading is a journey, just as our lives are a journey. Toni's tips on how to build a prosperity mentality will greatly enhance not only your trading but also your life as a whole.

As its title suggests, *Short-Term Trading in the New Stock Market* reminds us that the market has been on a roller-coaster ride since the more gentle bull market of the prior two decades. If you believe, like I do, that the decade ahead is likely to be more volatile and less consistently biased to the upside, then this book will show you a wealth of strategies to capitalize on short-term swings to the upside and the downside.

Toni manages to blend so many elements together smoothly in this book. She educates you on traditional technical analysis techniques used in the Western world, and the candlestick charting formations that originated in the Far East. Toni also incorporates sentiment analysis, teaching you about measures of crowd opinion such as the put/call ratio and volatility indexes that I find so useful on a daily basis. Toni also draws on a wide range of outside influences that add to the depth of this book, pulling in quotes from many sources that really make you think. Just as this book is lively and entertaining in the presentation of the material, I was making notes as a trader of fifteen years on areas where I could use some additional work, too. So both novice traders and more experienced market veterans can find many useful insights here to take their trading to the next level.

One of the relatively untapped areas within trading is the internal, psychological dimension. If I gave the same system to ten different traders, the results would be widely different, based on the internal state that each trader cultivated. As Toni says in one of her many useful Center Points, the three barriers of resistance are thoughts, words, and actions, and the internal mindset will lead to the external results, whether positive or negative. The unique Trader Personality Quiz developed by Dr. Brett Steenbarger shows that Toni is willing to incorporate useful ideas from other sources to help you get to know your own internal strengths and weaknesses.

I always tell traders it's important to know where your blind spot is when you drive. If you are unaware of your blind spots as a trader, then you can be run over by a nasty eighteen-wheeler before you know what hit you. Awareness is the first step, and then the next step is developing a plan to maximize your trading edge while avoiding excessive risk. The ideas in this section of Toni's book are well worth the cost many times over, and can help point you to the road to trading success.

The challenge of any excellent book is that when you finish, you often feel inundated by so many great ideas that you don't know where to begin. Toni makes this easy for you: start at the beginning. With her Action Items in each chapter, you should make sure that you have addressed each Action Item as you develop your trading plan. I find that fewer than 10 percent of traders I see in seminars have a written trading plan. With Toni's Action Items, you have the tools needed to craft a plan that fits you. While creating a plan may seem like work to you, realize that those who treat trading as a business have much greater odds of success than those who are in it only for excitement or action alone.

After the success of Toni's first two books, *A Beginner's Guide to Day Trading Online* and *A Beginner's Guide to Short-Term Trading*, I had a hard time seeing how she could top herself. Here Toni has succeeded greatly. I hope you enjoy this book as much as I have.

Price Headley, CMT
Founder & Chief Analyst, BigTrends.com
Author, *Big Trends in Trading*

INTRODUCTION

A Rip-roaring Roller-coaster Ride

If you've caught a ride in the financial markets during recent years, your knuckles have surely turned white by now, and you're probably gasping for breath. We've ridden a bull market straight up, a bear market straight down, another move back up and lots of gasping for breath in-between.

Think back to when our roller-coaster stock market chugged out of the mid-nineties. Remember how she glided forward in a smooth, almost languorous ascent?

Suddenly—overnight, it seemed—the Internet exploded into a wealth of financial information, and online brokers offered cut-rate commissions to "self-directed" traders and investors. Our delighted market sped higher. She enticed more and more participants to climb aboard, promising lofty profits.

When day traders started piling into the cars, the stock market grew feverish with attention. She shoved the pedal to the metal, and by 1997, she hurtled rapidly into her skyward climb. Racing faster at every turn, she whipped through spins and twists at a breathless pace.

Savvy traders learned how to ride and stay balanced at the same time. They laughed and held their arms in the air at every turn, exhilarated by their profit-stuffed wallets.

Others, lazy and giddy with greed, leaned out of the fast-moving cars while ignoring their seat belts (read: knowledge and discipline). When the coaster whirled into loop-de-loops, these unfortunates got dropped on their heads. Later gaining consciousness, they skulked away, hands jammed into empty pockets.

Our market soared to her pinnacle in February 2000, with her occupants squealing for more. But then, as roller coasters have a way of doing, our lady paused . . . curled her lip in scorn . . . and plunged downhill in a near-vertical drop.

Traders and investors gulped for air, while choking back pride and fear. Only the cleverest riders saw the market grin and wink at the drooling bears who paced the ground below.

Since that time, our roller-coaster market has continued her hair-raising ride, shooting skyward, diving downward, then rocketing up once again. Scores of riders have jumped for their lives. Others have tightened their seat belts. Newcomers approach the market with excitement lighting their eyes, sure that as the ride spirals and soars, they can sway in perfect timing with her turns.

Though the riders and spectators change, the delicious volatility that feeds greed and exhilaration will continue to lure riders to leap on board to experience the world's most exciting ride . . . today, tomorrow, and long into the future.

The New Market of Opportunities

Since my previous two books, *A Beginner's Guide to Day Trading Online* and *A Beginner's Guide to Short-Term Trading*, were published in March of 2000 and January of 2002, respectively, the world of online trading has undergone an exciting metamorphosis.

Certainly trading technology has made a giant leap forward. New software offers tools that range from proprietary oscillators (overbought/oversold chart indicators) to sophisticated stock filters and scanners. Direct-access order entry platforms are faster than ever, offering split-second fills to nimble traders.

The market itself has transformed and grown. Recognizing that the self-directed trader is healthy and here to stay, exchanges have also developed nifty new products designed for everyone from high-adventure adrenaline addicts to feet-on-the-desk, slow-is-better devotees.

What's Your Pleasure?

For those of you who want to trade or invest in an entire index or industry group with one keystroke, Exchange Traded Funds, or ETFs, are the way to go. ETFs are single equities that represent a basket of securities. You can buy or sell an entire benchmark, such as the S&P 500 index or the NASDAQ 100 index, or an industry group like the biotechs, or the leading companies in a foreign country. ETFs that represent commodities stocks such as gold and oil are currently on the drawing board.

ETFs appeared in our marketplace in 1993, and have since become household trading and investing vehicles. For example, the behemoth QQQQ, the ETF that represents the tracking stock for the NASDAQ 100 index, now trades upwards of 100 million shares per day.

You can buy and sell (and sell short) ETFs, just as you do a stock, through your online or direct-access broker. Many trade on the American Stock Exchange, and to date, more than 120 reside there.

Another highly popular trading product has been brought to us courtesy of the Chicago Mercantile Exchange (CME). The CME offers E-mini futures, or electronically traded futures contracts that represent smaller versions of the Standard & Poor's 500 index futures. The exchange is also the single source of liquidity for the E-mini NASDAQ 100 index futures contracts, as well as other mini-versions of index futures. The Chicago Board of Trade (CBOT) offers the mini-sized Dow index futures, which represent a smaller, more nimble version of the standard Dow futures contract.

One Chicago began offering *single stock futures* trading in November of 2002. As of this writing, single stock futures are still in their infancy, but average daily contract volume is rising, as is their popularity.

Some hardy folks are venturing into the international currency markets by dabbling in the spot, or cash foreign exchange market, known as the forex or FX. With a current turnover of $1.5 to $2-trillion daily, the forex is highly liquid, and it trades virtually 24/7. Most forex brokers make their own markets, so they charge no commissions. In addition, margin leverage is sizeable.

Of course, where you find a spot or cash market, you can usually find a related futures market. *Currency futures* trade on exchanges around the world, including the Chicago Mercantile Exchange's Globex electronic trading platform. Currency futures do not presently have the massive liquidity (volume) of the currency spot markets, nor all the glitzy "no-commission" type perks, but they certainly offer volatility. And that's what we, as individual traders, feast on.

Why I Wrote This Book

In our dynamic and exciting world of global finance, each day presents a new market of opportunities. As traders, we strive to stay in lockstep with the future.

If trading technology, money-management perspectives, financial products, and the texture of the market itself have evolved and grown, so have I. As I progress on the path of trader, writer, and trading instructor, my continuing objective is to stretch and reach into new dimensions. I'm confident you are on the same path.

I wrote this book to update you on the current financial marketplace, the way it works, and ways you can profit from it. I trust that whether you are a novice in this game, or a more experienced trader, you will learn new information that will enhance your skills and bottom line.

As in my previous two books, I'll talk to you about trading as though we are good friends, chatting over a cup of coffee.

And guess what? We're going to have *fun*. While I realize that the discussion of trading skills and techniques can be intense and complicated, I firmly subscribe to the belief that enjoyment is an important part of any learning process.

One of my readers wrote to me, "I appreciate your humor. [It seems to me that] it is a necessity when working through tough short-term trading material." Thank you, kind reader. I agree that humor is a necessity—and should be an ingredient in *all* parts of our lives. Laughter keeps us sharp, yet relaxed and balanced.

Finally, during the extensive traveling I've done over the past few years, I've been gratified to meet many of you along the way. To every one of you who has grabbed my sleeve at a financial conference, or attended my classes or presentations, *thank you*. I've enjoyed meeting you. And I've learned from your shared perspectives. To those of you I haven't met as of yet, I look forward to doing so.

Trading in the New Stock Market . . . Is It for You?

If you've already started your trading career and mastered success, you have confirmed your commitment to this business. You know that it's a tough but rewarding road that demands excellence, perseverance, and tenaciousness.

If you are new to the markets, here's a reality check. Trading will surely represent one of the biggest, most difficult challenges of your life. It's not an easy game. Traders do *not* "make nice."

In fact, every trader worth his or her profits depends upon undisciplined traders and thoughtless investors to pad our pockets by buying and selling at exactly the wrong times. What do we call them? They're known as "dumb money."

Did the term "dumb money" ever apply to me? You bet! Early in my career, I had more guts than brains. As a successful investor, I thought I knew enough to trade. I didn't. Investing and trading are two different animals. While I was learning that lesson, the tuition I paid in hits to my trading account and my self-confidence were titanic.

Even so, I survived.

I studied hard, wrestled with the devils of my own emotionality, and waded through trade after trade. When my mistakes smacked me to the floor—and I made some big ones—I struggled back to my feet, wiped off the blood, and took another swing.

Then finally . . . *finally* . . . the profits outnumbered the losses.

In my subsequent years as a trader and instructor, and in observing literally hundreds of people on the trading journey, I can say with authority that to succeed in this business, you have to love it. You have to be committed, 100 percent. It's definitely not for everyone.

At MarketWise Trading School (marketwise.com), they tell the story about a man who attended their weeklong trading class. At its completion, this gentleman approached the head instructor and said, "Great course. The instructors were fantastic, the content was organized and comprehensive, and I learned a lot about trading. And now I know one thing for sure. Trading is not for me."

Smart man. *Very* smart man! He had the insight to realize that for his personality, his risk tolerance, and his lifestyle, trading in the financial markets was definitely not the road he wanted to travel.

Trading Is a Journey, Not a Destination

If you are new to trading, ask yourself: Am I *truly* ready to commit the time, money, and dedication needed to proceed on the trading journey?

If you decide your answer is "yes," know that a maze of trails lead, into the financial forest. Will you trade stocks? Index-tracking stocks and exchange-traded funds? E-mini futures contracts? Single-stock futures? Currencies or currency futures? Or a combination?

Will you fire off scalping trades that range in length from seconds to minutes? Or will you shoot for intraday trend trades, multiple-day swing trades, or short-term investments? Will you rely strictly on charts and technical analysis? Or will you factor in news and/or earnings? Will you trade using a top-down or bottom-up method?

Perhaps you've been trading stocks for a while, and you've decided to research the other products on the market, either to hedge your account or to speculate. You'll apply these questions to the new trading products that attract your interest.

Wherever you are on your journey, search for direct and honest answers to your questions. Please don't assume you are ever going to get *too* comfortable, for this road leads to constant achievement as your only destination.

Let's Head into the Future

Are you ready to jump aboard the new stock market?

The price of a successful rider's ticket includes long hours of study, patience, and planning, with a surtax of time and money.

The ride is a fast and volatile one, with no signs of slowing. Once you climb on board, you'll find that Mother Market takes more delight than ever in carrying us to new and breathtaking highs, then dropping us to heart-stopping lows.

So, fasten your seatbelt and hold on tightly. This ride will be the most exciting one of your life!

Short-Term Trading in the New Stock Market

CHAPTER ONE

The New Stock Market

In democracies, nothing is more great or brilliant than commerce; it attracts the attention of the public and fills the imagination of the multitude; all passions of energy are directed towards it.

—Alexis de Tocqueville,
statesman and author (1805–1859)

Welcome to the new stock market!

It formed from the Big Bang of 1990s market mania, when Wall Street shot up, ballooned, exploded, and then imploded on itself.

After a three-year cooling period—a black hole stretching from 2000 through 2002 that devoured corporate dynasties and those who chose to tout them—our stock market emerged transformed, renewed. Now, as it spins into the future, it remains a churning mass of energy that feeds from its own fiery core of human emotions and the nonstop whirlwind of global events.

While our sizzling orb may slow again and even cool, it will never grind to a halt. For as long as we, as market players, profit from guessing the future, we will continuously nurture this crackling power sphere . . . and keep it alive and expanding.

The Birth of Short-Term Traders: A Brief Time Line

Until the last decades of the twentieth century, trading equities in the U.S. stock market remained largely the province of institutions.

As early as the 1960s, only about one-fifth of the U.S. population owned stocks. Indeed, well into the 1970s, a wide chasm of unfamiliarity lay between most American households and the mysterious world known as the stock market.

Then several catalysts occurred, which encouraged investors to take their financial lives into their own hands.

In May of 1975, the Securities Exchange Commission (SEC) lifted the standardized broker commissions. By the 1980s, discount brokers were luring customers to open accounts by offering two-digit commissions, instead of the usual three-digit or higher, charged by full-service brokers. As more and more

Americans started to explore the equities market, the shift into stock ownership was born.

The 1980s produced three major events that, although largely unnoticed by the American public, shortened the technology timeline immeasurably for traders and investors. First, in 1983, discount broker Quick & Reilly's introduced DOS-based software for private traders. Next, 1984 brought the NASDAQ's electronic SOES (Small Order Execution System), which gave private traders the ability to electronically execute small orders against the best quotations from institutions. Finally, in 1985, Charles Schwab & Company unveiled the Equalizer, linking PCs directly to the discounter.

Enter 1993. The World Wide Web, an electronic maze known only to valiant techno-geeks, suddenly became more accessible to the public, via a new browser called Mosaic. Traffic on the Web increased that year by 289,000 percent.

In 1997, discount broker Ameritrade launched an online price war, and lowered its commission to $8 per trade. Other brokerage firms joined in, slashing their commissions.

Suddenly, we realized that we no longer had to depend upon our stockbrokers to provide us with financial reports or information. We could jump online and access our own portfolios, at our broker's Web site. We bought and sold stocks with a mouse click, paid cheap commissions, and then viewed the transaction seconds later. Life was good!

From "Yippee" to "Yikes" in a Heartbeat

As the Internet puffed, it birthed dot-coms by the dozen. The dot-coms "went public" (issued stock as publicly held corporations) at the speed of light. Excited Americans jumped onto their new online brokerage accounts, happily buying any NASDAQ stock that breathed. Many of the tech issues went ballistic, soaring to dizzying heights by skyrocketing twenty to thirty or more points a day.

The frenzy increased, as people quit their jobs to become day traders. Normally complacent investors stayed glued to their computer screens. The stock market and its daily gyrations soon dominated all walks of life. Indeed, "What's the market doing today?" was a typical opening comment heard on many television morning talk-shows.

Ambitious CEOs soon realized that "shareholder value" held higher importance than a well-run business. Lush pay packages—adorned with generous stock options—came quickly to those slick Armani suits who could spike their company's stock prices. Soaring share prices fueled mergers and a spending boom, and many company employees chose stock options over salaries.

Came the autumn of 1999, and we thought the merriment would never end.

The Amazon.coms and Yahoos! of the newest global culture boasted "Earnings: Nonexistent" as badges of honor. Indeed, Mary Meeker, noted analyst at Morgan Stanley, reputedly wrote in a report, "We have one general response to the word 'valuation' these days: 'Bull Market.'"

Stoic, bespectacled market technicians, knowing the parties would gleefully kill any messenger who muttered the words "Nothing goes straight up forever," stared glumly at their charts and, for the most part, kept their suspicions to themselves.

If the concerned clucking of a few old-timers managed to interrupt our reverie, we pooh-poohed them with New Economy super-speak. We were profit druggies and the market was our supplier.

As we dashed around town in our new Porsches sporting license plates emblazoned with "QCOM," it plumb slipped our minds that industrialized economies expand and contract. We ignored the fact that this universe of ours progresses in natural cycles of action and reaction. Or what goes up . . . eventually comes down.

When the year 2000 streaked out of the gate, the U.S. stock market rocketed to new highs. Euphoria reigned.

Then, out of nowhere, the piper appeared. He sneered and demanded payment.

Beginning in February of 2000 and continuing through the year, the bull market that created our dazzling "wealth effect" unceremoniously yanked that wealth away, leaving stockholders stunned. Tech stocks toppled from their majestic heights, seemingly in free-fall. Dot-coms exploded into dot-bombs, their ashes tossed to the winds and disintegrating without a trace.

Technology stocks weren't the only casualty. We watched, bewildered, as our traditional value stocks—paraded as "Strong Buys" by major brokerages—shriveled to a fraction of their former worth.

When 2001 stumbled in, we prayed the hand-wringing was over. It wasn't. Like Humpty-Dumpty, the market continued its "great fall," and neither the king's horses (politicians), nor the king's men (Greenspan & Co.) could glue the economic numbers back together again.

By March 2001, the economy began to slide into a recession. An excess of inventories lined manufacturers' shelves. Companies found it nearly impossible to increase their sales or force up their stock prices.

The tragic events of September 11, 2001, shook our nation to its core. Surprisingly, though, after an orderly sell-off that pushed major indexes into bear territory, the stock market rallied in October and continued to soar into January of 2002.

In fact, our courageous, resilient country had just struggled back to its feet when the Houston-based energy trading company named Enron, a market and media star, collapsed in a mudslide of crooked accounting and phony transactions. Its auditing firm, Arthur Andersen, soon followed. Then Citigroup and J.P. Morgan Chase, two of our nation's largest banks, fell under regulatory investigation for allegedly aiding in arranging some of Enron's shady deals.

Next, K-mart, huge retailer and home of the all-American "Blue Light Special," declared Chapter Eleven (reorganization bankruptcy). Hot on the heels of K-mart's misery, WorldCom, one of the country's most successful long-distance phone companies, admitted to billions in major accounting fraud.

The fast and furious domino effect shot forward relentlessly. One after the next, tycoons toppled from their pedestals, pausing only to be filmed by hungry, ever-present media crews. Tyco International chairman Dennis Kozlowski resigned after being accused of tax evasion. Merrill Lynch absorbed nasty allegations of misconduct by its analysts. And founders of cable-television Adelphia Communications starred on network news, shackled in handcuffs.

Spring melted into June's summer heat, and the former CEO of biotech company ImClone, Sam Wacksal, was arrested for insider trading. But the nation went slack-jawed when Wacksal's friend, Martha Stewart, fell under SEC scrutiny related to the sale of her holdings in ImClone stock.

How could our diva of American homes and hearths, the goddess of "weave your own slipcovers," pull the wool over our eyes about dubious stock transactions? Heaven have mercy. Were skeletons shivering in *everyone*'s closet?

Lawmakers and the SEC moved quickly to establish fiscal reform. In the midst of a sweltering July, the Sarbanes-Oxley Act became law. It introduced legislative changes to the regulation of corporate governance and financial practice and established new rules to "protect investors by improving the accuracy and reliability of corporate disclosures made pursuant to the securities laws." Chief executive officers were required to sign financial reports published by their companies, attesting to their accuracy.

As 2002 waned into fall, the SEC continued their roundup of corporate scallywags and other folks who misused fiscal responsibility.

October pulled the Dow and NASDAQ to deep lows. But before it drew to a close, the sound of hooves was heard. The bulls were back! They charged into the market, and soon shooed most of the grumbling bears back to their caves.

Very slowly . . . very cautiously . . . we began to exhale.

If It Doesn't Kill You, It Makes You Stronger

Now, as we blaze into the future, those of us who played in the ill-tempered bear market—and lived to talk about it—feel stronger for the experience.

Investors steeped in the buy-and-hold-no-matter-what tradition learned that bull markets don't climb endlessly. They discovered that good fundamentals don't always support a company's stock price during a falling market, even if that company is a bona fide blue-chip.

They also realized that while handling the reins of portfolio control to a professional financial adviser can be wise, it's important to stay aware of market action and take responsibility for risk management by selling or standing on the sidelines in cash.

As short-term traders, we learned how successful trading tactics change in bull and bear markets, due to the obvious differences in demand and supply.

For example: In bull markets, a stock trading in an uptrend (daily chart) that closes at, or near, the price high of the day on strong volume will many times gap up (trade higher than the previous day's close) when the market opens the following day. Buying such a stock right before the closing bell and selling it at the following day's open can yield quick profits. In bear markets, however, this setup is unreliable. Stocks that close on highs with strong volume can just as easily gap *down* the next morning.

Another example: In bear markets, breakouts to the upside have little momentum and so they usually fail, or fall back to their prior support area. Why? Because when a stock shows *any* signs of positive life or strength, in most cases, terrified investors immediately dump their supply on the market (sell) in an effort to save a portion of their portfolio value.

Also, in bull markets, stocks that climb to fifty-two-week highs will often push higher. In a bear market, stocks that struggle to the same pinnacle can attract profit-taking bullets soon after.

The New Breed of Traders

There's a brand-new breed of trader, and you may be one of them. Whether you traded through the bull market/bear market cycle, or are an investor-turned-trader, or whether you are a novice trader, a new attitude about trading has emerged.

Individual traders participating in today's market project a different profile from those who dove in during the mid-90s mania. Most are eager to learn before they leap. Instead of the "buy-it-and-it'll-go-up" mentality displayed by novice traders during the go-go years of the late 90s, newcomers feel content to paper-trade for a month or two before they ante up real dollars. They are willing to study market psychology and apply personal discipline. In other words, they want to learn instead of burn!

The wild daily price swings—and possible profits—of the late 90s are now relegated to the memory attic. In today's market, daily price moves in a tighter, more realistic range.

Since we currently operate in smaller-price playgrounds, we know that the carelessness we got away with in earlier days can now trigger sizeable account drawdowns, or losses. In today's market, *precision* must form the heart of each trade. We must locate setups that adhere to well-thought-out criteria, then execute *precise* entries and exits.

Does precision trading take more time and effort to learn? Absolutely. It also produces more profits, more often, and is the hallmark of the new breed of trader.

What Traders Know . . .

More and more market participants have come to realize that whatever the time frame and channel targeted to make money, the powerful techniques utilized by traders are extremely effective and valuable.

First, as traders, we use charts as our primary tool. A basic chart gives us a complete picture of a stock or other derivative. With a quick glance at a price pattern and volume participation, we can instantly evaluate the current health of the stock, and its value as a worthwhile target.

It's no wonder that when the conversation rolls around to the stock market and someone offers a "hot tip," a trader's immediate retort is, "I'd have to see the chart." Indeed, for us traders to throw money into the market without seeing a picture of what's going on would be like driving a race car blindfolded.

We Be Trend-watchin'

Ask any trader worth her mouse where the market is today, and she will usually begin her comments with, "The S and P (Standard & Poor's 500 Index) is still climbing in an uptrend," or "The NASDAQ's rolled over into a downtrend."

The prevailing market trend represents one of the most important factors *anyone* involved in the financial arenas should know. It follows that those holding stocks for any length of time would also monitor price movement of that trend for signs of a reversal or deterioration.

I often think of all those disheartened souls who plunked down their hard-earned dollars for high-priced stocks in the bull market—stocks that soon plummeted in the bear market. *If only* those people had known about price uptrends, downtrends, and how trends "break." If only they had known what we traders can so clearly see on a chart . . . when a stock tops out, "rolls over," and then makes a lower low, it's time to sell.

I recently attended a dinner party, where a guest, a big, burly man, purchased a biotech stock that had slid to a fraction of his purchase price.

The guest pounded on the dinner table and boomed, "I'll stay in that stock until the end!"

I bit my lip to stop myself from blurting, "Why?"

Why would anyone ride a stock to zero, or even close to it?

If only our disgruntled dinner guest could have seen a simply daily chart of his stock, with the price diving into a downtrend, making lower highs and lower lows. Perhaps he would have "gotten the picture" and sold the stock while he still had some cash to rescue.

As traders, we eat and breathe trends. One glance at a chart, and we immediately know whether the market, indexes, stocks, or futures we are trading are trending up or down, consolidating or range-bound (vacillating between two approximate prices).

We also watch trends on volatility indicators, such as the VIX—the Chicago Board Options Exchange (CBOE) market-volatility index—and the VXN—the CBOE NASDAQ volatility index. The trend of these indexes can be revealing, as they move in the opposite direction of the broader markets. (We'll talk more about these indicators in later chapters.)

As well as monitoring current trends, we also look for signs of trend reversals. For anticipating a trend change correctly—whether on a weekly, daily, or five-minute chart—is one of the most important skills a trader can develop. Why? Because when the trend reverses as supply overcomes demand, or demand overwhelms supply, that's when we jump into a position and ride the initial momentum that the trend change provides. Many times, from those entries, the juiciest trades are made.

We Know When to Ante Up

For years, folks gobbled up equity shares with little or no forethought as to whether it was really an appropriate time to buy or not. And, mostly, they got away with it.

Today's market calls for different methods. As traders, we are in command of these stock-selection methods. If we're going to hold a position for a few days or even weeks, we like to buy stocks trading in the early stages of an uptrend, or sell short in the early stages of a downtrend. That gives us the most room for acceleration to the upside or downside, and thus the highest odds for profits.

Once we identify a stock with favorable trend movement, we zero in on current price action to see if a setup (auspicious set of conditions that warrants taking a position) is forming. If the setup plays out in our favor, we enter a position. If it doesn't, we don't.

Similar situation: You plan a picnic at the beach, and pack up the van with towels and food. But just as you start to back out of the driveway, a torrential rainstorm arrives. Do you still head for the beach? No, you make alternate plans. And if a stock or other trading instrument is moving in a nice trend—but it's too early or too late to enter, according to your risk analysis—as a savvy trader, you switch to a better opportunity.

We traders spend a great deal of our time scanning for high-probability setups (or shorten that time with scanning software) that will give us the most bang for our bucks in the fastest period of time.

We Know When to Hold 'Em, Know When to Fold 'Em

As just mentioned, traders define their risk *before* they enter a trade. (If you're a trader, I'm sure you're nodding your head in agreement!)

This strategy sounds like a no-brainer, yet how many market participants dive headlong into a stock position—on someone else's advice or their own fundamental research—and have no idea when to dump that position if it doesn't pan out? The answer: a boatload.

As successful traders, we plan for possible price movements, again, *before* we enter a trade. Our reasoning goes something like this: *If the setup unfolds as I expect, then I buy shares of my targeted stock in the price window I have designated. If the trade goes against me, I'll sell it at this price as a protective stop. If the price moves up, the next price resistance is at this point. That price represents my first profit target. If the stock hesitates at that price, I may sell half or all of my position. If it flies through that resistance, I will keep it and raise my stop to guarantee that profits stay intact.*

Reasoning along those lines is a process well known to traders, and one that can minimize losses and help keep profits safe. And while investors may not want to wade through that entire procedure, they would surely find their portfolios fatter if they placed initial protective stops on all of their equity positions, then turned them into trailing stops after the stock starts moving up.

Bottom line: Anyone with funds in a brokerage account can buy and sell stocks, options, and futures. Success boils down to pre-trade planning and knowing when to hold 'em and when to fold 'em.

This Is a Trader's Market

Volatility (rapid price swings) is becoming the norm. With global events inciting heightened emotions in all corners of the earth, and the media's ability to report those events—sometimes *as* they occur—our markets seemed destined to shoot up rapidly, then crumble just as fast.

As traders, we are nimble. We know that in volatile markets, time equals risk. So, we acquire the knowledge and tools that give us the ability to jump into positions, seize profits in a timely fashion, and leap out just as quickly.

We recognize the signs of changing markets and trends. If a market looks "toppy" or "frothy," and indicators signal that it's overbought, we take profits. Then we stand aside in safety to avoid the stampede of the panicked masses when prices start their slide.

We can profit in bear markets. We have the skills to sell short and profit from a stock's plunge off a price cliff.

We know how to "hedge," or leverage risk and offset losses by selling short and by trading alternative "weapons" of choice that include options, ETFs, or stock index futures.

As discussed earlier, our skills at identifying trending—or trendless—markets give us the ability to define the most profitable environments. Naturally, clearly trending markets are pleasurable for all traders, short-term and long-term.

Range-bound markets that churn in a sideways pattern (daily chart) are generally unprofitable for intermediate-term (days to weeks) and swing (two-to-five-day hold) traders. Choppy price movement delivers uncertain profit opportunities, so holding overnight may be risky.

During these periods, active traders have the edge. Why? Within the space of a single trading day, a tradable, intraday trend may emerge.

What if the intraday price movement is choppy and volatile? That can "whipsaw" active traders and result in losses with positions on both long and short sides. In this environment (example: options expiration day), scalpers who hop into positions from seconds to minutes, snatching profits from a fraction of a point, can benefit.

With those examples, you can see why your ability to identify overall market trend coupled with daily trading environment remains an important part of your skill set. Develop your trading style according to your personality and strengths. If the environment does not support your style, keep your profits intact by waiting until it does.

If you are an investor and have never executed a short-term trade, please understand that traders don't hold the only set of keys to making money in today's financial markets. Still, the principles that result in consistently winning trades are founded on sensible and intelligent guidelines that help you keep your principle protected and your gains intact, regardless of your preferred time frame.

The key-points review that follows will help you revisit content in this chapter.

Then, in chapter 2, we're going to begin the text version of my popular seminar, Seven Steps to Successful Trading. See you there!

Key Point Review

1. In May of 1975, the Securities Exchange Commission (SEC) lifted standardized broker commissions.

2. In 1993, the World Wide Web became more accessible to the public via a new browser called Mosaic; traffic on the Web increased that year by 289,000 percent.

3. In 1997, discount broker Ameritrade launched an online price war, dropping commissions to $8 per trade. Other online brokers quickly slashed commissions.

4. In February 2000, the three-year bear market was born.

5. In January 2002, Enron began its collapse due to crooked accounting and phony transactions. Numerous corporate scandals and securities-fraud accusations followed.

6. In October 2002, the bulls finally flexed their dormant muscles and sent the bears back to their cave.

7. The bear market taught investors that while obtaining professional financial advice is wise, it's important to stay aware of market action and take personal responsibility for risk management.

8. Trading tactics that deliver profits in bull markets don't necessarily work in bear markets, and vice versa.

9. For trading success, current markets demand that *precision* entries and exits must form the heart of each trade.

10. Traders utilize a skill set that can profitably serve all market participants. These skills include chart analysis, trend identification, scanning for high-probability setups and entries and the application of strict money-management criteria.

An Introduction to "Center Point"

In keeping with a custom established in my last two books, and one that received favorable feedback from readers, I will conclude each chapter with a "Center Point."

Please let me explain . . .

When I was a novice trader, I experienced days when I felt the market had used me for a punching bag. Stinging and sore, both my account and self-esteem suffered from multiple bruises on multiple occasions!

Still, I refused to "stay down for the count." Each time I stumbled, I struggled back to my feet and managed to throw another punch.

Now, more than ever, the financial markets present a rough-and-tumble environment where the pace is fast and furious. Only the toughest survive.

The "Center Points" you will find at the conclusion of each chapter represent concepts that encouraged me to stay the course early on. These core beliefs continue to remind me of the balance necessary to stay focused on my goals, both in the markets and in other areas of my life. It is my sincere hope that you find the ideas within each to be enriching and empowering, and that they help speed you on your journey to success!

CENTER POINT

Begin with the End in Mind

The secret of making something work in your lives, is, first of all, the deep desire to make it work: then the faith and belief that it can work: then to hold clear definite vision in your consciousness and see it working out step by step, without one thought of doubt or disbelief.

—Eileen Caddy, author

One of the most powerful principles you can use to promote personal and business achievement is to visualize each goal clearly and concisely *before* you start toward its completion.

In *The 7 Habits of Highly Effective People*, Stephen R. Covey says, "Begin with the end in mind." He states, ". . . *all things are created twice*. There's a mental or first creation, and a physical or second creation to all things."

To use this effective principle, start with a *clear* image, or picture, of your objective.

You may be thinking, "That's a no-brainer. Of course I know what I want" But stop and think for a moment. How clear and succinct is your vision?

Perhaps you have a vision of "being a successful trader." While that's a noble goal, the description may be too general to motivate you strongly.

To transform it into a compelling "first creation" that will lead to the second—and real—creation, try this: Go to a quiet place and clear your thoughts. Now, using your imagination, picture yourself as a "successful trader." Would you look any different? What would you be wearing? Would you carry yourself differently? Would you be more fit? More self-assured? Appear more affluent? What does your office or workspace look like? Have your surroundings changed? (Stay conservative, so that your goal remains attainable. There are no "wrong" thoughts. Different answers lead to different outcomes.) Perhaps you imagine yourself sitting at your desk, studying your trade sheet . . . your profits show you are disciplined and in command of your skills.

When your mental creation is complete, describe it on paper, in detail.

Next, determine the first step you can take to start your journey. Write it down, and others that come to mind. Review your "first creation" regularly, and progress with action steps.

For the fastest and best way to achieve your goals, *begin with the end in mind*. Then work consistently to make that image a reality!

Seven Steps to Trading Success

If I had my life to live over again, I would elect to be a trader of goods rather than a student of science. I think barter is a noble thing.
—Albert Einstein

Not too long ago, I found myself with a rare and wonderful luxury—a tiny pocket of daydreaming time.

With my feet propped up and a mug of steaming coffee in my hand, I soon let my mind wander back to my early, trial-by-fire trading days . . .

It was the mid-90s . . . and I remember friends and stockbrokers who pleaded with me *not* to jump into the world of trading. I ignored them.

I recalled the mistakes I made . . . my cockiness when I made a good trade, my pain when I rang up nasty losses.

I vividly remember taking one halting step after another, never quite knowing whether I would step on an exploding "land mine," or actually alight on fertile ground. In those days, day traders were scarce, and when I finally located a group of other novice traders like myself, they suffered from the same "what should I do now?" malady.

If only we'd had a set of guidelines and objectives that instructed: "To take the first steps on the path to a trading career, first research *this*, then study *this*, then do *that*." We would have saved a tremendous amount of time and money, not to mention interim losses of self-esteem!

From the feedback I've received in e-mails and at trading conferences, that need still remains. Many of you have written or spoken to me at trade shows, asking for a structured trading program that tells you how to create and develop a thriving trading career, step-by-step. You wanted to know *what* to learn, *when* you should learn it, *how* to learn it, and *where* to find it!

The next three chapters are my reply to that request. The Seven Steps to Successful Trading focuses on seven broad-spectrum steps, each with its own set of action items. Each action item lists topics that you can work through at your own pace to build a foundation of trading knowledge.

Think of the steps and action items listed in each as an architectural blueprint—and you are the head contractor. You'll study the plan, then bring in your own crew (broker) and suppliers (research materials). You'll begin with the concrete foundation (funded trading account), then build the framework (discipline), install the plumbing (technical analysis), and wire the electrical through-out (market machinations).

In other words, the seven steps list mostly *what* you can do to advance your trading career. *How* you go about it is stated in the action items in one of three ways: 1) in current text, 2) in a later chapter, or 3) in resources referred to in the text.

Have I listed every single, solitary aspect of trading known on planet Earth? Nope. Couldn't. Don't have that much paper. Still, if you are a novice trader, these steps can help jump-start your trading career. If you are a more seasoned trader, you may spot new aspects of trading you haven't explored, or would like to revisit.

Suggestion: Read through the Seven Steps in their entirety in this chapter, chapter 3, and chapter 4. Then return to Step One and progress through the steps at your own pace.

As you do, please rearrange the steps and add your own to suit your current ability and personal goals. You may breeze through some areas, or even skip them. Others may capture your attention for an extended period of time.

Note: Topics in a few of the action items were discussed in my prior books. Although it's necessary to touch on them briefly for the sake of new readers, fresh information has been added.

Now, let's get started!

Step One—Find Your Place

Action Item One: Explore, Discover, Analyze, Decide

Newspapers, magazines, books, Web sites and financial television networks showcase our exciting markets and pour out an endless and powerful stream of information.

Investor's Business Daily (IBD) and *The Wall Street Journal* are two of the daily newspapers most widely read by traders and investors. Go to *investors.com* and/or *wsj.com* and sign up for the free trials of print or online editions of *Investor's Business Daily* and/or *The Wall Street Journal*, respectively. *IBD* is great for traders, because it is geared toward technical analysis. Of course, the *Wall Street Journal* presents comprehensive coverage of global news with the focus on finance.

Two additional periodicals I enjoy are *Barron's* and *The Economist*, both pub-lished weekly. Go to: *barrons.com* and/or *economist.com* to find subscription infor-mation.

Magazine-wise, four choices that target traders are: *Active Trader* (active trader.com), *Stocks, Futures and Options (SFO)* (sfomag.com), *Futures* magazine, futuresmag.com, and *Stocks & Commodities* (traders.com). The contents of these magazines are well worth the price of the subscriptions.

You'll want to build a library of trading books to use as learning references. There is a recommended-reading list at the end of this book.

For a large selection of trading books and videos, go to the Web and check out *traderslibrary.com*. (You can also access Traders Library by going to my Web site, *toniturner.com*, and clicking on one of my book covers.) Or hop onto *amazon.com* and search for "day trading" or "stock trading" books and videos.

Like books, a gazillion financial Web sites populate the Web. You'll find pertinent Web addresses listed in some of the steps that follow. And, because Web sites and their names can change over time, check out my Web site, *toniturner.com*, and click on "Financial Links" for a list of current recommended sites.

Finally, you'll want to tune into the financial networks—CNBC, Bloomberg, CNN, or CNNfn—for news coverage and updates.

Action Item Two: Check Out Trading Schools

Will Rogers once said, "There are three kinds of men: The ones that learn by reading. The few who learn by observation. The rest of them have to pee on the electric fence."

The political sage might have also agreed that there are two ways to learn how to trade: you can either learn from competent trading professionals, or you can let the stock market teach you. And, trust me, the market is a tough coach (think "electric fence").

First, you'll need to locate a well-established trading school with a good reputation and skilled instructors. Know that most reputable trading schools offer discounted commissions with an affiliated broker or some form of rebate, if you attend their school. That's not necessarily a bad thing, and some excellent trading schools work this way.

Your job is to make sure the school focuses on teaching the fundamentals of trading—instead of dwelling on "how to get rich by Friday" tactics. If you call a school and someone assures you in a slick voice that even with a small account "you can rake in six to seven figures a year"—excuse yourself and hang up *fast*.

I maintain that the most reliable recommendations for trading schools come from word-of-mouth, by way of a trusted friend or mentor.

Before you go:

- Ask the school representative to define the level of experience targeted by the course to make sure it's a proper fit for you. Inquire if they publish an online syllabus.

- If you sign up for a course, ask for suggestions that pertain to reading or research materials that you can study ahead of time.

- If Course + Hotels + Food + Airfare = More Than You Can Spend Right Now, ask if the school has a selection of online courses. Most do.

Speaking of online courses and tutorials, you'll find a dizzying array of them on the Internet. Many will be offered free of charge. And, yes, the sponsors of these complimentary courses usually spend anywhere from a few minutes to a sizeable amount of time promoting their software or services. If the quality of the course is high, though, that should be acceptable. I've presented numerous online tutorials for companies that do a great job of keeping the educational content high and the advertising low-key, informative, and professional.

Action Item Three: Mind Your Own Business

Trading is a business. So, before you dive into actual trades, please define what your goals are and exactly what you are trying to achieve. Bonus: you'll attain success faster if you trade with the mindset that having the responsibility of your own business produces.

As a shrewd trader, you'll put a business plan on paper, even if it's loosely formulated. This will give you a "road map" and keep you on track. You'll modify it as your trading career evolves.

Considerations:

- If you plan to trade full-time, you may want to explore the benefits of establishing your business as a corporation.

- If you want your trading account to generate "capital gains," you will target longer-term trades and hold them from weeks to months. To create "income," you will trade in the short-term with intraday and swing trading time-frames.

- Budget for expenses, including office supplies, trading courses, and the services of an accountant or CPA.

- The money that you use to fund your trading account will need to be "disposable." Label it "high risk," and make darn sure that if you lose every penny of it, the loss will not affect your style of living or that of your family and loved ones.

- Start with, and maintain, enough money in your account to act as cushion for early losses. If you intend to day-trade stocks (open and close stock trades during the same trading day more than three times in a five-business-day period), SEC defines you as a "pattern day-trader," and its rules dictate that you must have at least $25,000 minimum account equity. If your account falls below $25,000, some brokerages freeze it. Therefore, consider opening your account with $30,000 or more, to provide a minimal cushion against losses. If you are opening a futures account to trade E-minis, or an account with a forex broker to trade currencies, minimum account equity is lower.

- Initial learning stage: Expect to take from six to eighteen months to wade through typical stages from 1) mostly losses, to 2) break even, to 3) consistent gains. (*Question: How long will it take me to learn how to trade? Answer: Five years if you're smart, ten years if you're **really** smart.*" Strangely enough, traders who have been mega-successes in their "other" lives sometimes have a difficult time in initial learning stages. They are used to being obeyed and accustomed to deals going their way. Mother Market, on the other hand, *never* obeys and rarely goes anyone's "way." So, strange as it seems, these big-brained folks can endure a thorny trip through trading's early learning curve.)

- You may want to list simple hedging strategies you intend to explore, which can protect—and add to—your gains. Examples include selling short, basic option plays such as writing covered calls on core trades, selling puts, shorting ETFs (exchange traded funds) like the Dow Diamonds (DIA), S&P 500 SPDRS (SPY), or NASDAQ 100 Trust (QQQQ). Some traders hedge with stock index futures, the E-minis.

- You can state your primary approach to the market, for example: "I will trade midpriced stocks with a share price exceeding $10, and specialize with these setups: 1) stocks breaking out of bases, and/or 2) breaking out of the first pullback in an uptrend. My risk:reward ratio (explained in upcoming text) will be at least 1:2 on intraday trades and 1:3, or better, on swing trades." Note: If you are a novice trader, stick to one style of trading. Mixing swing trades with day trades in the same account can be confusing.

- Define your overall loss strategy: "I will risk no more than 2 percent of my account equity on a single trade." (Example: If your account equity is

$20,000, then structure your trading plans so you never lose more than $400 on any trade.)

- Many traders like to specify a dollar amount that they intend to earn in daily or weekly profits. In the entry stages of trading, however, this applies too much pressure and promotes losses in forced trades. Try this on: You will strive toward the goal of making 40 percent . . . then 45 percent . . . then 50 percent . . . of your weekly trades as winners. (Sounds easy? It isn't!)

- If you plan to trade full-time, consider hiring the services of a competent CPA (certified public accountant) familiar with trading tax laws.

- In the book *The Richest Man in Babylon,* Arkad, the richest man in that ancient and prosperous kingdom, counseled his followers: "If one-tenth of all you earn is as much as you can comfortably keep, be content to keep this portion." In other words, when you become a consistently winning trader, take a portion of your profits each quarter and place them in an alternative investment.

The following represents a jump start on a basic, fill-in-the-blanks business plan for trading stocks. You can alter it and use it to suit your needs.

Please "build out" this plan to suit your personal goals. Once your plan is complete, schedule a weekly appointment with yourself to review it. What's working well? What needs tweaking? What can you add? In itself, the process of reviewing your tactics and improving your plan will motivate you to become a better trader.

Action Item Four: When and What Will You Trade?

The following trading time frames briefly define the types of trades we will talk about in this book. They are significant, as the length of time you hold a stock or other trading entity has a great deal to do with your lifestyle, your tolerance for risk, and how much attention you can devote to the market on a daily basis.

We can divide trading into four styles, which fall into four holding time frames. Ranging from micro to macro, they are: scalping, momentum, swing, and position trading.

Each method fits into your lifestyle in a different way. Besides the varying time frames, each style demands a different mindset, different lot sizes, and different risk-reward applications. The account size can also vary, depending on your objective.

JUMP-START BUSINESS PLAN

The primary goal of this _____ (sole proprietorship or corporation) will be to generate income and capital gains (including dividends, when applicable).

Initial budget of $_____ allows for a home office that includes a new _____ (brand) computer and _____ (number of) monitors. (Author's note: full-time traders should consider using at least two monitors.) The primary Internet service will consist of _____ (DSL or cable modem) The back-up Internet service will be provided by _____.

My account will be opened with _____ (brokerage name) and initially funded with $_____.

Time strategy: I will paper-trade for the first two months and gather expertise in becoming familiar with my trading software and execution system. For six months thereafter, I will trade with 200-share lot sizes. Assuming losses and gains are reasonable by the end of that period, I will enlarge share size as appropriate.

No monthly income from trading is *expected* for the first year. Percentage of profitable trades should begin to increase after six months of trading to 40 percent or higher. I will reassess the scale of winning/losing trades at that time and advance the share size accordingly.

Future hedging tactics may include _____.

After twelve to eighteen months of trading, 10 percent of the profits (if this is a capital gains–focused account) will be pared from the trading account on a quarterly basis and transferred into _____ (alternative assets or investments of your choice).

Scalping is for those who are fleet-fingered and have rapid reactions. True to its moniker, it describes a trader who runs up to a "victim," slices off a small reward, and then darts away. Scalpers buy or short a stock with the goal of taking a fraction of a point profit. They work on the tightest time frame of all, holding a position from seconds to minutes.

In the bull market of the late 1990s, when the daily price ranges yawned wider and wider and decimalization was still only a gleam in the regulators' eyes, many scalpers executed from hundreds to thousands of trades per day. The good ones slunk around town in shiny, new convertibles and bragged about spending a million bucks per year in commission fees. Now, though, with penny spreads between the bid and ask (or offer), and tighter daily trading ranges (average intraday price movement), scalpers have dwindled in numbers.

Momentum traders, day traders, active traders . . . all refer to those of us who open and close trades within the span of the trading day, while capitalizing on intraday trends in equities, stock index futures, or ETFs. Firmly planted in our chairs, we hold our positions for minutes to hours, unless we get stopped out. Focus is our game. We know how to ignore ringing phones, gnawing hunger pangs and other nagging bodily demands.

Most momentum traders trade for a living, because—besides scalping—this style represents the most time-intensive approach to the market.

Swing trading, in which the position is held on an average of two to five days, has emerged as one of the most popular trading styles. Swing traders strive to ride up or down price "swings" made by a stock or other trading instrument in the development of a strong uptrend, or downtrend.

Swing traders represent all lifestyles and ages. Many hold full-time jobs and complete their research before or after work, or on the weekends. Since intraday charts and market internals are not 100 percent imperative to swing trading success, some swing traders mosey along with the charts and research info provided to them by their online broker or end-of-day charting software (as compared to direct-access trading platforms and software).

The time-intensity involved in swing trading comes in the form of research. Trends are the name of this game, so most swing traders stay aware of overall market trends, along with sector, industry group, and, of course, stock trends.

Position trading, core trading, or trend trading could be described as short-term investing. The basic tactic is to buy a stock springing out of an established base on a daily chart and hold it for the duration of the uptrend. Or the trader sells short a stock falling into a downtrend on a daily chart and holds it for the duration of the downtrend. As you can imagine, the holding time for these positions can evolve into weeks or months.

As you also can imagine, core trades take the least amount of attention. Once in a position, you establish an automatic trailing stop (automated order to close your position at a certain price) with your broker and check it daily to make sure it remains in the context of an uptrend or downtrend.

Nowadays, many position traders are reformed (transformed?) investors who got backhanded by the bear market. Disgusted and disheartened by the untrust-worthy nabobs who told them to "hold" during the wealth-walloping down-turn of the early 2000s, they decided to take the reins of their financial future in their own hands.

Here's a list of common-sense criteria for each style of trading.

- *Momentum or intraday trading* (following criteria also applies to *scalping*)

  —$30,000 minimum account size (regulations listed below)

  —Open and close all positions during a trading day; no overnight holds

  —Average daily range of stock (ADR) = at least one point

  —Average daily volume (ADV) = at least one million

  —Profit objective: fraction of a point and higher

  —Risk-reward objective—1:2

  —Large share size, 500–1,000 shares or larger

  —Tools: market internals including S&P 500 and/or NASDAQ 100 index futures, possibly the TICK and TRIN (both discussed in chapter 3), in-dices, direct access account with Level II screens, "Time & Sales," daily and intraday charts

  —Time-intensive

- *Swing trading*

  —Intended hold time: 2–5 days

  —ADR and ADV not *as* important

  —Profit objective: One point to multiple points

  —Risk-reward objective—1:3

  —Small lot sizes of 100 shares and higher acceptable

  —Tools: weekly, daily, intraday charts

  —Level II screen optional

  —Smaller account size okay

  —Less time-intensive than day trading

- *Position, core, or trend-trading, or short-term investing*

   —Use in trending markets

   —Intended hold time: 2–4 weeks, or duration of trend

   —Profit objective: multiple points

   —Initial risk-reward objective—at least 1:3

   —Tools: broad market + sector environment, plus weekly, daily, possibly intraday charts

   —Small account size okay

   —May be least time-intensive of all styles

Bullet list explanations: As traders, we crave volatility. Rapid price movements provide our bread and butter. That's why we want *at least* a one-point average daily range in stocks we trade short-term, especially intraday. Stocks that trade less than a point provide a too-slim-to-bother-with profit potential.

As a smart trader, you will also prefer to trade stocks that attract a high volume. Thinly (low volume) traded stocks can still have a wide spread between the bid and the offer, or ask, of several cents. That makes the stock dangerous to trade, especially intraday, because price levels may be held up by a few—or no—participants. Translation: these price levels can disappear in a heartbeat, and a stock can drop a point or more before you can yell, "Help me! Get me out at any price!"

Therefore, when you day-trade, consider trading only stocks that attract an average daily volume of a million shares or more. A little less daily volume is fine for swing trades, where the entry/exit price doesn't have to be *quite* as precise. Ditto for position, or core trades.

If you are not familiar with the bulleted term "risk-reward objectives" know that risk-reward analysis represents an extremely important part of pre-trade planning. Here's a basic explanation:

You spot a good setup and intend to buy Fickle Freightways if it reaches your entry price of $20 per share. You've designated the trade as a swing trade, so your established risk-reward objective should be 1:3. That means one-part risk to three-parts reward.

Next, you decide that if Fickle goes against you, and falls through nearby support at $19, you'll sell. Therefore, $19 represents your initial protective stop and is one point away from your entry price.

Finally, you determine your profit target. You look for resistance, which, in this case, is the prior high on Fickle's daily chart. Prior resistance is $23. Since your profit goal needs to be at least three points higher than your entry, this price target meets your criteria and adheres to your risk-reward objective.

To summarize: Entry price: $20

Initial protective stop: $19

Profit target: $23

In this simple example, you can see how your risk is one point away from your entry price, and your potential profit is three points away from your entry price, yielding a risk-reward ratio of 1:3.

As you can see, the longer the time frame of your trade, the higher the reward portion of your ratio should be. Why? Because the longer your capital is at risk, the larger potential reward you should expect.

That's why the recommended risk-reward ratio for swing trades is 1:3, with 1:2 being the minimum. With day trades, a risk-reward ratio of 1:2 is acceptable, but whenever you can find a trade that offers a greater rewards ratio, it's preferable.

Why don't we enter trades with a 1:1 ratio? With slippage and commissions, you're many times operating at a loss when you first enter a trade. The price has to go your way for a percentage of a point just to move to even. Over time, a 1:1 ratio delivers odds of success that are minute.

Bottom line: Calculate your risk-reward ratio *before* you enter each trade. If it doesn't work out to *at least* one-part risk to two-parts reward—and 1:3 is better—don't take the trade!

When you are new to trading, I recommend you stick with one trading style at a time. Many people start with swing trading, as it is not quite as intense as day trading, and the $25,000 account minimum is not mandatory.

Note: When you tackle trading, focus on *your* needs. Just because your neighbor makes big bucks by scalping eBay, Inc. (EBAY) on one-minute charts, doesn't mean you can—or should. Your optimum style might be entirely different.

After you determine the trading style that suits your personality and lifestyle, check out the different trading vehicles. Just the nature of some of these critters dictates the trading style that best suits their characteristics.

The most popular categories include: stocks, ETFs, stock index futures (E-minis), single stock futures, spot forex (currencies), and currency futures.

Trading instruments and suggested time-frame applications:

- Stocks are versatile trading instruments, and generally work well in all trading time frames, or styles.

- Highly liquid (high volume) ETFs, such as the Semiconductor Holders Trust (symbol SMH), can be day-traded. ETFs that trade less than 600,000 to 800,000 shares per day on average are better suited to swing or core trades.

- Stock Index Futures trading (E-minis) can be time-intensive and are well-suited to active trading. Many E-mini traders do not hold contracts overnight.

- Spot forex (cash currencies) trading attracts scalpers, active traders, and "arbs" (meaning "arbitrageur" who simultaneously buys a security in one market and sells it, or a derivative of it, in another market to profit from the price differential).

- Night owls and early birds may enjoy trading spot forex and currencies futures, as they trade around the clock.

Action Item Five: Opening Your Account

Generally speaking, you'll open an online account with a discount broker if you plan to trade part-time. If, however, you intend to make more than twenty or twenty-five trades per month, and/or if you intend to trade intraday, consider opening an account with a direct-access broker. They cater to active traders, and will provide you with software that includes comprehensive, real-time quotes, charts, news, and dynamic market, position minders, and futures and other internals quotes.

Account type overview . . .

- Equities account: you can trade stocks, options, ETFs, single stock futures, bonds, and mutual funds

- Futures account: you can trade index futures, single stock futures, currencies futures, interest rate futures, energy futures, commodities futures, metal futures, treasury (bond) futures, and futures options

- Forex account: you can trade the spot forex or cash currencies.

As of this writing, a few brokers offer "one-stop shopping." That means you can open an equities account, futures account, and forex account with their company. Other brokerages specialize in equities, futures, or currencies alone.

Those action items conclude step 1. Let's move into step 2, where the action heats up!

Step Two—Stretch and Warm Up

Action Item One: Avoid Thrashing in the Sea of Information Overload

Thomas Gilovich, professor of psychology at Cornell University, said, "The mind can organize and prioritize only so much information."

While Dr. Gilovich states the obvious, surviving in the tumultuous seas of information overload remains a constant source of stress and frustration to most Americans in general, and traders in particular.

The first-place contender for our time is the Internet, which offers thousands of financial Web sites just a Google-search away.

Next, "How to Beat the Stock Market" books pop out from publishers daily, along with financial magazines that tout "What to Buy Now." Newspapers wait in our driveways each morning—with headlines that clamor for our attention.

When we click on the financial networks, talking heads natter over news that ranges from the price of palladium to the newest Microsoft anti-trust suit, from the current tango between the dollar and the euro to the latest unemployment numbers.

Good grief. How do you lasso this tornado of constant in-your-face information and convert it into practical knowledge?

First, accept that neither you, nor I, will *ever* know everything there is to know about the financial markets. *No one does.* The good news is we don't have to "know everything" to make money. We do, however, need to filter out the unneeded information that muddies up our minds, so we can focus on the input that supports our trading goals.

Quick fix: Many traders enjoy day-trading the E-mini stock index futures, because they can focus just on the technicals, meaning the chart and intraday trends. Most individual company news can be ignored. That's a valid approach and you may want to explore it. (Remember, trading futures is high risk; your losses can exceed the equity in your account.)

If you choose to trade stocks and are determined to maintain your sanity in the swelling sea of information overload, the following ideas may help keep you afloat:

In a bull market, *concentrate on a limited number of leading industry groups,* for example: banks, semiconductors, and Internet stocks. (In a bear market, target laggards for shorting opportunities.) Then create a focus list of five to seven of the strongest stocks in each group. Stay updated on your list's earnings news, and except for global news that affects the broad markets, ignore the rest.

Scan focus stocks for position (core), swing and/or day trading setups. (You'll become familiar with the way they trade. "Fire" them in favor of more orderly issues, when they become unruly.)

Limit your opening-bell trading targets to five solid setups and trading plans. Once the market opens, the setups will unwind in your favor—or they won't. Let market internals and stock price action tell you if, and when, to enter targeted positions.

Use a high-quality stock scanner, if you prefer. (RealTick, *realtick.com*, offers free and paid-subscription scanners with its software.)

Remember, even though a scanner may give you buy/sell signals, you still need to be able to read charts. Why? Say your scanner alarm beeps with a swing trade entry on a semiconductor stock. And say thirty seconds later, CNBC announces that chip sales are falling. You may want to reconsider taking the trade offered by the scanner.

Keep your charts simple. If you drape three oscillators, six moving averages, and a concoction of volume indicators on top of your chart, the price pattern will disappear under what looks like a clump of tangled fishing line! Keep it simple. Three or four moving averages, one oscillator, and one volume indicator will display high-quality entry signals.

Finally, *clutter makes stress.* Research shows that the more clutter you have piled around your workspace, the more stress you will feel. If the clutter relates to unfinished projects, efficiency experts call this "subliminal screaming," because the projects "call" for your attention. Good idea: during trading hours, clean off your desk except the materials you need for trading. Complete other projects outside of trading hours.

Action Item Two: Focus on Technical Analysis Fundamentals

Study:

- Cycles

- Stage Analysis

- Support and Resistance

- Trends and Trendlines

- Price Patterns

As traders, we use charts as our primary tool in the study of technical analysis. Charts give us a fast picture of a stock's health at any given moment.

The bulleted points just listed represent the vital framework upon which technical analysis originates. Each of these chart components builds on the next, so you'll want to study them in the order given. You'll find them discussed in chapters 5 and 6.

(As an additional reference, check out Stan Weinstein's *Secrets for Profiting in Bull and Bear Markets*. It's an "oldie" but still very much a "goodie" that focuses on technical analysis. For novice technicians, my previous two books, *A Beginner's Guide to Day Trading Online* and *A Beginner's Guide to Short-Term Trading* are also good resources.)

Action Item Three: Develop Your Pre-Market Analysis Routine

In *The Art of War*, legendary philosopher and general Sun Tzu states, "If you know the enemy and know yourself, you need not fear the result of a hundred battles. If you know yourself but not the enemy, for every victory gained you will also suffer a defeat. If you know neither the enemy nor yourself, you will succumb in every battle."

Like war—and many traders insist "trading *is* war"—preparation is key to victorious trading. Know that the brightest minds in the world are waiting to take your money. If you rush to your desk each morning and jump into trades without forethought, you are placing your account in deadly jeopardy.

As a successful trader, you will develop a pre-market schedule that's comfortable, efficient, and effective. You'll conduct your pre-market analysis, establish your opening bias (when the opening bell rings, does the market look poised to rise or fall?), and establish your focus list so that you are organized when the opening bell rings.

Note: You'll want to tune into one of the financial television networks that broadcast news coverage, such as CNBC, Bloomberg, or CNN.

- First, are the S&P futures (E-mini quotes are fine for this) trading up or down? (If you don't receive futures quotes from your broker, financial television networks display them before the market opens.) This futures contract is a leading indicator for the market, and will tell you whether the market is opening higher or lower from the previous day's close. Those who trade NASDAQ stocks may want to check the Nasadq 100 futures quotes, as well.

- Assess financial and global news. Have Asian and European markets closed positively or negatively? How are the U.S. index futures reacting to these events?

- Which, if any, economic reports have come out, or are expected? (Most come out at 8:30 a.m. EST, others at 10:00 a.m. EST.) Depending on current economic conditions, the reports can affect the markets enough to pump stocks higher, or push them lower.

- Evaluate broad market indices, such as the Dow Industrials, S&P 500, and the NASDAQ 100 or NASDAQ Composite. Are their long-term (weekly/ monthly chart) and/or short-term (daily chart) trends bullish or bearish?

- Check sector-specific news and trends.

- Move to stock-specific updates (re: your focus list) on financial Web sites. Look for news or upgrades/downgrades (*briefing.com* is a good resource) by brokerage firms that may affect stocks on your focus list or current open positions.

- How does your opening focus list—meaning setups you've chosen earlier for possible entry—align with your opening bias? Example: If you plan to trade software stocks (most software companies reside on the NAS-DAQ), and the NASDAQ futures look down and dirty, rethink your entry strategies.

- Active traders: When the opening bell rings, you'll have your target stocks and their setups lined up on your screen on one- to five-minute charts. You'll also watch index futures, plus a chart(s) of the index of the industry group with which your stock is affiliated. Additional market internals you may want to access include the NYSE and/or NASDAQ TICK and TRIN, the VIX or VXN (market volatility indicators published by Chicago Board Options Exchange, cboe.com), put/call ratio (also published by CBOE), and bond prices. (The TICK, TRIN, VIX, VXN, and put/call ratio are discussed in chapter 4.)

You've surely figured out by now that planning and preparation take up a big chunk of a trading career. I know of no shortcuts.

Despite lessons learned in the buy-it-and-it-will-go-up market of the late 1990s and early 2000, I still meet trader "wannabees" who cut corners and try to "steal home base." And just as before, when Mother Market sees them coming, she dons her napkin, licks her lips, and polishes her knife and fork!

From exploring markets and trading tools that support your personality and trading style, to research, homework, and morning groundwork, you must study hard, work hard, endure the learning curve, and survive a few "trial by fire" trades. If you're prepared, you'll come through relatively unscathed, and much, much wiser.

Action Item Four: Practice Paper Trading; It Isn't "Sissy," It's Smart!

None of us popped into this world preprogrammed with computer skills. In fact, those of us over the age of forty-five grew up with the belief that a mouse was a tiny gray rodent who wouldn't stand still long enough for anyone to get a firm grasp—much less shove around a fuzzy, green pad.

If you've opened an account with a direct-access broker, the software can initially appear to be tricky, confusing, and even overwhelming. It's not sissy—it's *smart*—to trade with a demo account (the broker should provide it for you), until you get up close and personal with all aspects of the trading platform. Nothing spells "agony" like fumbling an order entry when your stock is crumbling.

When you use paper trading early on, to get the feel of the market and how it works, remember to enter every trade just as though you were trading with real money. Plan your trade and trade your plan, including trade sheet entries and journal entries.

Keep in mind that when you trade with a demo account, your broker rigged it to make executions user-friendly. That means you might slide into a long position at a slightly more favorable price than actual specialists or market makers would hand to you. Or you will skate into a short position in a tanking stock with ease; in the "real world," a tanking stock may not offer enough upticks (with most equities, you must enter a short trade on an uptick) for you to sell short at an optimum price.

Paper trading is also a great "drop back and punt" tactic. Every trader, no matter his or her account size, runs into losing streaks. One cure for a losing streak: stop trading for a period of time, until your confidence returns. Then, paper-trade for a time until you "resync" with the market.

Finally, remember that when you trade with "funny money," you are executing trades minus your biggest challenge: your emotions. Please reserve your giddiness if you make a zillion bucks on paper. It's a different ball game when you load real money into your trades.

In chapter 3, we're going to blaze through steps 3 and 4 in the *Steps to Trading Success*®. First, though, for future reference, you may want to copy the key point review that follows. It summarizes steps 1, and 2 and their accompanying action items.

Key Point Review

Step One—Find Your Place

Action Item One: Explore, Discover, Analyze, Decide
Newspapers, magazines, books, Web sites, and financial news networks provide an ongoing resource to traders.

Action Item Two: Check Out Trading Schools
You can obtain a good trading education, or you can let the market teach you how to trade. The latter is easier and far less expensive!

Action Item Three: Mind Your Own Business
Create and develop a business plan—be it simple or comprehensive. It keeps you focused and responsible.

Action Item Four: When and What Will You Trade?
Choose the trading style and time frame appropriate to your personality and lifestyle. Then investigate various trading instruments to find one, or more, that makes a "good fit."

Action Item Five: Opening Your Account
Choose your broker carefully. Different brokers serve different trading needs.

Step Two—Stretch and Warm Up

Action Item One: Avoid Thrashing in the Sea of Information Overload
After you investigate different learning and news resources, control the amount of input you absorb each day. Keep your focus list narrowed down to a limited number of the strongest trading opportunities.

Action Item Two: Focus on Technical Analysis Fundamentals
Study

- Cycles

- Stage Analysis

- Support and Resistance

- Trends and Trendlines

- Price Patterns

Charts are the primary tools used by technical analysts. Cycles, stage analysis, support and resistance (think "demand and supply"), trends and trendlines, and price patterns create the foundation for technical analysis.

Action Item Three: Develop Your Pre-Market Analysis Routine

Create your personalized morning setup schedule that begins at least one hour before the market opens. Concentrate on a few well-chosen information resources, organize your focus list, and begin your trading day calmly and confidently!

Action Item Four: Practice by Paper Trading; It Isn't "Sissy," It's Smart!

Until you become familiar with the trading environment, your broker's online order entry form, or Level 2 order entry screen and charting software, you'll be wise to paper trade, or trade without real money.

CENTER POINT

Time Enhancement: Are You Efficient and Effective?

The time which we have at our disposal every day is elastic; the passions that we feel expand it, those that we inspire contract it, and habit fills what remains.
—Marcel Proust (1871–1922)

As members of a frantic society, most of us fall victim to the "busy, but not productive" syndrome. At day's end, we feel a nagging sensation of unfulfillment, as we shake our heads and wonder what we actually *did.*

The On-Purpose Person[i] is a terrific little book with a big message about achieving our purpose in life. In one chapter, it spotlights two simple concepts that enhance time management. When we're more productive, we have more time to work on important personal goals (or relax!). The author, Kevin McCarthy, states, "Efficient is doing things right. Effective is doing the right things."

When we are efficient, we become the masters of our own time. Besides the standard time-management strategies, such as preplanning schedules, prioritizing objectives, delegating appropriately, and cultivating a polite "no" reply to needless requests, efficiency means we learn new,

[i]Kevin W. McCarthy, *The On-Purpose Person* (Colorado Springs: Pinon Press, 1992), p. 59.

more proficient ways of accomplishing old chores. We learn how to make rapid, high-quality decisions by applying ethical considerations, trusting our instincts, and, when appropriate, seeking consensus from others.

When we apply efficiency techniques to "the right things," we become highly effective. And what are the right things? They are your personal "wants," including your needs, goals, desires, and visions for the future.

Think of the different sectors in your life, then write them down by listing headings such as: Career, Family, Health/Fitness, Finances, Social, and Spirituality. Next, jot down your short-term (present time to one year) and long term (five to ten years) goals and desires under each heading. Finally, prioritize *those* goals, create a time budget for each, and plug them into your schedule, starting today!

When we practice "doing the right things right," the payoffs and rewards are monumental. We grow more as human beings. We are happier, and we have more time to spend on relaxation, friends, and loved ones. Furthermore, we achieve the goals that move us forward on the road to fulfillment and success.

Point 'Em Downhill!

Spend at least as much time researching a stock as you would choosing a refrigerator.

—Peter Lynch

I admit it. I'm addicted to downhill snow skiing. I'm the happiest when I have two boards strapped to my feet and I'm flying down a white, powdery slope at Mach 2, with my hair on fire.

After a series of skiing lessons many years ago, one particular instructor stuck in my mind. The handsome, blond Nordic, Sven (all ski instructors seem to be named Sven, don't they?), skied behind me, all the while calling, "Point them downhill, Tooo-neee. Point them downhill!"

In this chapter, we're going to move through steps 3 and 4 of the Seven Steps to Successful Trading. These steps represent the vital functions for virtually every trading time frame and vehicle, and include practical applications you will perform many times over in your trading career.

So . . . let's point 'em downhill!

Step Three—Ready, Set, Trade

Action Item One: Study Key Chart Components

- Candlestick Reversal Patterns

- Volume Signals

- Moving Averages

In chapter 2, we zeroed in on trends, support and resistance, and price patterns. Now we're going to build on that knowledge and add analysis that shines with a bit more glitz and flash, namely candlestick reversal patterns, volume and its On-Balance indicator, and moving averages. Once you understand how these key chart components work together, you'll have a firm foundation of technical analysis you can use to support your trading plans and money-management skills.

The techniques used to create candlestick reversal patterns were initiated by a sixteenth-century Japanese rice trader, So-kyu Honma. It was said that this wealthy farmer made one hundred winning trades in a row.

Candles themselves involve no calculations. They consist of the bar used on traditional Western charts, with the space between the opening and closing prices filled in. Just as with a bar chart, each candlestick represents one period of data.

Many technicians color positive (closing price higher than open) candles green, and negative (closing price lower than open) candles red.

In this book, positive candles are clear, and negative candles are black.

Whether you use candle charts or prefer to stay with traditional bar charts is a matter of personal choice. I enjoy using candle charts because they give me early reversal signals, broadcast market psychology, and act as great money-management tools.

In chapter 7, you'll find an overview of candle theory and several examples of candle reversal patterns.

Friendly warning to bar chart holdouts: Candle charts and references to candle reversal patterns will be used throughout this book.

After you become familiar with the basics of reading candle patterns, you'll want to grow adept at reading volume. Because it represents the total number of shares or contracts bought and sold during a given time frame, volume is a highly powerful communicator, and holds court as a narrator extraordinaire.

Joe Granville, noted market technician of the 1960s, stated, "Volume precedes price." Volume transmits important signals because, unlike most chart indicators, volume is not a derivative of price.

Consequently, when you add volume information to other chart indicators and reach a single "buy" or "sell" signal, volume strengthens the signal.

High or low volume spikes tell us whether market players are interested in a stock. Basically, high volume driven by fear causes supply to overcome demand; price will fall. Strong volume bolstered by greed causes demand to absorb and overpower supply. So prices rise.

Think of volume as a multipurpose trading tool. Its signals confirm entries, fine-tune risk strategies, and validate exit decisions.

We'll talk about volume in chapter 7. We'll also explore the On-Balance Volume (OBV), a dandy momentum indicator created by Joe Granville. You can use OBV signals on all time frames.

Next on our hit parade of trading tools is the ever-popular, ever-reliable moving average. Brought to us in the form of a single line that connects closing prices in a given time period, moving average serves as a support and resistance marker for price action. The longer the time frame measured by this dependable device, the more compelling its message becomes.

Chapter 7 discusses moving averages, as well.

I know traders who use only candles, volume, trend lines, and moving averages on their charts. And they make money in all time frames. Their methodology is proof that you don't have to drape dozens of indicators on your charts to pull gains from the market.

Before you head into the next action item, become familiar with the interaction among candles and their basic reversal patterns, volume and the OBV, and two or three major moving averages of your choice. This knowledge will serve you well when you jump into high-probability setups.

Action Item Two: Focus on Basic Setups

Imagine yourself in a sprawling public library. Long aisles stretch in all directions, lined with shelves that hold thousands of novels. Each novel has a different story. Each is populated with different fictional characters who strive to overcome huge obstacles in order to reach their goals.

As you glance at the shelves, how many themes would you say exist? Hundreds? Thousands? Nope. The answer is *three*. Three central ideas form the structure of all of those novels. They are: 1) man against man, 2) man against nature, and 3) man against himself.

"Why, that's fascinating," you murmur, scratching your head, and wondering how this trivia tidbit relates to trading. ☺

Here's how: Despite the proliferation of setups published, many with proprietary indicators, the fact remains that only *four basic setups* exist. They are: 1) breakout from consolidation in a base or uptrend, 2) breakout from a pullback in a base or uptrend, 3) breakdown from a consolidation in a reversal pattern or downtrend, and 4) breakdown from a rally in a downtrend.

A setup is a price formation that, when identified on the chart time frame of our choice, provides an opportunity for profiting by taking a long or short position. Figure 3–1 shows basic setup patterns with buy and sell (short) entry points.

Again, these are plain-vanilla setup patterns. You'll come across many variations of these patterns that add decisive factors such as price movement, volume criterion, moving average, and oscillator conditions.

Budding traders should be aware that just as it's not necessary, or even desirable, to trade every financial product available, it's also unnecessary to memorize or actively trade every intricate setup encountered in books and seminars.

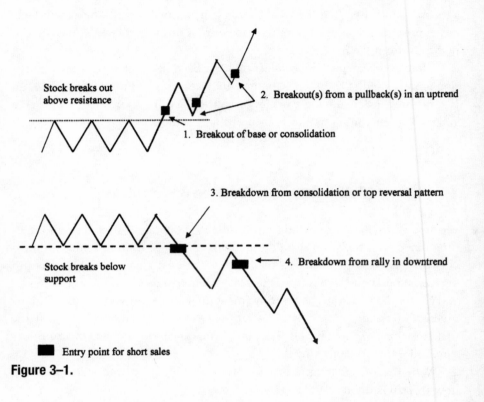

■ Entry points for long positions

Stock breaks out above resistance

2. Breakout(s) from a pullback(s) in an uptrend

1. Breakout of base or consolidation

3. Breakdown from consolidation or top reversal pattern

Stock breaks below support

4. Breakdown from rally in downtrend

■ Entry point for short sales

Figure 3–1.

Some of the most successful traders I know camp on one or two simple set-ups. Instead of knowing a little about a lot of setups, they've mastered a select few, and profit nicely from their expertise.

Here's an added benefit: specializing in one or two setups reduces information overload. If, for example, you scan for stocks or ETFs that are consolidating in a base and possibly heading for a breakout on high volume, it eliminates the remaining universe of stocks.

The bottom line with setups: you'll be a wealthier trader if you understand how and why setups progress into either good entry opportunities, or failed nonevents. Knowing how price action unwinds keeps you operating in a confident, yet cautionary zone.

Finally, if you use a scanner to spot your setups, please remain aware of broad market environment. As mentioned earlier, scanners are great tools as long as you have a foundation of trading knowledge and discipline to confirm their signals.

Action Item Three: If One "Buy" Signal Is Good, Three Are Better! Correlating Multiple Time Frames

Say you're looking for a setup, for either a swing or day trade, that's ripe for the picking. You spot one and check it quickly for an entry point. Wouldn't you be tickled happy if instead of *one* buy signal appearing for the play, you saw *three*?

If you're backing away because you think this sounds too complicated, please listen up. Spotting three distinct buy signals, on three separate time frames—for the same trade—is easier than it looks. An optimum setup on a longer time frame will many times lead naturally to a single signal on shorter time frames. Plus, knowing that you have signal confirmation from the macro time frame to the micro time frame contributes to your confidence in your trading plan.

Here's an example in capsule form: One morning early, before the opening bell, you scan daily charts for a long swing trade or day-trade entry. You spot Bitty Broadband, which has risen nicely out of a base in a new uptrend and is now consolidating on price and moving average support.

If Bitty opens at a price zone around yesterday's closing price, it will present a buying opportunity. You bring up a sixty-minute chart of Bitty. On this "close-up" of the daily chart, you can see the orderly consolidation candles more clearly. They, too, form a "buy" signal.

When the opening bell rings, you have a five-minute chart of Bitty on your screen. The stock opens nearly even with yesterday's close, and starts edging up on strong volume, in a positive market. A few minutes after the open, you buy a position and quickly enter your initial protective stop.

Now you can see how to segue from a setup into the reassuring realm of *multiple time frames* that agree on either a "buy" or "sell" signal. Typically, you'll find a setup on a daily chart, then zoom closer to a sixty-minute chart and check its signals, then zoom even closer to a fifteen-, ten-, or five-minute chart to fine-tune your entry.

Optimally, you'll want identical "buy" or "sell" signals on at least three time frames to heighten the odds of a winning trade.

Is it *absolutely, positively necessary* to trade from multiple time frames? If you enter long-term trend or core trades, and use end-of-day charting software, then the multiple time frame methodology may not be necessary, or even feasible.

When you execute short-term trades, however, correlate signals on multiple time frames. You'll heighten your odds of success and take one more step toward protecting your capital.

Action Item Four: Sharpen Your Money Management Skills: Predetermine Share Size, Perform Risk-Reward Analysis, and Execute Protective Stop-Loss Strategies

You've heard it a gazillion times over: "Plan your trade, then trade your plan."

Kind of brings on a yawn, doesn't it?

Guess what chokes a yawn? Going broke. Or a string of zeroes where your trading account balance used to be. Not only does *that* reality clog up a perfectly good yawn—the line of zeroes is a real attention-getter!

So, let's get excited about the money-management skills that lead into "plan your trade, then trade your plan." Utilizing the information in this action item will separate you from the herd of traders and investors referred to as the "dumb money."

Predetermine Share Size

Before you enter each trade, determine your share size and calculate the risk-reward ratio that includes your entry price, your initial protective stop, and your profit target.

Before you enter a trade, you'll have established a predetermined share size based on your account balance, your trading criteria, and your experience. Obviously, you won't max out your account with only one or two stock positions, or other financial instruments. A good rule is to commit no more than 25 percent of your account to a single position. Consider diversifying your positions into varying industry groups. And know that it's always a good idea to keep a stash of cash in your account as a safety net.

Some traders plug one share size (for example five hundred shares) into their order-entry screen, and use that as a default for every trade.

Here's an alternative method: assign a moderate dollar amount relative to your account size, and apply that to the majority of your trades. Adjust the share size to fit the dollar amount.

You may wish to adjust your share size for other reasons, as well. Those reasons include price or market volatility, low liquidity, or time of day. Why adjust your position size for time of day? Because trading during the midday period (lunchtime in New York), when liquidity sinks to lower levels, holds higher risk. Unless a lunchtime rally known as a "noon balloon" is in force, the time period from 11:30 a.m. to 2:00 p.m. EST can produce limited follow-through on setups, and low volume levels that restrict precision entries and exits.

Perform Risk-Reward Analysis

Next, calculate your risk-reward analysis. This process is of the utmost importance in planning each trade *before* you enter. We discussed risk-reward analysis in chapter 2; we'll bring it up again in upcoming chapters.

Execute Stop-Loss Strategies

Remember the old song, "Fifty Ways to Leave Your Lover"? Nearly that many techniques exist for calculating *protective stop strategies*. There are percentage of account stops, technical stops, percentage of price stops, and time stops, to mention a few.

You'll figure your initial protective stop for each trade as an essential ingredient in your risk-reward analysis. Once you are in the trade, manage your risk by adjusting your stop.

If you are highly disciplined, you can use mental stop-losses. I prefer setting electronic stop-loss orders with my broker, as it frees me to attend to other matters and takes "the worry out of being close."

Can you think up a boatload of reasons why setting stops is wrong for you? (*The market-makers know where my stop is, and they stop me out on purpose,* or *The stock could hit my stop and then reverse,* etc.)

Try this line of thinking: You buy health insurance, automobile insurance, and home insurance to protect yourself against catastrophic losses. Now, you're adding another form of insurance—stop-loss insurance—to protect yourself and your hard-earned trading account against losses that would severely diminish chances of success. Makes good sense, doesn't it?

Stop-loss strategies can be based upon:

- Percentages of the equity in your account
- A technical approach
- Percentage of share price
- Time in the trade

Protective Stops as a Percentage of Equity

As suggested in chapter 2, please risk no more than 1 to 2 percent of your account on any trade.

Next, especially when you're new to trading, consider setting limits on losses to a prespecified amount for the day, week, or month, based on a percentage of your account equity. For example, establish a daily loss limit of no more than 0.5 to 1 percent of your account. If your account equity is $20,000, your maximum daily loss limit should equal no more than $200. Adjust the percentage at the end of each trading day, according to your account balance.

You can also set a daily loss limit in a fixed dollar amount that, again, should be relative to your account size.

Here's another idea: When you approach your loss limits, decrease your share size. For instance, say you have an open position of five hundred shares. As you approach your loss limit for the day, decrease your share size from five hundred to three hundred shares, while keeping your stop-loss order intact. This lowers your shortfall.

Once you've reached your maximum designated loss for a given time frame, *stop trading*. Reassess market conditions, your trading criteria, and your mindset. Remember, preservation of capital remains your number-one priority.

Technical Protective Stops

When you place a technical stop, you place it by looking at your target stock's chart and pinpointing key support or resistance relative to price levels, trend lines, and/or moving averages. Again, the initial risk (the spread between your entry price and your stop price) should be smaller than your profit potential.

Generally speaking, you'll want to place a technical stop a few cents under a nearby prior support (potential buyers) area for a long trade, and a few cents over nearby prior resistance for a short trade.

Swing traders use daily, hourly, or short-term charts to identify key support or resistance levels that will serve as strong stop-loss points. Day traders use intraday charts to locate support and resistance levels that point to stop prices.

Percentage of Price Stops

Some swing traders place stop orders derived from a percentage of the price of the stock they are entering. If this appeals to you, consider using a stop based on 2 to 3 percent of the price. For example, if you are buying a stock for a swing trade that costs $20 per share, you would risk no more than 3 percent, or $0.60. That means you would set your initial stop at $19.40.

Of course, if you use a 2 to 3 percent stop loss, you'll want to use at least a 4 to 6 percent profit target strategy. Please make sure both percentage points line up with key support and resistance levels. If you're long a position, and nearby resistance (potential sellers) perches a few cents away from the current price, you cannot assume that the stock will break through the resistance just because you've set a profit target at a loftier level!

Time Stops

Active traders are famous for using "time stops." Swing traders use them as well.

The theory is: When you plan your trade, you expect the stock or trading product to move in a certain direction. If it doesn't do so within a certain amount of time (adjusted to the time frame you are trading), you may want to exit the trade early.

Here's an example of an intraday trade using a time stop: You locate a high-quality intraday setup for a long day-trade. You plan your share size and complete your risk-reward analysis. The setup unfolds favorably, and you buy the stock as it breaks out of a consolidation area on high volume.

Within minutes, though, the upward momentum decreases. The stock drifts down and begins to churn sideways. Although it does not touch your technical stop, time erodes. Momentum and volume fade. Realizing the stock isn't as strong as you imagined, you close the position.

If you're swing-trading and you enter a position that doesn't act as you anticipated within a day, or two—even though it doesn't touch your stop-loss price—you may decide to "time it out" and scale back or close the entire position.

The bottom line with time stops: If you enter a position and the stock does not act the way you thought it would, you can manage potential risk by exiting a portion, or all, of your position. This confirms the wise market axiom, "When in doubt, get out!"

Step Four—Fine-tune Your Approach

Action Item One: Create a Trade Sheet with a Conscience

Now let's move into step 4 of the Seven Steps to Trading Success. As you progress through the diverse action items in this step, you'll fine-tune your approach to trading and strengthen your foundation of knowledge and experience.

If you haven't already done so, this is the perfect time to create a detailed trading sheet that will help to increase your trading skills by tracing the progress of your trade in black and white.

The trade sheet illustrated in Figure 3–2 is designed to assist trade planning and management.

It takes guts to use this trade sheet. Its end-point objective is to make you a better trader. I'll bet you my duck slippers (those of you who know me know I

Trade Sheet with a Conscience

Commissions of $10 per trade have been added into the Total Amounts.

Entry Date 2004	Symbol and Type	Number Shares	Long or Short	Entry Price	Total Amount	Initial Stop	Profit Target	Risk: Reward Ratio	Adjusted Stop	Adjusted Profit Target	Exit Date	Exit Price	Total Amount	Profit / Loss
3/24	PCLN Swing	500	Long	23.20	11,610.00	22.60	25.00	1:4	3/25 - 24.70	25. 50	3/26	25.90	12,940.00	1,330.00

only bet my duck slippers on sure things) that if you take the time to fill it out completely with each trade, you'll find that your trading skills *and* bottom line improve rapidly.

Action Item Two: Study Momentum Indicators

- MACD (Moving Average Convergence Divergence Oscillator)

- Stochastics Oscillator

- ADX (Average Directional Movement Index) with Plus and Minus Directional Indicators (+DI and −DI)

As you can see in action item two in step 4, we're heading back into the study of technical analysis. Earlier, you focused on the four stages of a cycle, trends, and reversal patterns. Next, you worked and traded with charts that show the basics, including candlesticks, volume and the OBV, and moving averages.

Now you'll add momentum indicators to your charts—one at a time. These may include the MACD, or moving average convergence divergence indicator (say that fast three times!), the stochastics oscillator, and indicators from Welles Wilder's directional movement system, the ADX with +DI and −DI.

Momentum measures the velocity, or pace, of a price move. Identifying this momentum is extremely important to traders. Momentum indicators, such as those just mentioned, act as decision support tools to predict trend continuation and reversals. We also refer to them as "oscillators," because their lines oscillate, or form alternating peaks and troughs between top and bottom boundaries.

They are most helpful when they move to overbought or oversold extremes in conjunction with a trend. Next, the price continues in the trend direction, but the indicator refuses to confirm price movement and even reverses direction. This is called a "divergence." At this point, the oscillator becomes a leading indicator; price momentum may begin to decelerate and even reverse.

Momentum indicators add to the predictive power of candles, volume, moving averages, etc. Since each uses different calculations, each moves at a slightly different pace. We'll discuss these momentum indicators in chapter 8.

You may want to study and experiment with additional momentum indicators. For more information on additional momentum tools such as the RSI (Relative Strength indicator) and Momentum indicator, go to my Web site, *toni turner.com*, and click on the tutorial.

Action Item Three: Target Gap Strategies

With current market volatility rising and showing no signs of calming, nearly all trading vehicles experience price gaps on daily charts.

A gap commonly occurs when a stock, for example, opens higher or lower than the previous day's close. An imbalance in supply-and-demand order flow (more buy orders than sell orders, or the other way around) causes the price to skip levels.

Intraday gaps, especially in stocks, are less common. Still, if mega-dramatic news hits the market, it can cause incremental gaps in stocks and futures.

The Japanese call gaps "windows." That's a good descriptive analogy, as gaps, like windows, are closed sooner or later.

Markets that habitually fill their opening gaps quickly, such as ETFs and the E-minis, attract traders who attack like piranha fish and "fade the gap."

Definition of "fade": to trade against the prevailing trend. So, if a stock (or futures contract) gaps to the upside at the open, traders immediately sell it short. If the stock gaps down, traders buy. When the stock fills the gap, or "closes the window," those traders exit the position.

Beware of fading gaps that open on extremely strong volume. You could get stopped out—and fast! Strong volume can ignite a stock with a spurt of momentum that continues to push it in the direction at which it opened.

Conversely, low volume on a gap open presents a better fading opportunity. Since low volume equals low levels of enthusiasm, the odds are better that the gap will close sooner and faster.

If you are an experienced trader, you may jump into gap plays routinely. If you are a novice, please avoid fading gaps until you study and paper-trade the strategy extensively. *Again, all gaps do* not *close right away*. In fact, in a bull market, a stock may gap up a point or more and not close that gap for days, or even weeks. Please learn before you burn!

We'll discuss additional gap strategies in upcoming chapters.

Action Item Four: Are You a Top-down or Bottom-up Trader?

We've talked quite a bit about trading styles. Here are two more techniques you can try on, to see which one fits. By and large, they apply to all trading time frames.

If you are a "top down" trader, you consider macro market trends first, then broad index trends. Next, you check out sector and industry group trends, then the relative strength of the top five (for example) stocks in that group. Now, from that group, you narrow your focus list to the best two or three setups. Here's a bullet list that shows an example of how your top-down assessment might turn out:

- Macro trend: bull market

- Dow and S&P index: in strong uptrend; bullish

- Bank index (BKX.X): in uptrend, bouncing up from fifty-day moving average, bullish

- Leading stocks in BKX: Bank of America (BAC), Bank of New York (BK), Citigroup (C), Fifth-Third Bankcorp (FITB), and J. P. Morgan Chase (JPM)

- High-probability setups for long trade: C and FITB

The "bottom-up" method involves less analysis. You simply choose a stock based on the quality of its trend direction and setup.

This style works for stocks that swim against the market tide. Many times, low-priced or small-cap stocks will buck the broader trend.

Quick caveat: The majority of stocks eventually follow the direction taken by major indices, especially in bear markets. Exceptions to this rule show up in commodities stocks, such as oil, oil services, and metals.

We've covered a lot of territory in the past two chapters.

Soon, you'll turn to chapter 4, which moves through the final three steps in the Seven Steps to Trading Success®. The action items we'll target include ways to identify trading environments, intraday indicators (for active traders), and sentiment indicators. In the technical-analysis arena, we'll add Fibonacci retracement lines and more indicators to our charts.

If you've traded for any time, you know that your mindset is one of *the* most important aspects of trading. To that end, step 7 turns the spotlight back on you. It includes the psychological test we mentioned earlier, created especially for this book by Brett Steenbarger, Ph.D.

Dr. Steenbarger's Three-dimensional Quiz is fun and easy to take. It will help you penetrate your psyche and will act as a personal "system check" for emotional strengths and challenges related to trading. We trust you will find this enjoyable exercise an insightful experience that will help you boost your bottom line.

First, though, here's a review of the steps in this chapter and their action items.

Key Point Review

Step Three—Ready, Set, Trade

Action Item One: Study Key Chart Components

- Candle charting techniques

- Volume and volume indicators

- Moving averages

Candles, volume, and moving averages represent important chart components. Team up their signals with support and resistance, trend analysis and price patterns, to arrive at a confluence of signals that point to a "buy" or "sell" signal.

Action Item Two: Focus on Basic Setups

Basic setups provide entry opportunities. Two basic "buy" setups and two basic "sell" (short) setups exist. Most others are variations on those themes. It is important to learn the principles that transform setups into solid entry opportunities.

Action Item Three: If One "Buy" Signal Is Good, Three Are Better! Correlating Multiple Time Frames

The ability to spot a "buy" or "sell" signal on three or more time-frames correlations is an important tool in your trading skill-set. When you have, for example, a "buy" signal on a daily, sixty-minute, and five-minute chart, it heightens the odds of a successful long trade.

Action Item Four: Sharpen Your Money Management Skills: Predetermine Share Size, Perform Risk-Reward Analysis, and Execute Protective Stop Strategies

As a savvy trader, you plan your trades by applying risk-reward analysis *before* you plunk your money on the line. Once in the trade, you establish your protective stops immediately.

Step Four—Fine-tune Your Approach

Action Item One: Create a Trade Sheet with a Conscience

Turn your trade sheet into more than a record of your entry and exit prices, by adding columns that help you plan and manage your trade.

Action Item Two: Study Momentum Indicators

- MACD

- Stochastics

- ADX with +DI and −DI

We add overbought/oversold indicators such as the MACD, stochastics, and the ADX to our charts for their predictive value related to trend velocity and reversals. Translation: If you're long a stock, and the trend's gonna end, I'm sure you'd like a heads-up. These momentum indicators are designed to tell you just that.

Action Item Three: Target Gap Strategies

Price gaps or "windows" (skipped price levels that occur mostly at the market open) offer experienced traders the opportunity to "fade," or trade against, that move.

Action Item Four: Are You a Top-down or Bottom-up Trader?

Top-down traders measure the mood and manner of the entire market, the exchanges, sectors, and industry groups, and take applicable stock index futures into consideration before entering a trade. Bottom-up traders zero in on a single stock or trading vehicle and ignore surrounding market noise. Either approach is valid—the choice depends on your personal trading style.

CENTER POINT

You Are in Control—You Are Proactive!

I know of no more encouraging fact than the unquestionable ability of man to elevate his life by conscious endeavor.

—Henry David Thoreau

In our quest for personal excellence, one characteristic that serves us more powerfully than perhaps any other is the ability to be *proactive*.

Those who are proactive take responsibility for their lives, their relationships, and their environments. They take the initiative and they act, instead of "being acted upon."

Naturally, events come into our lives that hurt us, physically and/or emotionally. But if we stay proactive, these events need not steal our core identity. In fact, how often have unwelcome events, when resolved with courage and honesty, resulted in eventual blessings and sturdier life skills?

The opposite of "proactive" is "reactive." Those who react to their environments usually give their power away to the person or situation in which they find themselves. This passivity is easier in the short run, but plays severe havoc in the long run.

Victor Frankel raised proactivity to heroic levels. Psychiatrist and Jew, he was imprisoned in a death camp in Nazi Germany. He suffered torture and indignities. Yet this hero decided that no matter how badly he was treated, he would remain in control of his responses and maintain his values. He was determined to keep his behavior as a function of his own decisions, not those of his captors. Frankel became an inspiration to the other prisoners, including many of the guards. He emerged from the death camp as a hero.

Monitor the situations in your life and start making a conscious choice to handle them on a proactive level. You and you alone are the master of your destiny!

Spend Quality Time with Your Money

Averaging down in a bear market is tantamount to taking a seat on the down escalator at Macy's.

—Richard Russell

One snowy evening in New York City, I was riding in a taxi on my way to a dinner meeting, and a billboard caught my eye. It said, "Spend quality time with your money." *Wow*, I thought. *What a fantastic statement!*

We all spend quality time on our priorities. We paint our homes, put gas and oil in our cars, hug our kids, and work hard at the office. Yet, when it comes to money, some folks hand their savings over to a well-meaning stranger (financial consultant), ignore it completely, and then expect it to thrive and grow. Go figure.

As traders, we *do* spend quality time with our money. Excluding the foolhardy, who jump into the market with no knowledge or discipline and disappear in a flash, most of us eat, sleep, and breathe the stock market on a daily basis. We know *exactly* how our money is—or isn't—performing at every moment.

In order for you to gain additional knowledge that will make the time spent with your trading account more effective in this chapter, we'll work through the final three of the Seven Steps to Trading Success®. The items cover a broad range of topics, from identifying market environment, intraday market internals, and economic reports, to the quiz created especially for this book by Brett Steenbarger, Ph.D.

Step Five—Polish Your Performance

Action Item One: Trade When the Gettin' Is Good!

Learning how to evaluate the trading environment is one of the most important tools in your trader's skill-set. It will keep you trading when Mother Market feels generous, and safely on the sidelines when she acts onerous. This is one area of trading where your ability to define trend direction, both long and short-term, plays a crucial role.

As we said in chapter 1, trending markets, on any time frame, serve up the most delicious profits. Choppy, sideways environments are hard to crack, and yield little, if any, gains. In fact, by the end of the day, they usually hand you a loss.

To evaluate the markets effectively for trading opportunities, target the time frame you trade.

- *Intraday:* The S&P 500 futures generally lead the markets; the NASDAQ 100 futures point the way for tech stocks. (A mini-discussion of stock index futures follows this section. For a broader explanation of the futures indexes, their symbols, and how to subscribe to them, see chapter 10.) You've already established your opening bias. After the opening bell rings, watch an intraday chart—a five-minute chart is fine—of the index futures. Observe them for a few minutes to see if they etch a series of higher highs and higher lows that develop into an uptrend, or draw a series of lower highs and lower lows for a downtrend. If they grind sideways, chopping up and down with no discernible trend, intraday trading opportunities with stocks that track the index futures will be high-risk. Wait until a trend begins before taking a position. Trading the E-minis themselves may also be tough going. Your choices: 1) again, wait for an intraday trend to begin, 2) hang it up and go to the beach, or 3) find a stock that defies market action and is trending on its own steam.

- *Swing trades:* When the broad markets rise in a robust uptrend on a daily chart, that's swing-trading paradise. If they crumble in a nasty downtrend, we can sell short and *still* rake in the gains. During trendless markets, however, when the markets churn sideways for days, or weeks, especially after an extended uptrend or downtrend, swing-trading entries get dicey and carry high risk. Wait for direction to appear.

- *Position, core, or trend trades:* When you hold stocks that track market trends, and the market flounders after making a multiweek uptrend, or stabilizes after a multiweek downtrend, check current positions for possible profits. You will also want to start looking for new trading opportunities that may take advantage of the market's reversal.

Action Item Two: Active Traders: Target Intraday Indicators

- Stock Index Futures

- NYSE and NASDAQ TICK and TRIN

As just mentioned, if you are an active trader, you will keep a real-time intra-day chart of the S&P 500 futures on your screen when you trade. If you focus on NASDAQ stocks, you may want to add an intraday chart of the NASDAQ 100 index futures. These futures contracts are a leading indicator, because they tell us (especially the S&P futures) whether market players feel bullish or bearish on America's economic outlook.

About S&P 500 and NASDAQ 100 futures quotes:

- Direct-access brokers cater to active traders and offer streaming stock index futures quotes; brokers usually pass on exchange fees to the customer.

- Most online discount brokerages *do not* furnish streaming stock index futures quotes.

- The E-mini quotes for both the S&P 500 and the NASDAQ 100 futures work well for this purpose and are less expensive to access than standard "big" futures contracts. Plus, they show the volume of contracts traded.

- If you do not have an account with a direct-access broker and want to access mini stock index futures quotes, subscribe to them at the Chicago Mercantile Exchange at *cme.com*. Monthly fees are reasonable and definitely worth the price.

Please know that day-trading successfully, without these index futures quotes would be akin to walking into a desert without a bottle of water! Why? The index futures markets digest global events as they happen. Then they reflect the impact those events will have on our economy in the immediate future. Although commodities stocks like oil, gold, lumber, etc. can take off on their separate paths, the majority of stocks rise and fall with the index futures.

The TICK and the TRIN also provide dynamic information to active traders about market direction. Again, direct-access brokers offer streaming TICK and TRIN quotes; online discount brokers may not.

While TICK and TRIN quotes are not absolutely necessary to execute money-making day trades, they do offer predictive value relating to intraday market direction, especially when they soar or slide to extreme readings.

Every stock exchange has its own TICK and TRIN. As they represent the

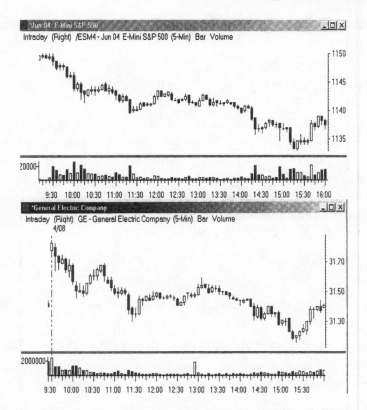

Figure 4–1. The top chart displays a five-minute chart of the S&P 500 index E-mini futures contract for a single day. The chart below it shows a five-minute chart of General Electric (GE). Notice how behemoth GE closely mimics the futures contract movement.

broadest scope of market action, the NYSE and NASDAQ TICK and TRIN offer the most potent information.

First, let's talk about the TICK. The following guidelines apply to both the NYSE and NASDAQ version.

The TICK is a market-breadth indicator that measures the difference between the number of stocks *ticking* up and the number of stocks *ticking* down, at that moment.

For many stocks, a tick equals a $0.01 move up or down. Say a stock is trading at $30 even. If the next trade takes place at $30.01, it's "ticking up." If it then trades at $30.00 again, it's "ticking down." (A zero-plus tick means the transaction was at the same price as the one before, but still higher than the nearest preceding price. A zero-minus tick indicates the stock traded at the same price as the prior trade, but still lower than the nearest preceding price.)

The TICK median line is zero, and the TICK quote will usually be a number higher or lower than zero (a zero reading means it's unchanged on the day).

Figure 4–2. The top chart in this illustration is a five-minute chart of the NASDAQ 100 futures E-mini contract. The chart below it displays a five-minute chart of software giant Microsoft (MSFT) for the same day. Note how MSFT follows the general pattern as the NASDAQ futures contract.

So, if the NYSE TICK, for example, reads +120, it means 120 more stocks are ticking up than are ticking down. That's a positive sign. Maybe the TICK displays a reading of −745. That means 745 more stocks are ticking down than are ticking up, which is a negative reading.

When the TICK stays mostly above zero, it suggests a trading environment favorable to long trades and short covering. A TICK that dives below zero and remains in the minus zone implies an environment favorable to selling short and taking profits on long positions, when applicable.

Most of the time, you'll use the TICK as an overall positive or negative measurement for the market environment. Remember that the NYSE and NASDAQ TICK numbers change every other nanosecond. Just because a TICK falls from +3 to −40 in a heartbeat, don't yell "YIKES! GET ME OUT AT ANY PRICE!" and dump your long positions.

If you notice the TICK(s) dropping below zero and continuing to slide, however, check the futures and other market internals for a possible market shift. Then you may want to check your protective stops and possibly take some profits.

Intraday TICK extremes predict overbought/oversold conditions that transform the indicator to contrarian. When the NYSE TICK shoots to 1,100 or higher, the market's overbought. Nine times out of ten, the market will make a quick U-turn and slide south for a bit. (Again, that doesn't mean you *have* to sell all your long day trades, unless you're scalping. But you *should* monitor protective stops closely and take profits where appropriate.)

When the NYSE TICK dives to *minus* 1,000 and lower, it signals an oversold market. Once it plummets below −1,200 or so (catastrophic news can hammer it much lower), it usually bounces, at least temporarily.

As I write, the NASDAQ TICK tops out at an overbought area of about 900, and finds support in an oversold level of about −1,000.

The NYSE TICK serves as an informative indicator for trading the S&P 500 E-minis, as well as broad market stocks. The NASDAQ TICK works as an indicator for NASDAQ 100 E-mini traders, although some traders also like to reference the NYSE TICK.

Most traders read the TICK in conjunction with its chum, the TRIN. The TRIN, which is an acronym for "traders' index," was developed by Richard Arms in conjunction with NYSE data. Some quote services refer to it as the Arms index, or the MKDS.

Now, the other exchanges publish their own TRIN. It's a dandy volatility indicator that combines both breadth (advancing stocks compared to declining stocks) and volume measurements.

The calculation:

$$\frac{\text{Ratio of advancing/declining stocks}}{\text{Ratio of volume of advancing issues/declining issues}}$$

Fortunately, we don't have to sharpen our pencils to compute the TRIN. Again, your direct-access trading software should include that quote.

The median line for the TRIN is 1.0. When the TRIN rises above 1.0, market action focuses on declining stocks—a negative sign. When the TRIN falls below 1.0, rising stocks receive more attention—a positive sign. So, if you see the TRIN reading at 1.2, for example, it's giving a mildly negative signal. A TRIN reading of, say, .72 is positive.

By now you've noticed an important characteristic of the TRIN: It moves in the opposite direction of other momentum indicators. As you'll see in a moment, when the TRIN moves to its lowest extremes, it tells us the market is oversold. Fear goads sellers to dump stocks like crazy. At high readings, the

TRIN warns us the market is overbought. Buyers are floating in Euphoriaville and gobbling up everything in sight.

When the NYSE TRIN reads in the range of .5 to 1.0, market players feel affable and relatively content. The environment favors long positions.

If the NYSE TRIN rises to 1.20 and higher, though, you'll see major indexes and stocks head south and the market dip into oversold territory.

Days when the TRIN slides below .50, the market climbs into overbought territory. Look for an upcoming pullback.

The roguish NASDAQ TRIN tends to skip up and down between wider extremes. At the present, you'll see it skid to overbought levels as low as .10 before it bounces. And it can shoot to 2.0, or even more extreme overbought levels, before it turns downward on profit-taking.

Although you can observe the TICK and TRIN independently, I pair them together. Typically, they each head in opposite directions. When the TICK boogies happily above zero for a period of time, the TRIN usually sidesteps below 1.0. Again, that environment favors long positions.

If the TICK slogs around below zero, look for the TRIN to use the 1.0 level and above as its stomping ground. A negative TICK and TRIN that reads 1.0 and higher suggests a market conducive to short trades.

Do the TICK and TRIN *always* move in opposite directions and thus confirm each other's signals? Nope. They don't. Occasionally—especially in slow, negative markets and during options expiration day (third Friday of every month)—they get catawampus to each other—especially the NASDAQ TICK and TRIN. Still, they give great clues to market direction much of the time.

I keep both the New York Stock Exchange and NASDAQ Stock Exchange TICK and TRIN quotes on my screen when I trade. The quotes themselves give me enough information. You may prefer to chart them.

Idea: Create them as line charts, instead of bars or candles. Line charts show clear direction without any clutter.

Figures 4–3 and 4–4 display ten-minute line charts of the TICK and TRIN for both the NYSE and NASDAQ.

Action Item Three: Monitor Market Pulse with Put/Call Ratio and VIX

Two more indicators you may want to add to your trading arsenal come to us courtesy of the Chicago Board Options Exchange (CBOE). They are the put-to-call ratio and VIX.

If you are an active trader and can watch another indicator, or two, without

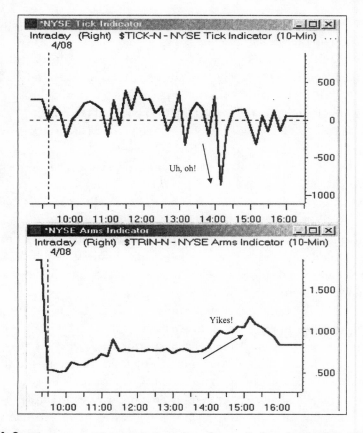

Figure 4–3. These two 10-minute intraday charts display the NYSE TICK and TRIN. Notice how the TICK stayed above the zero line (positive) until just after 2 p.m. (14:00) EST, then dove to nearly −1,000 for a few minutes before it revived. Also at 2 p.m., the TRIN, which had been dozing under 1.0 for most of the day, etched a mini-trend higher, to about 1.25. Before the closing bell, however, the TICK settled back into positive territory, and the TRIN fell back to just below 1.0.

going cross-eyed and alarming your optometrist, stay with us on this discussion of sentiment- and fear-based indicators. Day traders can use these intraday as decision support tools. Swing and position traders will check these indicators on daily charts to monitor the market's pulse. Interpreting the signals these indicators give should help keep you on the right side of trends.

In the long term, business environment and economic conditions drive the financial markets.

Short-Term, however, emotions ranging from greed and euphoria to fear and outright panic stimulate market motion. Indeed, the markets soar because participants feel confident about the future and think prices will rise. The markets crumble if players feel panicky about the future and expect prices to fall.

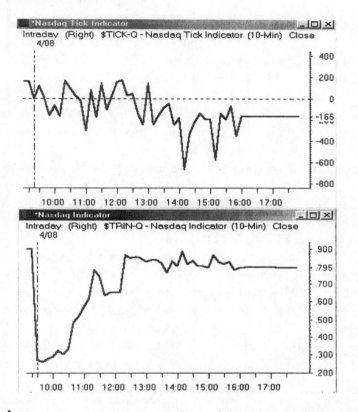

Figure 4–4. Here you can see 10-minute charts of the NASDAQ TICK and TRIN. These charts display the same day's indicator action as in Figure 4–3, the NYSE TICK and TRIN. The NASDAQ TICK wiggled above *and* below its zero median until about 2 p.m. EST, when it took a dive similar to the NYSE's. The NASDAQ TRIN started in oversold territory (the dotted vertical line denotes the market open of a new day), then climbed all morning to hover in the 0.90 area in the afternoon. Check out the NASDAQ index futures in Figure 4–2, and note how they moved lower much of the day, as the NASDAQ TRIN moved higher.

The put/call ratio is an excellent indicator with which to quantify crowd emotion, or sentiment. Options players buy calls when they feel bullish and think the underlying stocks will increase in value. A "call" is an option contract that gives the holder the right to buy the underlying security at a specified price for a certain, fixed period of time.

Conversely, options players buy puts when they feel bearish and believe the market will fall. A "put" is an option contract that gives the holder the right to sell the underlying security at a specified price for a certain fixed period of time.

The p/c ratio equals put-option volume divided by call-option volume.

The CBOE calculates p/c ratio for stocks, indexes, and the combined total traded on their exchange. The stock ratio generally states public sentiment. The index, or OEX (S&P 100) ratio, relays the outlook of institutional players. Since institutions play bigger share size, and as they tend to use options as hedging tools, the index p/c ratio portrays readings different from the stock ratio. Bottom line: We'll use the CBOE p/c ratio, which combines them both.

If you have a direct-access trading platform, you can observe the total p/c ratio intraday. Or go to *cboe.com* and click on "Market Data" and "Intraday Volume." As of this writing, the CBOE updates put/call volume and the total ratio every half hour during the trading day.

Swing traders and position traders can use the end-of-day data posted on the CBOE by going to *cboe.com*, clicking on "Market Data," then "Market Statistics."

The p/c ratio is a contrarian sentiment indicator that is most useful when it reaches extremes. The theory assumes that options players are overly emotional. They buy puts when they should be buying calls, and vice versa.

Although extreme readings alter slightly in different market environments, it's safe to say that when the ratio moves above .60, market mood is bearish. When it penetrates 1.0 and higher, the already fearful bears become panicky. If you have open short positions, start peeling off gains. Then scan for long setups so you'll be ready in case the market bounces off lows and reverses to the upside.

If the p/c ratio moves below .50, market environment is bullish. But if it keeps heading lower, and falls below .40, it suggests traders are living in La-La Land, and overdosing on calls. A market top may be in the offing. You'll want to pinpoint long positions for possible profits, then keep an eye out for short setups.

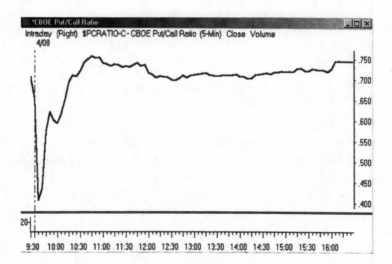

Figure 4–5. In this intraday line chart of the CBOE put/call ratio, which displays the same day's market action as in Figures 4–1 through 4–4, you will note that this contrarian sentiment indicator pedaled along the same general track as the TRIN. As the broader markets edged down, the ratio moved up, as more market participants bought puts (bearish).

Figure 4–5 shows an intraday line chart of the p/c ratio.

Figure 4–6 displays daily charts of the Dow Jones Industrial Average and p/c ratio.

The p/c ratio works best in trending markets. When a market top is in the making, bulls and bears can change sides in a heartbeat. The p/c ratio readings are not at their most predictive during these periods.

Also, please keep in mind that the p/c ratio—or any other indicator, for that matter—is *not* the Holy Grail. Use the p/c ratio in conjunction with other market indicators.

Finally, know that one day's extreme reading doesn't ensure a market top or bottom. Track several days of readings and compare them with market highs and lows, to see the complete picture.

The final indicator in this action item, the VIX, also comes to us courtesy of

Figure 4–6. In these daily charts of the Dow Jones Industrial Average and the CBOE p/c ratio, you will note how the ratio started climbing in March, as bearish options players bought more and more puts. At the same time, the Dow Jones Industrial Average began to fall. By the last week of March, however, that fear escalated to extremes and drove the p/c ratio to 1.33 (arrow). That contrarian signal told traders to look for long setups. A week later, the Dow Jones Industrial Average etched a relative new high (arrow).

the CBOE. The CBOE launched the VIX—volatility index—in 1993. This index measures market expectations of near-term volatility conveyed by stock index option prices. Since volatility often signifies financial turmoil, VIX is often referred to as the "investor fear gauge," or a "fear-based" indicator.

Like the TRIN and p/c ratio, the VIX is a contrarian indicator that tracks in the opposite direction of the broader market.

Since 1997, the VIX has traditionally traded in a range between the 15 and 40 levels. A VIX of 15 percent suggests that options traders in the S&P 500 Index (SPX) options expect the SPX to move in a 15 percent range over the next 12 months.

Conversely, a VIX reading of 40 percent or higher implies an expected market movement of 40 percent from low to high during the next year.

Translation: When the VIX dives to 20, or below, look for the market to get too complacent. Television announcers will prattle that the market is "toppy" and "frothy" (meaning lots of high-priced bubbles with no substance).

Conversely, if the VIX shoots up through 30 and ramps north to the 40 mark, a market bottom may soon appear.

Figure 4–7 shows weekly charts of the S&P 500 Index and the VIX.

As you can imagine, VIX made a multi-year high of 43.74 on September 16, 2001, the first day the markets opened after 9/11 (not shown on chart).

Although plotting the VIX on daily charts is sufficient for swing and position traders, Figure 4–8 shows a five-minute chart of the S&P 500 Index over a five-minute chart of the VIX. When you are day-trading and using the VIX as an indicator, think of it as an inverse indicator for price movement. Again, this is the same day used in prior illustrations in this chapter, so you can compare the VIX's movement to that of the TICK and TRINs, and p/c ratio.

FYI: If you enjoy watching the VIX, you can now trade VIX options and futures. Go to the CBOE Web site for more information.

NASDAQ traders: The VXN is the CBOE NASDAQ Volatility Index, which came on the market in January 2001. Like the NASDAQ, it is volatile. VXN readings have risen to highs (oversold) in the 70s and 80s, and current lows (overbought) in the 20s. On September 16, 2001, the first day the financial markets opened after 9/11, it spiked to 99, but we'll consider that to be an anomaly. As of this writing, the VXN has trended downward since its inception, and not found a trading range. If you'd like to use it in conjunction with your NASDAQ trades, check out current highs and lows at the CBOE Web site to determine overbought/oversold levels.

By now, some of you surely feel like you are up to your eyeballs in indicators. I bet my duck slippers I know the question perched on the tip of your tongue: "Holy Moly, I'll end up in Pecan Manor (the nut farm) if I have to watch *all* of those indicators at the same time. Which ones do I watch, when?"

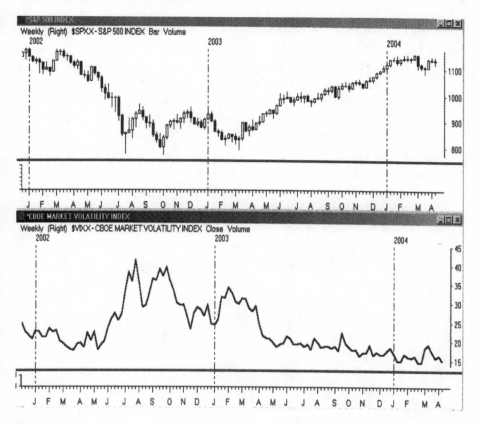

Figure 4–7. The two charts shown in this illustration are weekly charts of the S&P 500 index, stretching for more than two years, with a corresponding weekly line chart of the VIX, below it. You can clearly see how the S&P and the VIX tend to move in opposite directions, with the VIX bottoming below 15 and topping above 40. For many years, the VIX was calculated from options traded on the OEX, or S&P 100 index. In 2004, however, the CBOE began calculating VIX from options traded on the benchmark S&P 500 index.

Answer:

- **New active traders:** Start with an intraday chart of the S&P 500 E-mini futures on your screen. Then add *either* quotes or a line chart in the same time frame of the NYSE (and/or NASDAQ) TICK and TRIN, *or* the VIX or VXN. (Use the p/c ratio for longer-term trades.) When you become comfortable with one set of blinking numbers, add or substitute others and decide which adapt well to your personal trading style. Above all, keep your screen simple enough that you avoid feeling overwhelmed.

- **Swing and position, or trend traders:** You do not *have* to watch intraday charts of the stock index futures, although the S&P and/or NASDAQ

Figure 4–8. On this five-minute chart of the S&P Index and corresponding chart of the VIX, note how both sidestepped through the morning hours. After the midday doldrums, the S&P tumbled downhill, marked by an uphill climb by the VIX. The two charts clearly show that when prices fall, volatility rises.

E-mini futures can help you refine your entry. Nor do you need to observe intraday TICK and TRIN movements. You may want to plot daily charts of the p/c ratio and the VIX and/or VXN to use as decision support tools. Now and then, flip to weekly charts of these indicators to obtain an overall view of market action.

Action Item Four: Develop Your Watch List

A question I hear the most often from stock traders is, "How do I develop my watch list?"

One way to find stocks to trade is to go to my Web site, *toniturner.com*, and check out the "Sectors & Stocks" page. There, you will find a list of sectors and industry groups with a selection of prominent companies under each. Please understand that these lists are not "buy" or "sell" suggestions. They are a reference guide to stock selection.

Another avenue: Go to *holdrs.com*. The HOLDRS are ETFs, or single stocks that represent industry groups. Click on "HOLDRS Outstanding" and you'll see a list of HOLDRS, including Biotech (symbol BBH), Internet (HHH), Regional Banks (RKH), and Wireless (WMH).

Now, for example, click on the Wireless HOLDRS and you'll see a list of the stocks represented in that group, with their weighting. For the WMH, the stocks weighted the most highly are presently QUALCOMM Inc., Motorola, Inc. (MOT), and Verizon Communications (VZ). If you want to add wireless stocks on your watch list, you may choose to add these companies.

If you trade with direct-access software, you should be able to access a comprehensive list of indices, such as the SOX, the Philadelphia Semiconductor Index; the MSH, or Morgan Stanley High Technology Index; and the DRG, the Amex Pharmaceutical Index and their equity components.

Of course, you can find industry groups and stocks that reside in them at Web sites like *marketgauge.com*. Please choose stocks to trade that have a minimum average daily volume of at least 300,000 shares for swing trades, and 800,000 to 1 million shares for day trades. Trading low-volume stocks equals high risk.

Once you develop a basic watch list, scan your stocks for setups. Next, narrow down the setups to a focus list of candidates that represent the highest probability of success. Overall, I look for leading stocks in leading industries when the market trends up, and lagging stocks in weak industries to sell short when the market trends down.

I keep my watch list separated into sectors or industry groups, with five or so stocks under each heading. If you are a novice, start your watch list with ten stocks you get to know well. When you feel comfortable, add more and "fire" the issues that turn disorderly and unstable (no trend, no follow through, and lots of gaps on a daily chart).

Stocks are like people. They each have different personalities and they each act differently during the trading day. If you are brand-new to trading, please don't jump into hot-tempered stocks, especially for day trades. Tech stocks remain the "bad boys" of the market, and certain issues dart all over pricewise on an intraday basis.

Look for stocks that "chart well." That means they make orderly patterns and trends with few gaps, and keep their erratic behavior to a minimum. Volatile, unpredictable stocks have a tendency to zig when you thought they would zag. Lots of zigs equal lost money.

Step Six—Strategize Your Success

Action Item One: Become an Expert on One or Two Setups

Say you were going into the hospital for heart surgery. Aren't the odds of successful surgery higher if it's performed by a cardiologist rather than a general practitioner? Heck, yes! The doctor who spends years specializing in heart functions knows more about them (we hope) than the physician who treats heart conditions sporadically.

That's why it makes perfect sense, especially early in your trading career, to become a specialist in one or two setups. Those who are "jacks of all setups, king of none," have a difficult time of it.

You already know why the ability to identify solid setups is so important. No matter what trading vehicle you use, it takes three basic steps to execute a trade. First you locate the setup, then you decide on the entry, and assuming you enter the trade, the final step is to exit the trade. Without a high-quality setup in place, the other actions are null and void.

Fortunately, your knowledge of technical analysis will work well to help you spot good setup opportunities in all time frames, with all trading vehicles.

As we mentioned in chapter 3, virtually all setups emerge from four basic patterns. By way of review, they are: In the context of an uptrend, 1) breakout from a consolidation, 2) breakout from a pullback. In a downtrend (reverse the image), 3) breakdown from a consolidation, and 4) breakdown from a rally.

A zillion variations on these themes make up the universe of setups. Glance over the selection of setups listed on most scanning software, and you'll see what I mean. Taking price action as a given, setups are based on lists of criteria that include candle reversal patterns, volume, moving averages, momentum indicators, Fibonacci retracement levels, and, for some folks, the current position of the moon and stars (really!).

As a shrewd trader, you'll concentrate on setups that match present-time market flow. For example, if the market (reference the Dow Industrials index,

S&P 500 index, and NASDAQ 100 or NASDAQ Composite index) has slid in a downtrend and appears to be finding a bottom, keep an eye on stocks and their industry groups that unwind in orderly bases and form setups ripe for a break-out. When these issues scoot to the upside and climb through prior price resistance on the wings of strong volume, that's your entry.

Or perhaps the market has flown up in an uptrend and is now rolling over into a downtrend. You may study the characteristics of a throwback rally (initial lower high) in a downtrend. When a rally moves up to price resistance, then falters and starts to fall, that's your shorting entry. You can also focus on reversal patterns, such as the double top, double bottom, and so forth.

If you are confused, worry not. We'll be talking about characteristics of setups all the way through this book, with plenty of charts included.

Bottom line: Traders who become expert at one or two setups and trade them well minimize losses and enhance their odds of easier profits.

Action Item Two: Add the ADX and Fibonacci Retracements to Your Technical Analysis Toolbox

The ADX (Average Directional Movement Index) is a nifty chart indicator you can use to gauge the strength of a trend. It's a popular component of the Directional Movement system developed by market technician Welles Wilder. We'll discuss the ADX and other momentum filters in the Directional Movement system in chapter 8.

Along with most indicators, Fibonacci retracement levels are a derivative of price. These percentage ratios, however, add a different dimension to support and resistance, as they represent three basic proportions present in nature.

Fibonacci retracement levels were born, literally, from a mathematical problem posed by a twelfth-century Italian mathematician, Leonardo Fibonacci Pisano, regarding the romantic antics of two rabbits. I promise, it's true. You'll discover in chapter 8 how the rabbits and the number of offspring they birthed resulted in important percentages that make great decision support tools.

Action Item Three: Brush Up on Economic Reports

When economic reports are released, the market ingests them, and the index futures immediately reflect whether they like "the numbers" . . . whether they don't . . . or whether they consider them with nothing more than a bored yawn.

Reports come out every week of the month. Most are released at either 8:30 a.m. or 10:00 a.m. EST, and are broadcast immediately by the financial networks. These reports include retail sales, the PPI (producer price index), the CPI (consumer price index), ISM (Institute of Supply Management), housing starts, and the GDP (gross domestic product).

To the degree that the report relates to a vital segment of the current U.S. economy, it may or may not deliver a wallop that moves the market higher or lower.

For example, if the economy is floundering, and workers are being laid off, the unemployment report (released the first week of the month at 8:30 a.m. EST) gains critical attention. If inflation rears its ugly head, traders watch the core PPI (core = calculated without volatile food and energy prices), which measures prices of goods at the wholesale level. Traders also follow Retail Sales Ex Autos (excluding automobile sales) as a timely barometer of consumer spending habits, particularly over the Christmas holidays.

Here's the trick with economic reports and, indeed, all economic and financial news: *You don't play the news. You play the market's* reaction *to the news.* As you've probably discovered by now, Mother Market's reaction to events and how she interprets them can seem illogical. So don't try to predict her reaction. Wait for it.

As a sharp trader, you'll want to remain aware of the economic reports released each week. For an explanation of major economic reports and their release dates, go to *toniturner.com* and click on "Economic Reports."

Action Item Four: Your Success Journal—Give Yourself the Gift that Keeps on Giving

We all know the definition of insanity: we repeat the same action over and over again—and expect different results!

Most of us repeat trading mistakes several times over. Then we wonder why our account total remains stagnant—or worse.

Some people have a habit of entering trades too late; some get in too early. Some take profits too soon. Others wait too long—until the profit's come and gone.

Do any of those descriptions fit you? The sooner you start recording trades and their details in your journal—I call mine my "Success Journal"—the sooner you will identify your weak spots and replace them with good habits. Conscientious trading habits equal higher profits.

Streamline your learning process and create a simple but effective trading journal that lists:

- Date, symbol, share size.

- Why did you enter the trade? What were the signals? (If you don't have an answer for these questions *before* you enter the trade, please rethink your trading strategy.)

- Intended time frame: day trade, swing trade, position or core trade.

- Risk–reward objectives.

- Exit price, and reason for exiting.

- Print out a copy of the stock's chart(s), or capture it and include it in an electronic journal. Draw trend lines and make notes on the chart. Put arrows where you entered and exited. Did your plan make sense? How did the final price pattern play out after you entered?

- *Most important:* What did you learn from the trade that you can use in the future?

One night a week, or on weekends, when the market's closed, schedule a quiet time. Make a personal appointment with your journal—and keep it. Evaluate each one of your trades. As you read over the entries, you may find a common thread that cuts your profits short. Once you identify the problem, you can work on replacing it with a different action.

Of extreme importance: examine the sum of your losses, then the sum of your profits. As you progress, your profits should increase until they are at least twice your losses. Otherwise you'll want to revisit your risk-reward and money-management tactics, along with your overall approach to the market.

Remember to congratulate yourself every time you make a winning trade that you planned and executed perfectly. If you were "stopped out" of the trade and if your initial plan was a good one, congratulate yourself if you followed it from entry to exit.

Will you ever be such a mega-trader that you won't need to make journal entries? Maybe. If you are like the rest of us, however, you'll continue to expand your skills and experience the growing pains.

Maintaining a success journal keeps you on track for improving your trading skills at a rapid clip. Promise—and deliver—this gift to yourself. You'll thank yourself later, and so will your trading account!

Step Seven—Review, Renew, Reconnect

I call step 7 the "growth step." It serves as a reminder to examine your learning process and review your progress.

Study your mistakes with an honest eye, use them as learning tools, and re-calibrate your tactics. Next, scrutinize your victories, then decide how you can "raise the bar." Then you can decide how to raise your personal best to new levels.

Action Item One: Review Your Process and Progress

It's time to exhale. If you can, please take a week off from trading to complete the process in this step. Loosen up, take long walks, and take quality time *by yourself, with yourself*. Reflect on the actions you've taken, where you want to go next, and how you plan to get there. You are worth this time, and so is your trading career.

Ask yourself questions, such as:

- Does my business plan reflect my goals? Am I using it to its best advantage? How can I revise it to better suit my expectations and objectives?

- Does my trading style agree with my personality? Do I feel a sense of calm and confidence when I trade? Or do I feel uncomfortable and nervous?

- Have I planned my trades consistently well, and improved upon those plans? What areas of preparation do I need to revisit?

- How can I enhance my pre-market analysis to better serve and support my trades?

- Which areas of my technical analysis knowledge base are weak? Which are strong? What steps can I take to strengthen my skills?

- Are my trades ego-based or plan/system-based? How can I eliminate more of my ego and the "need to be right" from my trades?

- Do the results I've created point to a bigger investment in myself and my career by way of a trading course, school, or mentorship?

These questions will lead to others. Answer honestly. Then use your answers to create your own "action items" that will improve every aspect of your trading.

Action Item Two: Hey, Traders—It's Fear O'clock . . . Do You Know Where *Your* Emotions Are?

Novice traders, and occasionally experienced traders, become vulnerable to three fear-based syndromes that slither into their office and seemingly grab their computer controls and populate order-entry screens.

The first devilish condition is known as "chasing." This syndrome manifests itself in euphoric environments.

Say a stock has broken to new highs and is burning up a trader's screen with higher and higher prices. The trader watches, his heart racing, as the stock heads for the moon. Ignoring his conscience, feeling only the thrill of the chase, the trader keys in a limit order for a thousand shares of the stock at the offer price. The stock explodes higher. His order goes unfilled.

The trader pounds on his desk. Then he resubmits his order at "the market." His order is filled. Elation! The stock soars higher. The trader, his heart hammering in his ears, throws in another thousand-share market order.

Suddenly, the stock halts and trembles. After a mighty shudder, the price plummets straight down. The trader stares, disbelieving, his hands paralyzed on his keyboard. Finally—frantically—he fumbles for his mouse. With shaking hands he keys in the order to sell his shares at the market price. His trade confirmation soon stares back at him . . . validating his fears. The loss is a big one.

What will our trader do the next time he sees a stock screaming to the moon? He'll grin, shrug, and go hunting for a high-opportunity setup where he can buy into the birth of an explosion, instead of its leftover smoke and final, dying sparks.

The next malady common to those new to the markets is "revenge trading."

The author John Ford once wrote, "Revenge is its own executioner." And in trading, that statement holds mighty true.

Say Fickle Freightways rolls into a great setup for a long day-trade. You buy five hundred shares. But alas, Fickle soon makes a U-turn and heads south. When it hits your protective stop, you grit your teeth, sell the position, and take a loss.

You want revenge. You want it *now*.

Muttering, "Hey turkey, make my day," you quickly sell short five hundred shares of Fickle. It falls for a few moments . . . and you smile with satisfaction. Ah, sweet revenge.

Seconds later, though, Fickle finds support, quivers, and scurries higher. Faster and faster it flies. "Rats!" you yell, as it shoots through your entry price. Fumbling, you buy to cover at the market price. Then you stare glumly at your trade sheet. You've racked up another loss.

The next time a trade goes against you, please don't take it out on the stock. This kind of revenge is like taking poison and expecting your enemy to die.

The last habit that sneaks up on new traders is "overtrading." Dr. Brett Steenbarger, psychologist, author, and trader, whose quiz follows in the next section, says, "Overtrading is the most common source of losses among the traders I've interviewed. Traders overtrade when they feel internal pressures to make money that blind the trader to what is happening in the markets at the time."

Indeed, this syndrome is insidious, and can even go unnoticed until commission charges are tallied, or trade sheets are looked at as a monthly statement. It usually operates under the "hamster effect." The trader makes a zillion haphazard trades, and only his or her broker gets richer. Many involve chasing stocks, revenge-trading *those* trades, or averaging down (buying a stock as it tumbles, in hopes of lowering cost basis).

Early in my trading career, I remember one October in which I overtraded to the max. When I received my brokerage statement for that month, it was as thick as the Manhattan phone directory.

I still remember how I stared, slack-jawed, at the endless list of trades. What had I been thinking? I made a profit, but certainly not enough to justify my trading rampage, nor the commission charges I paid.

One well-planned trade will yield more profits than five badly planned, what-the-heck trades. The pros don't trade "just to trade." And as astute traders, neither do we.

Action Item Three: Take Dr. Brett's Three Dimensions (3D) Trader Personality Quiz

By now you've realized that your success as a trader is highly correlated with your mindset and your personality.

As previously mentioned, I am delighted and gratified that Brett Steenbarger, Ph.D., agreed to design a quiz specially for this book and its readers. Director of Trader Development for Kingtree Trading, LLC in Chicago, and Associate Professor of Psychiatry and Behavioral Sciences at SUNY Upstate Medical University in Syracuse, New York, Dr. Steenbarger is an active trader. He is also the author of *The Psychology of Trading,* which I highly recommend.

I trust you will find Dr. Steenbarger's personality quiz insightful, productive, and enjoyable.

Dr. Brett's Three Dimensions (3D) Trader Personality Quiz

by Brett N. Steenbarger, Ph.D. *brettsteenbarger.com*

When traders run into emotional difficulties with their trading, they often assume that they have deep, dark, underlying personality conflicts that require therapy. Sometimes this is true, but very often the source of the problems is different. Often there is a mismatch between the method or system that a trader is using and the trader's needs and personality.

Instead of berating themselves for a lack of "discipline," traders need to ask whether their challenges in following a methodology might be because the methods aren't right for them. Finding the proper fit between who you are and how you trade is a big part of finding success in trading.

The following questions are designed to help you assess facets of your personality that are related to the kinds of trading approaches that are likely to work for you. Please remember, *there are no right or wrong answers.* None of the questions are designed to evaluate your emotional stability or mental health. Rather, we are trying to find out your personal style, so that you can match it to your trading style. Each item consists of two statements.

Please choose the statement that best describes you:

1a) I often arrive early for appointments and events to make sure I'm not late.

1b) I'm not very time-oriented and often show up late to appointments and events.

2a) When a problem occurs in my trading, I first feel frustrated and vent my feelings either outwardly or at myself.

2b) When a problem occurs in my trading, I first try to focus on what went wrong and what I can do to fix it.

3a) When I go out to eat, I generally go to my favorite restaurants and order my favorite foods.

3b) When I go out to eat, I like to try new and unfamiliar restaurants and foods.

4a) I tend to be detail-oriented and try to get each aspect of a job done as well as I can.

4b) I focus on the big picture instead of details and don't sweat the small aspects of a job.

5a) If you could hear the thoughts in my head as I'm trading, you'd hear worried or negative thoughts.

5b) If you could hear the thoughts in my head as I'm trading, you'd hear me analyzing the market action.

6a) If I had a choice of car to drive, I would choose one that is comfortable and quiet.
6b) If I had a choice of car to drive, I would choose one that is fast and handles well.

7a) I would be good at following a diet or exercise program.
7b) I would often cheat on a diet or exercise program.

8a) It is hard for me to shake off setbacks in the market.
8b) I take market setbacks as a cost of doing business.

9a) I like vacations that are peaceful and relaxing.
9b) I like vacations where you see and do a lot of different things.

10a) I get routine maintenance done on my car when it is scheduled.
10b) I don't follow deadlines for routine maintenance on my car.

11a) Sometimes, when I'm trading, I feel on top of the world; other times, I feel depressed, or down on myself.
11b) I don't have many emotional ups or downs in the market.

12a) I would like a job with a stable company that pays a guaranteed salary and benefits, even if I might not get rich.
12b) I would like a job with a startup company that offers me a chance to get rich, even if I might get laid off if things don't work out.

13a) I try to eat healthy foods and get a good amount of exercise and rest.
13b) I'm very busy and don't always eat, exercise, and sleep as I should.

14a) I trade by my gut.
14b) I trade with my head.

15a) I avoid arguments and conflict.
15b) I like to argue and hash things out.

Dr. Brett's Scoring

Items 1, 4, 7, 10, and 13 measure a personality trait called "conscientiousness." A conscientious person is someone who has a high degree of self-control and perseverance. If you scored mostly a) responses for these items, you are high in conscientiousness. Conscientious traders are good rule-followers, and they often do well trading mechanical systems. Traders who are low in conscientiousness will have difficulty following explicit rules and often trade more discretionarily. Ideally, you want a style of trading that is more structured and detail-oriented if you are more conscientious. Trying to trade in a highly structured manner will only frustrate a trader who is low in conscientiousness. Such a trader would do better with big-picture trades that do not require detailed rules and analysis. Similarly, very active trading with rigid loss control will come easier to the conscientious trader; less frequent trades with wider risk parameters will come easier to the trader lower in conscientiousness.

Items 2, 5, 8, 11, and 14 measure a personality trait called "neuroticism." Neuroticism is the tendency to experience negative emotions. If you scored mostly a) responses for these items, you are relatively high in neuroticism. The trader prone to neuroticism tends to experience more emotional interference in his or her trading. Wins can create overconfidence; losses can create fear and hesitation. The trader who is low in neuroticism is more likely to react to trading problems with efforts at problem-solving and analysis. He or she will not take wins or losses particularly personally.

Neuroticism is a mixed bag when it comes to trading. Often the person who is high in neuroticism is emotionally sensitive and can use this sensitivity to obtain a gut feel for market action. The trader who is low in neuroticism may experience little emotional disruption with trading, but may also be closed off to subtle, intuitive cues when a trade starts to go sour.

In my recent experience, I have been surprised at how successful gut traders are often relatively neurotic traders. Very active trading methods are particularly challenging for such traders, as they don't allow much time for regaining emotional equilibrium after losses. This can lead to cascades of losses and significant drawdowns of equity. It is much easier for the non-neurotic trader to turn losses around, since these are less likely to be tied to self-esteem.

Items 3, 6, 9, 12, and 15 measure a trader's risk aversion. A risk-averse trader is one who cannot tolerate the possibility of large losses and who would prefer smaller, more frequent wins with controlled losses to larger wins with greater drawdowns. If you scored mostly a) responses for these items, you are a relatively risk-averse trader. Trading with careful stops and money management, and trading smaller time-frames where risk can be controlled with the holding period, will come most naturally for the risk-averse trader.

The risk-seeking trader is one who enjoys stimulation and challenge. Larger positions and longer holding periods are easier to tolerate for the risk-seeking trader.

Very often, the risk-seeking trader will be impulsive in entering trades and will have difficulty trading during periods of boredom (low volatility). The risk-averse trader often experiences difficulty hanging onto winning trades, and will cut profits short to avoid reversals. This trader will be challenged during periods of high market-volatility. Position sizing is key and often overlooked as a trading variable. Trading too small will bore the risk-seeking trader, who will then lose focus. Trading too large will overwhelm the risk-averse trader, who will also then lose focus.

Ultimately, it is the blending of these three dimensions of trader personality, and not any one in isolation, that is most important in shaping trading outcomes. In my experience as a psychologist, the traders who are most poorly suited to trading are those that are risk-seeking and who are low in conscientiousness and high in neuroticism. Such traders often take large gambles on impulse, and very often those impulses are driven by emotional frustrations. An example would be a trader who gets frustrated after a loss and doubles his position size on the next trade just to make the money back quickly.

Conversely, I have seen very few successful traders who were highly risk-averse. The risk-averse trader, particularly one who is high in neuroticism, is motivated more by a fear of loss than a desire for gain. This makes it difficult to sustain meaningful position sizes during promising trades. Often such traders berate themselves for being self-defeating or sabotaging, but the reality is that they might be better suited for investing than trading.

If I had to identify an ideal personality pattern for traders, I would say that such a person would be risk-tolerant, low in neuroticism, and high in conscientiousness. Such traders are generally good at following trading rules (entries, exits, money management) and disciplined in their preparation. They don't take losses personally, which gives them the perseverance to weather losing periods. When they see a good trade, they are comfortable trading in size, so that the average size of their wins exceeds that of their losses.

Finally, let me mention one other important dimension that is related to neuroticism and emotionality. I strongly suspect that cognitive style is just as important as personality style in trading. Some people process information intuitively, relying on gut cues and subtle, nonverbal information. Other people process information explicitly, through reasoning and analysis. Both cognitive styles can make traders money in the markets, but it is essential that one's cognitive style match one's trading methodology.

As one trades shorter and shorter time frames, moving from swinging to scalping, it is less practical to expect explicit analytical routines to guide trading. Very short-term trading is more about pattern recognition than historical research. Conversely, longer-term trades often benefit from modeling and statistical analysis that informs traders where the edge might lie. How traders process information most effectively is a neglected variable in selecting proper time frames to trade.

You can find Dr. Steenbarger's articles and trading strategies archived on his Web site, *brettsteenbarger.com*.

Action Item Four: Reconnect with the Market

By now you feel refreshed. You have taken a step back and cast a candid look at yourself and your progress. You've decided what works and what doesn't. You've used old challenges to create new opportunities. And, I trust, you feel energized and rejuvenated.

Take a few minutes each morning, before the opening bell rings, to close your eyes and prepare mentally for the day. Take a deep breath. Imagine yourself calmly and confidently executing trades. See yourself planning, executing, and exiting trades, both at stop points and at profit points, with poise and self-assurance. Declare . . . *know* . . . you are a successful trader. Then open your eyes, take another deep breath, and come back to reality. Sports figures use mental imagery before big events as a preparation tool. Try it—it works.

Congratulations. You've finished the *Seven Steps to Successful Trading*. I hope you've enjoyed the process as much as I enjoyed creating it.

Once again, the key point review lists the steps and their action items.

When you're ready, turn to chapter 5, and we'll head into the future!

Key Point Review

Step Five—Polish Your Performance

Action Item One: Trade When the Gettin' Is Good!

It's important to identify market environment accurately to make sure it agrees with your trading style. Here's where your knowledge of trend analysis comes in handy.

Action Item Two: Active Traders: Target Intraday Indicators

If you're an active, intraday trader with a direct-access trading account, you'll keep a chart of the S&P 500 E-mini futures and possibly NASDAQ 100 E-mini futures on your screen. You may want to watch the NYSE and/or NASDAQ TICK and TRIN, as well.

Action Item Three: Monitor Market Pulse with Put/Call Ratio and VIX

To stay on the right side of the current trend, swing and position traders will want to watch the put/call ratio, a good sentiment indicator, along with the VIX, a volatility indicator. Both are published by the CBOE.

Action Item Four: Develop Your Watch List

Create a watch list from leading stocks in leading industries in a bull market, and lagging stocks in weak industries in bear markets. Become familiar with the "personalities" of the stocks you monitor; choose stocks that chart well. When a stock's price pattern becomes disorderly and disorganized, fire it!

Step Six—Strategize Your Success

Action Item One: Become an Expert on One or Two Setups

Choose one or two setups that agree with overall market trend, then become an expert on those patterns.

Action Item Two: Add the ADX and Fibonacci Retracements to Your Technical Analysis Toolbox

Study and apply the ADX and "Fib" retracements to your trader's decision support toolbox.

Action Item Three: Brush Up on Economic Reports

The market's reaction to economic reports can apply very real force—positive or negative—to your trades. Brush up on which reports are important in current economic environments.

Action Item Four: Your Success Journal—Give Yourself the Gift that Keeps on Giving

Successful traders keep a journal of their trades, how they played out, and the lessons learned. This investment of time is an important part of an evolving trading career.

Step Seven—Review, Renew, Reconnect

Action Item One: Review Your Process and Progress

Ask yourself questions about every aspect of your approach to the market, from your business plan to your trading style to your emotions. Use the answers to these questions to make positive changes in the challenging areas and "raise the bar" on the strong areas.

Action Item Two: Hey, Traders—It's Fear O'clock . . . Do You Know Where *Your* Emotions Are?

Chasing stocks, revenge trading, and overtrading are monsters that creep into our trading offices and take over our order entry screens. If these monsters look familiar, take steps to eliminate them from your trading day.

Action Item Three: Dr. Brett's 3D Personality Quiz

It's important to your success that your trading style matches your personality.

Action Item Four: Reconnect with the Market

Now that you're refreshed and revitalized, reenter the market with your new foundation of knowledge and emotional discipline. Stop for a recheck whenever you feel it's necessary.

CENTER POINT

What Questions Do You Ask?

Quality questions create a quality life. Successful people ask better questions, and as a result, they get better answers.

—Anthony Robbins

How many times do we rush the week without really paying attention to our actions? How many times we attack our back-breaking schedules like frantic robots, stressed to the max with too much to do, and too little time to do it in?

When—if ever—do we stop and ask ourselves questions about our *busy*ness? "Is this project or chore *really* important, or even necessary? Could I use this time more wisely?"

If the project *is* important, when, if ever, do we think to ask ourselves questions that lead to a more fruitful outcome?

"What am I missing? How can I accomplish this task more efficiently and more effectively?" "How can I learn something new from completing this activity?" "How can I make this more enjoyable, more productive, more *fun?*"

If you paused during your busy day long enough to ask yourself questions such as these, followed by creative answers, could you engineer your time to be richer and more fulfilling? Good question, isn't it?

One of my favorite questions—and one that's pulled me through a number of challenges in my life (like writing three books!)—comes from Dr. Robert Schuller. He asks, "What would you attempt to do if you knew you could not fail?"

Try asking yourself that question. Your answer may be, "Hmm. If I knew I couldn't fail, I would do *this*, then *this*, and then *this*." All of a sudden, you'll find the fear of failure behind you, and a path of progress in front of you.

Keep asking yourself questions. Insightful questions. Creative questions. Encouraging questions. Lesson-point questions. Mind-broadening questions. Loving, powerful questions. If you concentrate on creating high-quality questions, and then come up with thoughtful and worthwhile answers, you will indeed raise the quality of your life!

CHAPTER FIVE

Cycles—The Wheels of Fortune

*In this game, the market has to keep pitching, but you don't have to swing. You can
stand there with the bat on your shoulder for six months until you get a fat pitch.*
                                                                    —Warren Buffet

Imagine, for a moment, that we've boarded a spaceship on a flight that carries us
high above planet Earth. From our vantage point in the stratosphere, we observe
with awe the exquisite sphere we inhabit. We continue to gaze, and it soon becomes clear—our world operates on a series of rhythmic checks and balances, or
cycles.

As our planet rotates on its axis, daylight dissolves into the night sky and
reappears hours later with satisfying predictability. Tides ebb and flow. Our seasons progress in phases from the summer heat to the brilliant, crisp months of
fall, into the cold quiet of winter, to the fresh breath of spring, into summer
warmth once again.

Cycles, which are generally defined as a series of events that recur regularly
and usually lead back to the starting point, have been observed and studied in as-
tronomy, biology, cosmology, commodities, economics, geology, geophysics, history, music, physics, society, and wars. In fact, the Foundation for the Study of
Cycles, in Wayne, Pennsylvania, has catalogued nearly twenty thousand cycles.

The Cyclical Nature of Financial Markets

Since cycles format our lives, it's easy to understand why business and financial
markets—which originate with humans, after all—churn through cycles on a
regular basis.

The cyclical nature of market prices first appeared in commodities prices,
with heating oil and agricultural commodities repeating seasonal ups and
downs. That makes sense, as weather cycles have a large impact on the supply
and demand of oil and food production.

You can spot cycles in the stock market on charts of every time frame—from
years to minutes. Longer cycles, however, generally depict clearer and more distinctive cycle patterns. Figure 5–1 illustrates how cycles move in a series of
peaks and troughs.

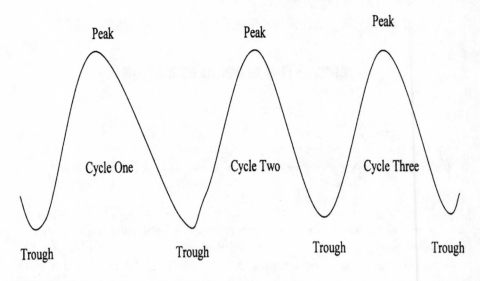

Figure 5–1. A cycle is an interval of time during which a series of recurring events is completed. Since cycles appear throughout our known universe, it makes sense that they emerge in the business and financial markets of industrialized nations. The movement from trough to peak to trough represents one cycle.

The U.S. business cycle makes a complete cycle from trough to peak to trough again, roughly every four years, with the stock market's primary trend revolving around that cycle. ("Roughly" is the operative word here. The cycle has varied between forty and fifty-three months.) Of course, U.S. presidential elections take place every four years and influence the cycle.

Figure 5–2 shows the Dow Jones Industrial Average on a monthly chart. You can see that a cycle started at the trough, or lows, in October 1998, rose to January 2000 highs, then fell back to 1998 lows by October of 2002.

The NASDAQ moved in a complete cycle from its lows in 1996, to moonshot highs in 2000, then back to those 1996 lows in October 2002. Since the NASDAQ is not representative of the entire U.S. economy, we can't hold it responsible for etching four-year cycles. Figure 5–3 shows the NASDAQ's trough-peak-trough cycle.

Now let's move to selected charts of Microsoft Corporation (MSFT), a weighty component of the NASDAQ 100 index. As you can see in the monthly chart displayed in Figure 5–4, Microsoft evolved through a multiyear cycle similar to that of the NASDAQ 100, although it didn't return to its 1996 lows. (Thank goodness!) Note the smaller cycles created in spans of months that form "Mister Softee's" (Microsoft's Wall Street nickname) larger cycle.

Figure 5–5 exhibits a weekly chart of MSFT, which moves in for a close-up. If you drew a horizontal line on this weekly chart of NASDAQ 100 Index

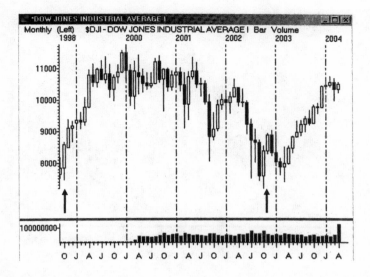

Figure 5–2. In this monthly chart of the Dow Jones Industrial Average, you can see how the Dow moved up from the 7,000 area in October of 1998, to its highs of 11,750 in January of 2000, then back to the 7,000 in October of 2002, in a four-year time span.

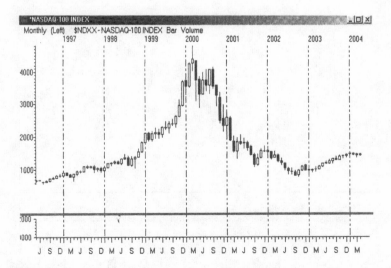

Figure 5–3. This monthly chart of the NASDAQ 100 index stretches in a time line that spans eight years. Notice how the index of top 100 NASDAQ stocks traced a near-perfect cycle from the sub-1,000 lows in 1996, to the March 2000 high of 4,816, then back down to the October 2002 lows of 795.

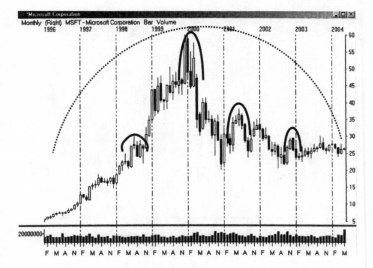

Figure 5–4. In this monthly chart of Microsoft Corp. (MSFT) that spans 8-plus years, you can see that the price has risen, topped out with the NASDAQ early in the year 2000, and rotated through a series of smaller cycles to present levels that match those of 1998. If you look closely, you can see many more minicycles in addition to those marked on the chart.

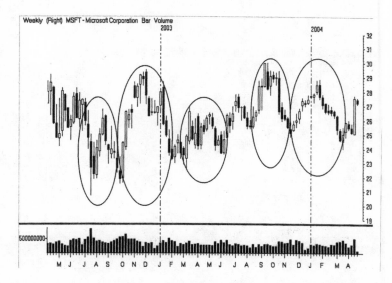

Figure 5–5. This weekly chart of Microsoft Corp. (MSFT) shows how several small cycles evolve in the context of the long-term cycle. In this case, MSFT has been grinding sideways for nearly two years, in what may turn out to be a long-term base. Of course, if the price breaks the July 2002 lows, Mister Softee may experience a downtrend.

component Microsoft Corp. (MSFT), starting at April 2002, and ending in April 2004, you'd find the beginning and final price to be $27. You could almost draw a straight line between those two dates. The price action between those two points, however, contained at least five minicycles.

Figure 5–6 shows a daily chart of MSFT. It zooms in to magnify the last price cycle in Figure 5–5, spanning November 2003 to March 2004. Again, you can spot short-term cycles that make up the larger one.

Figure 5–7 brings us to a ten-minute chart of our tech giant. It illustrates how microcycles participate in macro time-frames. Check out the larger cycle that begins on April 19 and ends on April 21. Then put on your reading glasses and find the smaller cycles that make up the larger one.

As you can see, we've gone from extended to short-term time frames, and cycles appear in all of them. Know that the longer time-frame you observe, the more complete cycles you will see. Longer time-frames show less "noise," or volatile interim price movement, so their structures are more apparent.

> **Hot Tip: Some equities adapt 28-day cycles (think "lunar cycle"). This time span refers to 28 calendar days, which contain about 20 trading days.**

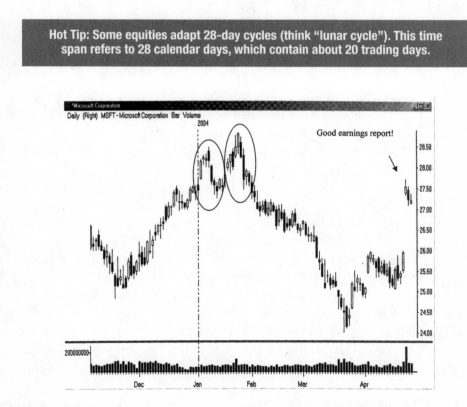

Figure 5–6. This daily chart of Microsoft Corp. (MSFT) shows two smaller cycles. If you look closely, you can find many smaller cycles in the context of the uptrend from November into mid-January, as well as in the downtrend that took place into the final week of March.

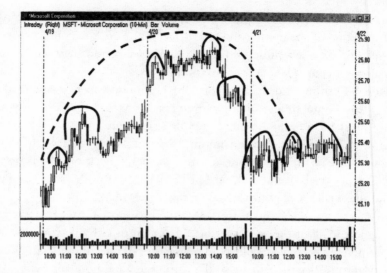

Figure 5–7. In this 10-minute chart of Microsoft Corp. (MSFT) that spans 3 trading days, you can spot one longer-term cycle over the course of 3 days (dotted line), plus many more, smaller cycles. If you were to move to a micro time-frame, such as a 1-minute chart (where each bar or candle represented one minute), you could see cycles there, as well.

Please don't assume that all cycles draw a complete, orderly arch, or bell curve. At a given moment, *price* represents consensus of opinion built upon expectations. Since those opinions change constantly, they influence the shape and time cycle of the markets.

That means cyclical price movement in an uptrend may not return all the way back down to the prior low. On the flip side, price in an uptrend may return to the low, slice through it, and skid even lower. This is especially true for minicycles formed by rallies in a downtrend.

Keep in mind that cycles also affect each other's momentum. For example, say you're trading a big-cap NASDAQ semiconductor stock. That stock's momentum and resulting price action will be influenced by the fluctuations of the NASDAQ indices, the NASDAQ 100 futures, the SOX (Semiconductor Index), the S&P 500 futures, overseas markets, and more.

You'll be hard-pressed to find a stock that moves strictly on its own steam with no outside intrusion. Exceptions are small-cap stocks or penny stocks that trade on thin volume, attracting little or no institutional representation (too small for the institutions to bother with).

Bottom line: At the very least, let this section on cycles serve to remind you of one lesson point—the market and its equities have elastic price action. When you're absolutely, positively *sure* the market you're trading will soar to the moon, the planets, and beyond . . . *forever and ever* . . . stop right there!

Remember, what goes up, *always* comes down—at least a little, and maybe a lot. For every up, there's a down. For every action, a reaction. That's the cyclical nature of our world and its operating system.

The Stock Market and Business Cycles: A Bi-cycle Built for Two

Two cycles track the U.S. economy: the business cycle and the stock-market cycle. While they move in tandem, the stock-market cycle many times speeds ahead of the business cycle. Why? Because again, people buy stocks based on expectations for the future. So the market cycle periodically acts as a leading indicator for the business cycle.

Let's look at the two cycles and how they evolve.

First, we'll raise the curtain on a typical stock-market cycle. Imagine, please, the stock market settling at its lows (trough) after a bear market, churning through the valley of a cycle bottom. Both bulls and bears occupy the valley. At the moment, the animals keep to themselves and tolerate each other's movements.

Suddenly, a large herd of bulls gathers on the horizon. The ground trembles as they stampede into the valley floor. Nostrils flaring, they stop to paw the earth and gaze at the mountain that looms in front of them. It promises rich fertile pastures, all the way to its glorious top.

Excitement courses through the veins of these mighty beasts. They begin their journey by charging up the series of ever-rising foothills at the mountain's base (early bull market). The enthusiastic herd attracts other bulls, and together they lope to even higher ground and a middle bull phase.

At that point, the bulls pause briefly to rest and graze in the lush pastures. But loftier ground looms before them. Excited and refreshed, they take off again, running faster and faster and reaching higher and higher altitudes. At last they arrive at the late bull phase, and soon after, the mountain's peak. Once there, they celebrate their strength and good fortune.

> **Hot Tip: In a bull market, three out of five stocks will chase the bull higher. In bear markets, as a rule, four out of five stocks follow the bears downhill.**

After a while, though, the bulls tire from their partying. Exhaustion takes over. They realize they have run out of ground, and the mountain top is strewn with rocks and chasms. Weary and hungover, the bulls lie down to rest.

But wait! Without warning, a large, burly bear appears on the horizon. Then another, and another. The bears have been in a long hibernation. Now, emerging from their caves, they feel irritable and hungry.

Spotting the heard of bulls and sensing the herd's weakened state, the bears give chase. The surprised bulls are out of shape from grazing too much on their recent mountain-climbing journey; they are no match for the ravenous bears. One by one, they fall prey to the sharp-clawed attackers (early bear market).

As the massacre progresses, a few surviving bulls spy a steep and narrow path that appears to lead down the other side of the mountain. They run to the trailhead in an effort to escape. A flock of bleating sheep, who had been shadowing the bulls and eating their leftovers, now joins the frantic bulls in their hasty retreat.

The bears stay hot on the heels of the fugitives. More bears charge out of their caves to gorge on faltering bulls and slow-footed sheep. The mêlée moves down the mountain hill en masse, fighting their way to the foothills and a late bear market.

After a time, the contenders find themselves in a new valley. The battle slows. The sheep have been slaughtered, and the now-tiny group of bulls who survived the conflict limp away to lick their wounds.

The bears, sated and burping from their feast, amble into a grove of large trees and lie down to rest in the shade.

Suddenly, without warning, the earth trembles with the sound of thundering hooves. A new herd of bulls, strong and stout, charges into the valley.

The sleepy bears, too bloated to fight, head into nearby forests to find new caves. Those who linger in the bulls' path are trampled and crushed.

The stampeding bulls head for the promising green foothills . . . and the cycle begins anew.

> **Hot Tip:** Markets fall faster than they rise. When considering the four-year business cycle, figure it will take longer to rise to its peak (ballpark estimate—30 months), than it will to tumble to its lows (18 months, plus or minus).

As you followed the battle market down the mountain, you may have wondered at the absence of the middle bear stage. Why wasn't that ground covered? Because fear is stronger than greed. Bear markets usually fall at a rapid pace, at an angle steep enough to skip a middle bear stage. Thus, bear markets many times fall faster than bull markets climb.

Now let's look at the business cycle. As you can imagine, it is propelled to a great degree by interest rates. Interest rates equal the cost of borrowing money.

Again, we'll start this cycle at the trough, or cycle lows. The trough of a business cycle represents stabilization after a recession; interest rates are low. This low lending rate boosts the economy, and the cycle moves up and into a recovery phase.

If economic growth continues, the cycle rises into a middle recovery phase.

Along the climb, prices of goods and services may inflate. In order to keep this inflation in check, the Federal Reserve Board raises interest rates to raise borrowing costs. Now companies have to pay more for the use of money, which dampens their earnings and lowers their incentive to borrow.

Momentum, however, will push the economic expansion higher and higher, to a point that will represent the peak.

Now the Fed will raise interest rates one too many times. The expansion stops cold in its tracks. The cost of borrowing money is too expensive. Hiring slows, and layoffs begin. The economy rolls over and tumbles into a recession.

The Fed winces and lowers interest rates to deflect a recession.

The effects of discounted interest rates, however, take time to flow through industry veins. With crimped earnings, mounting inventories, and employee cutbacks, business owners are in no mood to take advantage of cheapening money.

The downward spiral continues, and the recession deepens. The Fed continues to lower rates, maybe two, three, or four times. Everyone prays for a "soft landing."

At some point the economy does land—softly or not (think "valley or trough"). Finally, the reduced-rate environment soothes the weary recession. The now lean-and-mean companies start to eke out positive earnings, and signs of renewed hiring and manufacturing appear. Money is cheap, and lenders notice fresh lines of borrowers at their doors.

And, yes, you guessed it—the cycle starts over again.

What's Hot, What's Not—Sector Rotation

As stock market and business cycles churn through their phases, certain sectors of the economy profit from favorable conditions. This is called "sector rotation." As a shrewd trader, you'll have a distinct advantage knowing which sectors and industry groups are "hot" in recovering or recessionary economies, and which can be ignored or even sold short.

Study Figure 5–8 to see how sectors hand off the economic baton to each other as the market chugs up an economic recovery track to peak expansion, tops out and rolls over, then slides down a wall of economic contraction and into a recession.

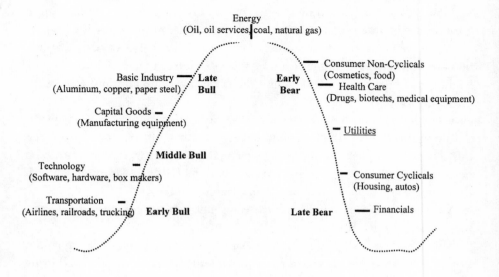

Figure 5–8. This drawing shows an overview of a stock-market cycle and the sectors that are strong in different phases of the cycle. Note that transportation and technology sectors thrive in the early bull market. Basic industry (think "aluminum, chemicals, copper, paper, steel") and manufacturing materials prosper as the market climbs to a late bull market. Energy stocks take the limelight at the bull market top. When the bulls see the bears charging in and signs of weakness appear, investors move into defensive equities, such as health care and consumer non-cyclicals (think "food, cosmetics, pharmaceuticals"). As the economy spirals down, utility stocks, which are interest-rate sensitive, jump into the spotlight. So do autos and housing, as discounted interest rates attract buyers of big-ticket items. In the late stages of a bear market, smart money moves into the financial sector. Lower interest rates support lending institutions, brokerages, and financial services.

At the beginning of a new bull market, check out industry leaders in transportation and technology stocks for trading and short-term investing on the long side. These stocks do well when the Fed rates are low. Choose established, reputable companies. They should move up nicely as new buyers move into the market, and short sellers buy as well, to cover and close their short trades.

> **Hot Tip: Transportation stocks typically rise when oil prices tank.**
> **Why? Lower fuel prices enhance earnings.**

As the market climbs, the Fed may start to raise interest rates, but the lending rate is still low enough for big money flow into capital goods. Look into the retail sector and cyclical stocks (aluminum, steel, paper) for good buying opportunities. Watch technology stocks spike to nosebleed altitudes.

When the economic expansion and bull market peaks, energy prices are red-hot. By this time, the Fed has hiked interest rates, probably from three to five times.

If you are holding long-term positions on the buy side, monitor the major indices for market fatigue and signs of distribution. Distribution is institutional selling. You can see it when the S&P 500 Index bangs up against resistance (supply) several times on a daily or weekly chart. If it can't rise above recent highs, and begins to slide south on heavy volume, start taking all or partial profits on your long positions. NASDAQ technology companies, who need low interest rates to survive, may already be weakening.

Let's say at this point the market crests and rolls over.

In an early bear market, you may want to take limited long positions in defensive groups. Check out drug companies and consumer noncyclicals, such as food and cosmetics. This makes sense, as prescription drugs and food are considered necessities.

Added to that, I can assure you male readers of one fact: No matter how bad the market, economy, or global conditions become . . . we women will *always* buy mascara and lipstick!

If the economy continues to grumble, the Fed will probably reverse its hiking habits and start to punch down rates. You'll want to scan the utilities sector for limited long positions. Utility companies have capital-intensive business models that are sensitive to falling interest rates.

The bear market deepens. This is the phase where news commentators frown more than usual and bark "soft landing" into the cameras at every opportunity. Financial gurus compare current bear market lows with lows from yesteryear.

Even though they may be wallowing in their lows, at this time, you may want to check out auto and housing stocks. If the Fed is still lowering rates, the "cheap money" helps these sectors to flourish.

As a rule, technology stocks are the most lucrative stocks to sell short in a bear market. Just be sure your heart is strong and your stops are well-placed. The ride down can turn your knuckles white!

> **Hot Tip: In bull markets, buy leading stocks in leading industries.
> In bear markets, sell short lagging stocks in lagging industries.**

In final phases of a bear market and early phases of a bull market, look for long opportunities in financial stocks such as banks, home-finance, and brokerage firms. Discounted interest rates encourage customers to refinance big-ticket items.

Whether we're experiencing a bull or bear market, you can understand why the ability to identify which sector is "hot" and which is not can add to your success as a trader. Research and preparation keeps you one step ahead of the crowd. You trade with the added support of the "smart money," and steer clear of the "dumb money" losses. It doesn't get any better than that!

Seasonality: Elections, Hemlines, and the Super Bowl

While we're on the subject of economic and market cycles, it seems a natural segue to hop into the study of stock-market seasonality.

As mentioned before, commodities were among the first critters in the financial markets to display seasonal ups and downs within the calendar year.

In the stock market, certain months have earned reputations for producing juicy profits on the long side. Other months tend to bully stocks lower. Summer months, for example, are notoriously nasty months for tech stocks. While you can't bank on that happening, it's a point of interest that converts into reality more times than not.

The study of market seasonality is interesting and fun. Wall Street pundits have applied seasonality to occasions from (mostly) straight-faced political events to whimsical happenings, such as the length of ladies' hemlines. (Shorter hemlines in style mean up market; longer hems in style mean down market.)

> **Hot Tip: The Super Bowl predictor insists that if the NFC team wins the Super Bowl, the market will go higher that year. If the AFC team wins, the market goes down. Use this indicator at your risk.** ☺

On a serious note, a great resource for yearly trends and seasonality is the *Stock Trader's Almanac* by Yale and Jeffrey A. Hirsch (stocktradersalmanac.com). As an organizer and work calendar chock-full of statistics, the *Almanac* is published annually, near the end of the fourth quarter.

Before we look at the monthly calendar, I want to inject one heads-up. Please don't ignore your stop-loss point because of seasonal probabilities.

For example, bank stocks habitually rise in January, especially as a continuation of a bull market. So, let's imagine that we're in the midst of a brawny bull market. And, say, you buy a hefty lot of bank stock J. P. Morgan Chase (JPM). If the trade goes against you, sell at your planned stop price. Don't cling to a losing trade using the excuse that bank stocks are *supposed* to thrive in January. As they say in Georgia, "That dog won't hunt."

Political Events Move Markets

U.S. presidential elections take place every fourth year. Overall, election years tend to support a positive stock-market environment. The incumbent works hard to "gussy up" the economy, while the opposing candidate counters with glittering promises of his own.

When incumbent administrations remain in the White House, Mother Market usually remains serene, and stocks tend to rise in March, June, October, and December. But if we shoo unpopular administrations out of power, the market pops to the upside in November and December.

Interestingly enough, October, the month we historically dread because of the 1987 market crash, held no major losses (except a fractional loss in 1984) during election years in which the incumbent party retained the White House.

Wars, recessions, and bear markets tend to occur in the first half of new presidential terms. Prosperous periods and bull markets more likely appear in the third and fourth years of presidential terms.

Monthly Monitor

Here's a list of the months of the year, and quick descriptions of their well-known characteristics.

Remember, use seasonality statistics as you would any trading tool. Combine it with other indicators and a big dose of common sense.

January— *"As January goes, so goes the market."* January is the birthing period for a spanking new year. We watch and talk about its performance more than that of any other month on the calendar.

Historically, the "January Barometer" indicates that the net gain, or loss, for the month of January dictates whether the market will close higher or lower by the end of the year.

Here's the reasoning:

- Most corporations conclude their accounting periods at December's end. This provides the company and Wall Street a starting point for sales and earnings forecasts for the following year.

- Both institutional and individual investors rearrange portfolios in January.

- Economic statistics begin a new foundation in January.

No wonder this month unwinds under the notion that if the baby is born pretty, it will grow even prettier. If it's born homely, however, it probably won't transform into a beauty queen as time goes on.

Another pleasant January phenomena, known as the "January Effect," arrives this month courtesy of small cap stocks. As a rule, small cap stocks tend to spike starting mid-December; they may continue to rise through January. This "baby stock" rally is probably due, in part, to the extra pocket money derived from year-end dividends, payouts, and bonuses.

If you invest in these low-cap equities, make sure they have good fundamentals. Low-priced stocks have a tendency to wake up and move skyward for a few days, usually on good news. Then they settle back to their lows and fall back to sleep for long periods of time, à la Rip van Winkle.

Finally, know that analysts have long touted November, December, and January as the "three best months of the year." When these three calendar girls honor their reputation, and you've profited from their upward movement, consider taking partial or all profits as the end of January approaches.

February— *"Pay the Piper Month."* Sharply soaring Januarys commonly lead to consolidations, or corrections, in February.

And although the market usually moves higher during the two days preceding *most* legal holidays, trading days leading up to February's Presidents Day historically slump to the downside.

March— *"Green Beer and Volatile Action."* Speaking of holidays, the days leading up to St. Patrick's Day frequently follow preholiday tradition and pop a wee bit to the upside. Once the day of green beer and smiling Irish eyes comes to a close, however, the last week or two of March can become erratic. Reason: onset of end-of-quarter fiscal news and reports.

April— *"Earnings Season."* The Dow traditionally experiences an upsurge in this spring month, as stocks anticipate first-quarter earnings announcements. Following the "Buy the rumor, sell the news" adage, many stocks will spike *before* earnings reports.

> Hot Tip: If you want to protect your capital, keep up with earnings announcements related to your open positions and take partial or all profits before the announcement takes place. Holding a position through its earnings announcement can result in big drawdowns (read: losses). What if you sell, then the stock pops higher? Shrug it off. "Buy the rumor, sell the news" holds true more often than not. Here's another truism: "Missed money is better than lost money."

While November, December, and January are known to be favorable months to the upside in a bullish environment, some analysts stretch the three best months to the "six best months." April marks the final month of the six best.

May—*"Leave in May and stay away."* This market adage advises investors to sit on the sidelines during late spring and summer months.

Of course, Mother Market delights in making fools of all of us on a regular basis! You can flip back to a chart of May 2003, to see that May was a very merry month indeed, for tech stocks, Dow components, and members of the S&P 500. In fact, each month from April through December (except September) bounced happily to the upside. If you had "left in May" in 2003, you would have left some swell profits on the table!

> **Hot Tip:** A century or so ago, beloved sage and humorist Mark Twain observed stock market seasonality by noting: "October is one of the peculiarly dangerous months to speculate in stocks. The others are July, January, September, April, November, May, March, June, December, August and February."

The 2004 *Stock Trader's Almanac* states that "Since 1950, an excellent strategy has been to invest in the market between November 1st and April 30th each year and then switch into fixed income securities for the other six months."

As traders who can profit from bearish markets as neatly as we can from bullish ones, most of us won't switch into fixed-income securities on May 1. Still, if it appears that a bullish winter/early spring move is on the wane, we can take profits or hedge core trades by selling short stocks, ETFs, or futures.

> **Hot Tip:** In bull market environments, the final few days of the month plus the first two of the following month tend to produce bullish bias.

June, July, August—*"Three-Month Whipsaw."* After stating the first days of the month usually propel the Dow higher, we're going to amend that by saying that's true for every month but August. For some reason, the first day of August refuses to cooperate.

Summer months, in general, deliver choppy trading days due to low liquidity. Many institutional traders desert Wall Street and head to the Hamptons for summer vacations; the rest of us forsake computer screens for suntan lotion. The resulting volume dip delivers whippy, volatile price patterns.

We've all heard of the seasonal event known as the "summer rally." Know, however, that if the summer rally emerges from the heat, it's historically the weakest rally of all seasons.

> **Hot Tip: Market axiom: "Don't sell stocks on Monday." In *bull* markets, many Mondays are positive and close on their highs.**

September—*"Bad news bear."* September is fast gaining a bearish reputation. Vacations end, and money and fund managers return after Labor Day to weed their portfolios of losing positions before preparing year-end statements. Investors initiate tax selling this month, by selling losing stocks in order to register a tax loss. September may open strong, but across the board, the Dow, S&P 500 and NASDAQ indices have ended lower during the last decade of Septembers. Exceptions are election years.

October—*"Bad news, good news."* October appeared to be jinxed for many years, due to dire market drops that took place on its watch. Certainly the crashes of 1929, 1978 and 1979, 1987, and 1997 gave a bad reputation to this leaf-changing month.

Now, however, we're noticing that although October can take the market to many important lows, it also tends to be the "turnaround" month for bear markets.

This happy ending, plus the fact that September has stolen October's "bad news bear" crown, transforms this fall month into an enjoyable—if highly volatile—time period. Keep an eye out for good tech stock/ETF–buying opportunities in October.

November—*"TGIN"* or *"Thank goodness it's November."* November takes the lead as the beginning of the "best six months" of the year. In addition, the 2004 *Stock Trader's Almanac* lists November as the top S&P 500 month for gains since 1950; it's the number two month for the Dow. It also reigns as the third best month for the NASDAQ since 1971 (December and January were a bit more positive).

Holiday-wise, the trading days before and after Thanksgiving are usually winners, with a few "turkeys" along the way. (Traders, use caution: The day after Thanksgiving traditionally plays out on low volume, which makes price patterns choppy and unreliable.)

December—*"Mixed Bag of Gifts."* This is the month of final year-end tax selling, the Santa Claus rally, "window dressing," and the onset of the "January Effect."

As we mentioned in the earlier section on September, year-end tax-selling refers to investors who sell losing equities in order to deduct their losses from that year's income tax. Since the deadline for tax selling is December 31, many weak stocks take a hit in December.

Then, however, if geopolitical events are positive and our economy is relatively stable, Santa usually arrives in his sleigh pulled by bulls to bring us "Santa Claus" rally for the last five trading days of December.

Portfolio managers (PMs) contribute to the rally by "window dressing." They snap up strong stocks during the last hours of the year to dress up their portfolios.

Again, remember to add high-quality small caps to your Christmas list. Part of the "January Effect" is supplied by small cap activity to the upside. That means the Russell 2000 index of small capitalization stocks may climb higher by mid-January. (If you want to buy the Russell 2000 index in one stock, i.e., the ETF, check out the iShares Russell 2000 Index Fund, with the stock symbol IWM. For more info, go to *ishares.com*.).

In chapter 6, we're going to dive head-first into chart analysis. We'll look at trends, trendlines, and support and resistance. Then we'll jump into candle chart basics, with a special introduction by candlestick guru Steve Nison.

Before you turn to chapter 6, though, check out the following quiz. It lists a series of questions and answers taken from the text in this chapter.

Studies show that we only retain a small percentage of material that we read. To counteract that (knowledge is *so* important in this business!), answer the questions and then check the answers. In comparing your answers to those listed, you may find areas you want to review. You may also notice nuggets of new information!

Quiz

Questions

1. From trough to peak to trough, the business cycle customarily lasts about _____ years.

2. True or false: The stock-market cycle many times leads the business cycle.

3. If the answer to question number two is "true," *why* is it true?

4. True or false: Complete stock or index cycles reveal themselves only on weekly charts.

5. Stock prices, in both the long term and the short term, usually fall faster than they rise. Why?

6. Give a simple definition for interest rates.

7. When inflation (increasing cost of goods and services) rears its ugly head, will the Federal Open Market Committee (FOMC) raise or lower interest rates?

8. Why do interest rates have a major impact on our economy?

9. What is the "January Barometer"?

10. Which months of the calendar year historically deliver the highest up-side gains?

Answers

1. The business cycle habitually lasts about four years, give or take a few months.

2. True. The stock market cycle many times rotates ahead of the business cycle.

3. The market cycle moves ahead of the business cycle because portfolio managers (PMs) and individual investors and traders buy stocks based on expectations of the future. If the "smart money" (PMs) suddenly forsakes tech stocks for pharmaceuticals and consumer noncyclicals, which are considered to be defensive sectors, these institutional managers may forecast a market turndown in the near future.

4. Price cycles appear in virtually all time frames, although they are more obvious on longer-term charts.

5. Stocks and other trading vehicles fall faster than they rise, because fear and panic are stronger emotions than optimism and greed.

6. Interest rate is the cost of borrowing money for a given time period.

7. When inflation (increasing cost of goods and services) rears its ugly head, the Federal Open Market Committee (FOMC) leans toward raising interest rates. When inflation stays in check, or the economy falls into a recession, the Fed lowers rates to encourage borrowing and growth.

8. In a high-rate environment, companies and manufacturers have to pay more to borrow money. For capital-intensive corporations, especially, dishing out more money for loans creates a negative impact on earnings. Lower earnings mean lower stock prices.

9. The "January Barometer" is a seasonal indicator that states if the stock market closes higher at the end of this month, then the stock market will close higher on the year. If the market closes lower on the month, the stock market will close lower on the year. Market axiom:"As January goes, so goes the market."

10. November, December, and January have gained the nickname "the three best months of the year."

CENTER POINT

Free Yourself from the Past

Passion costs me too much to bestow it on every trifle.
—Thomas Adams (1640)

How many times have you chastised yourself for past actions? How many regrets do you carry around with you, day in and day out? How many times this week have you shaken your head at personal situations gone awry and wished for different outcomes?

Nothing stops us from enjoying the present—and assertively advancing into the future—like hanging on to our moldy bundle of regrets. If we listed the thought patterns in our daily lives that "keep the brakes on" our advancement to new successes, our refusal to release regrets would rank among the top contenders.

Fact is, if we could have done things better, we would have. Most of us perform the best we can, with what we know, in every situation.

Here are three ideas that can help free us from the past.

First, if a painful memory haunts you, attempt to reframe it by asking, "Is there *any other way* I can look at this? Did it *really* happen the way I think it did? Is there an angle I'm missing that might cast a different light?" Search until you find at least one aspect of the experience that contributed to your current success.

Second, if your past disappointments lie in missed opportunities, believe that new commitment to a worthy goal will naturally draw fresh and even better opportunities to you, now. It's amazing how enthusiastic belief in a vision acts as a magnet to attract auspicious prospects and people into our lives.

Third, hit the delete key on endless ruminations about "the good old days." Truth is, some were good, some weren't so hot. More often than not, we brush those memories with "pretty paint" and drape fantasy over reality. Let's replace those thoughts—and the time they consume—with ideas to improve our present-day reality.

When we spend less time on dwelling in the past, and more time living in the present, we can see the opportunities that surround us, *right now*. Let's free ourselves from the past, take time to enjoy the present, and develop compelling plans for the future!

The Art of the Chart

There is only one side to the stock market; . . . not the bull side or the bear side, but the right side. It took me longer to get that general principle fixed firmly in my mind than it did most of the more technical phases of the game of stock speculation.

—legendary trader Jesse Livermore

The financial markets are becoming more and more volatile. As the media throws headlines at us faster and faster, the stock market reacts by shooting stock prices higher one day, then pounding them lower the next.

In order to take control of their financial futures and avoid the surprises of the past, more and more market participants, including traditional investors, are learning the art and science of reading charts.

Market participants generally use one of two methodologies to research equities for investing and trading purposes: fundamental or technical analysis. Fundamental analysis serves investors and institutional managers who hold equities positions for the long term. A company's "fundamentals," such as p/e ratio, market share, ROE (return on equity), and EBITA (earnings before interest, taxes, depreciation, and amortization), impact a security's valuation and price in the long run.

In the short term, though (excluding earnings announcements and news), temporary imbalances in supply and demand move equity prices higher and lower. To take advantage of these short-term moves, traders use technical analysis.

Technical analysis is the study of a stock or indices' price history, as plotted on a chart. Speed is of the essence when you trade, and charts give you an instant picture of a stock's health status.

> **Hot Tip: Your goal, is to capture the most amount of profit in the least amount of time. Time spent in the market equals risk exposure.**

Once we study the price behavior, we overlay various studies, most of which are derived from price, to glean added information that's predictive of future price movement. If history doesn't always repeat itself *exactly*, it many times rhymes in similar patterns that forecast probable future moves.

The art and science of reading charts is an ongoing educational experience. I've studied thousands upon thousands of charts, and to this day, they *still* reveal new and intriguing nuances of price action.

The next two chapters delve into the underlying principles and basics of chart analysis. That way, when we refer to charts in the chapters that follow, the "what-in-the-heck-is-that-doohickey, the-one-right-over-that-gizmo?" questions will have been answered.

Also, please know that in the discussions that follow, I will use the term "stock" as a reference point. You can substitute whatever you are trading, however, because principles of technical analysis and chart interpretation apply to all trading instruments that display high, low, opening, and closing prices.

The Price Is Right

Price patterns displayed on charts are not drawn by a capricious trading god on steroids. ☺ They are drawn by you and me, and other market participants who agree on a point of worth at a moment in time.

Price is consensus of opinion—an agreed-upon perception of value. You own shares of stock, and you want to sell them. You believe they will lose value in the future.

Conversely, your shares look attractive to me. I think they will gain in value in the short or long term. If we agree on a price, we exchange securities for money.

If logic ran the financial markets, and the future remained an unknown with no expectations attached to it, then I would pay you the amount your shares of stock were worth based on a company's fundamental information and perhaps book value.

Instead, I'm purchasing your shares of stock with an added premium tacked on for anticipated future value. (If the underlying company's fundamentals were terrible, and the stock wallowed at a low price, I would purchase the shares at a discount to the fundamental value.)

The variable in price between the *real* price determined by fundamental analysis, and the price traders and investors *expect* it will be worth in the near or long term, creates price fluctuation.

As our expectations for the future of the stock fluctuate, driven by our inner motivations of either greed or fear—so does its price.

Emotions: The Power that Drives Price Momentum

Our expectations represent the end point of two overriding emotions: greed and fear. These two emotions, and varying levels of each, drive the financial markets.

When market players feel optimistic about our economy's future and think prices will rise, optimism stimulates hope. Hope kindles greed. Greed explodes into euphoria. This expansion of emotion expands price ranges, and the market swells to new highs.

After a period of expansion, a period of indecision may set in. The market contracts into narrow price fluctuations. Conservative optimism supports price enough to hold it up, while cautious pessimism presses down. Equal buying and selling pressure propel prices sideways; they vacillate within a narrow range. If expectations for the future spout into solid optimism, and available supply within the horizontal trend disappears, then prices begin to rise. Soon, a rebirth of hope, greed, and euphoria once again expand the market to new highs.

In an alternate scenario, the market once again expands and contracts. But when it begins to churn sideways, pessimism creeps into the collective mindset of market players. As it gathers, anxiety spreads a hot, gray blanket over market action, and prices drift lower by inches. We say the market "gets heavy." Could this contraction or consolidation transform into the current "top"? Will the fat lady burst into song? Has Elvis officially left the building?

When that belief system takes control, anxiety rolls into fear. Prices head south. If optimism doesn't step up to the plate and absorb supply, fear escalates into panic. Now the market expands again, but this time it retraces a percentage, or all, of its prior gains, or even capitulates to relative new lows.

Do you see how you can analyze a chart by assigning predominant emotions? It's interesting, and true. Scan a chart of any active stock or trading instrument, and you'll see human emotion tugging price patterns into various shapes. From optimism to euphoria, from pessimism to panic, human emotions move prices across the chart, many times in repetitive patterns that are measurable.

As a consistently profitable trader, you'll want to become skilled at predicting how emotions evolve into future price action.

The Ever-tilting Scales of Supply and Demand

Alternating levels of greed and fear create imbalances in demand and supply. In the financial markets—indeed, all markets!—these imbalances push prices higher (demand), or drive them lower (supply).

Basic human nature dictates that we want what we can't have. And we fluff off what we *can* have. Or at least we acquire it at our leisure.

When high demand results in limited quantities of a desirable item, many of us happily pay higher and higher prices for that item.

If an abundant supply of a certain item floods the marketplace, however, the item loses its uniqueness and a portion of its corresponding value. We tend to ignore it, or demand sellers lower their prices if they want us to buy it.

Here's a quick example: Say you plan to attend the Super Bowl. While other pro football games take place across the nation during football season, there's only one Super Bowl. That means a limited supply of tickets go up for sale. Limited supply of a much-sought-after item equals high demand. So, ticket sellers spike prices for admission to this exciting, all-American event.

On top of that, let's say you insist upon enjoying the game from seats on the fifty-yard line. If available supply is limited even more, the price for tickets—if you can even find them—skyrockets. You'll probably pay thousands of dollars for each seat!

On the flip side, imagine that a new pro team started their first season in the city where you live. Maybe the quarterback can't throw worth a darn. And maybe in the last game, the receiver ran the wrong way with the ball. (Yes, I've seen that happen at a pro game!) Now, attendance is light, so the supply of tickets is huge. You can pay rock-bottom prices to attend a game, and even find reasonably priced seats on the fifty-yard line.

> **Hot Tip: Commodities markets showcase how price fluctuations dictate supply and demand. A quick lesson in supply/demand related to the price of oil: watch (lament?) the price fluctuations on the sign at your local gas station.**

Nowhere does price fluctuation created by imbalances in supply and demand show itself as clearly—and at such a rapid-fire pace—as in the financial markets. In time spans ranging from seconds to years, the alternating forces of greed and fear propel prices higher, then lower, with varying levels of momentum.

Figure 6–1 shows a weekly chart of the SPY, which is the ETF, or tracking stock, for the S&P 500 Index. You can see how fear and panic drove this stock down a steep price cliff in 2002, all the way to its October lows.

In March of 2003, the bulls decided to stay for a while, and their greed created enough demand to push the SPY to its relative highs in February. Shortly thereafter, pessimism alternating with smaller puffs of greed took it lower.

Figure 6–2 displays a five-minute chart of the E-mini S&P 500 Index futures. We've taken the time frame from the weekly, long-term time span in Figure 6–1, where each candle represents one week, to a short-term, intraday chart

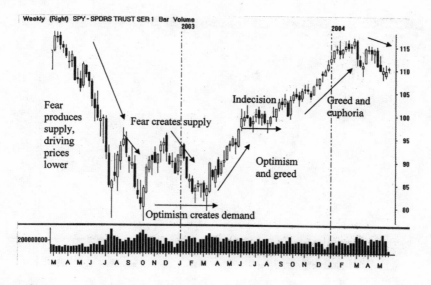

Figure 6–1. This weekly chart of the SPY, the tracking stock for the S&P 500 Index, shows how fear created supply and drove prices lower from March to mid-July of 2002. Then greed and fear, or demand and supply, alternated in a 20-point range until June 2003, when the SPY accumulated enough demand to carry it over previous highs. Indecision kept the SPY in consolidation in mid-2003, as it side-stepped through the summer months. In the first part of September, optimism finally pushed the SPY higher, and it flew to its relative high of 117 in February 2004. There, pessimism took over and drove the SPY lower.

in Figure 6–2, where each candle represents five minutes of price action. No mater the time frame, emotions trigger alternating imbalances in supply and demand, from long- to short-term time frames.

If you are skilled at analyzing emotions and their effect on the scales of supply and demand, you are leagues ahead of most market players. You'll know when you should capitalize on a trend—which is most of the time—and you will know when it's time to flip to the defense and prepare to run a countertrend tactic.

You will also know when it's time to hunker down in your bunker and preserve your capital by taking your account to cash. As mentioned in earlier chapters, knowing when *not* to trade ranks as one of the most important skills you can develop!

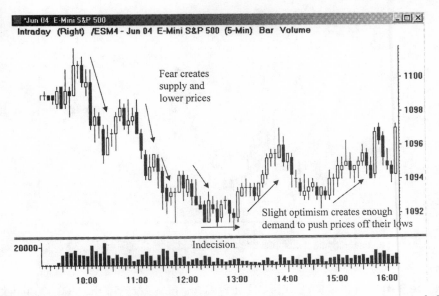

Figure 6–2. Emotions, whether fear-based or greed-based, create temporary imbalances in demand and supply and so move the markets on a moment-to-moment basis. This 5-minute chart of the S&P E-mini futures shows how fear mixed with intermittent spurts of optimism moved prices lower during morning hours. You would have been wise to stay on the short side of this mini-downtrend.

The Four Phases of a Cycle

In chapter 5, we discussed cycles and how they move. Now, to establish the basis for chart interpretation, we'll divide these cycles into four major segments, or phases. They are: 1) accumulation, 2) mark-up, 3) distribution, and 4) markdown. For traders targeting short-term charts, those phases also translate into a base, uptrend, rollover or top reversal, and downtrend.

Figure 6–3 shows a simple graphic that details the four phases in a cycle.

Figure 6–4 displays a weekly chart of Intel Corporation (INTC). Intel evolved through all four phases of complete price cycle from 1997 through 2002.

The consolidation, or basing period in a cycle, is also called the "accumulation phase." Since the term "accumulation" refers to institutional buying, it's more accurately applied to a daily or weekly chart. (When a stock forms a base on a five-minute chart, we cannot assume institutions are accumulating.) Therefore, we're going to use "base" and "basing action" to describe this area of a cycle, so we can apply it to all time periods.

A base forms at the trough, or valley, of a cycle. A close-up shows price moving sideways in a range, with alternating highs and lows. The amplitude (price swings) of the range depend on the individual stock's inherent volatility.

If you are a position, or core trader, you'll want to scan stocks that are work-

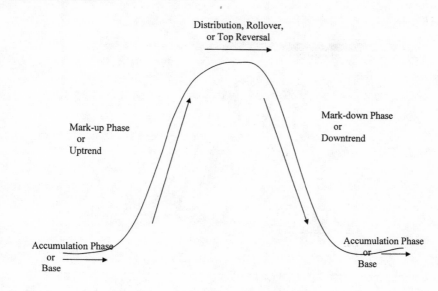

Figure 6–3. This drawing shows the four phases, or stages that make up a price cycle. The accumulation phase, or base, corresponds to the trough, or valley, mentioned in earlier cycle discussions. The rise to the peak is called the markup, or uptrend. The peak represents the distribution, rollover, or top reversal phase. When the price gives way to fall to a lower low, followed by a lower high, the price cycle is in a downtrend. Finally, when panic subsides and the sellers have exhausted their supply, buyers step in, and a new base begins to form.

ing through orderly bases on daily charts. (Position traders buy stocks as they rise out of a base into an uptrend.) Wild, disorderly price-spurts to the upside—which fall just as quickly back into the base area—tell you that when the stock finally *does* break to the upside, the odds of a reliable uptrend are "Slim and None, and Slim's just leaving."

For the most profitable position and core trades, scan for bases with orderly horizontal price movement and steady volume. In chapter 7, we'll study volume signals that take place in basing action and that give you a heads-up that institutional accumulation is probably taking place. A stock's momentum can be greatly enhanced by institutional favor, and if the stock looks like it's going to break into an uptrend, you'll want to go along for the ride.

> **Hot Tip: Longer bases (several weeks) tend to produce stronger uptrends than short ones.**

Orderly bases that form on daily charts also serve up great swing and active trading opportunities when the breakout to the upside occurs. We don't have to

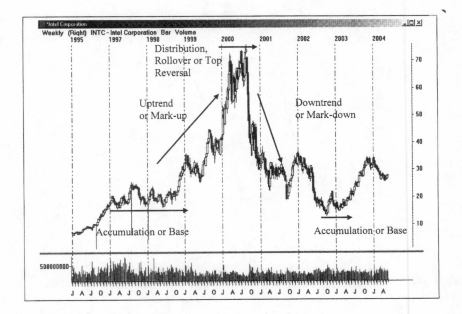

Figure 6–4. This weekly chart of Intel Corp. (INTC) displays a long-term price cycle labeled with four succeeding phases. In the accumulation or basing phase (1997 and most of 1998), buying and selling pressure alternate and price trades sideways, within a range. From October 1998 to March 2000, INTC's price more than triples, rising in a steep uptrend, or markup phase, from $20 + to a high of $72.69. From March though September of 2000, INTC endured a volatile distribution, or top reversal pattern, including a pop to a new high of $75.81, on August 28. After that, the tech giant crumbled in a markdown phase, or downtrend, which finally bottomed in October 2002. The short-lived base made a higher low in the beginning of 2003 and broke over its December 2002 high, in June 2003. The higher low and higher high initiates a new uptrend.

be quite as picky about the base's orderliness for these types of trades, especially day trades, because we are interested in short-term profits only.

As the base matures, bulls begin to outnumber the bears. Sellers see demand coming into the market and raise their prices. If enough buying pressure shoots the stock through the highest price level touched in the base, the stock breaks out of the base.

Now, ideally, the stock will continue to move higher and close at a price above the base highs. When it retraces, and then resumes its upward climb, the reaction low will be a higher low.

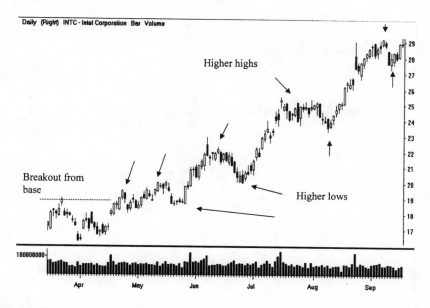

Figure 6–5. This daily chart of INTC shows the tech icon in a clear-cut uptrend. Each low was higher than the prior low, and each successive high touched a higher price than the previous one. Along the way, in June, July, and August, you'll see daily candles that gap open to the upside, then fall quickly. When stocks display volatile behavior, reasons include geopolitical news, earnings announcements, and options expiration days.

> **Hot Tip:** On all time frames, when prices break above the highs of prior basing action, then quickly retrench, the failed rally creates a "bull trap."

The definition of an uptrend (on all time frames) is: *price that rises in a series of higher highs and higher lows.*

Figure 6–5 illustrates a daily chart of INTC. This mighty semiconductor giant soared in a brawny uptrend for most of 2003. The structure of the uptrend is strong and positive, with higher lows and higher highs.

When the markets rise in a muscular uptrend, all trading styles thrive. Again, if you are a position trader, you buy as the stock rises out of the base, and they hold for the duration of the trend.

As a swing trader, you take advantage of the price "swings" to the upside, entering when the price breaks out of the base or successive retracements or consolidations (think "price rest-stops"). If you prefer intraday trading, a trending market produces solid, uptrending days for day trades.

The daily chart of INTC as in Figure 6–6 targets price swings that provide

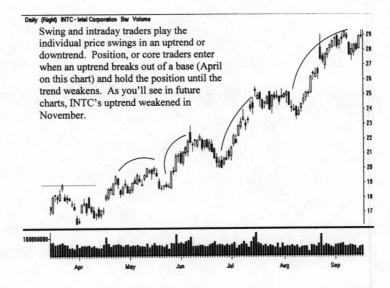

Daily (Right) INTC - Intel Corporation Bar Volume

Swing and intraday traders play the individual price swings in an uptrend or downtrend. Position, or core traders enter when an uptrend breaks out of a base (April on this chart) and hold the position until the trend weakens. As you'll see in future charts, INTC's uptrend weakened in November.

Figure 6–6. This shows the same daily price chart of the Intel Corp. (INTC) as Figures 6–5, but this time the price swings are indicated. These swings build a robust uptrend, offering profit opportunities to position, swing, and intraday traders.

trading opportunities to swing and intraday traders. (Position traders would hold for the duration of the uptrend.)

Figure 6–7 exhibits INTC as it rises in an uptrend on a ten–minute chart. You can see why an uptrend keeps the same definition, whether it's on a monthly, weekly, daily, or intraday chart.

Keep in mind that the lows touched in an uptrend are more important than the highs. A stock's price can test its own highs with one or two successive relative highs that don't rise above prior highs, as long as the retracements or pullbacks stay at least even. If the price falls to a lower point than the previous low, the uptrend is broken.

The third phase in a cycle represents the mountain peak. This phase is known as the "distribution phase," especially in the context of daily and weekly charts. Since "distribution" refers to institutional selling, and that may not be accurate on a very short-term chart, we'll use the term "rollover" or "top reversal," as they are interchangeable within all time frames.

Figure 6–8 shows INTC again, but this time we've advanced the daily chart to the rollover, or top-reversal phase. In this case, distribution certainly drove prices lower, as well. Notice how INTC tried in December and February to climb higher than November highs, but couldn't. That tells you that buyers refused to pay higher prices for the tech giant.

Figure 6–7. Figure 6–7 exhibits a 10-minute chart of INTC, over 3 consecutive days. Note how the first day's price action ground sideways, providing no real profit opportunities for intraday traders. The next day shows INTC opening a few cents lower and churning sideways for the morning hours. At noon, however, the semi stock retests 10 o'clock lows, then pushes into an uptrend, making higher lows and higher highs for the remainder of the day. The intraday trend offers clear-cut profit prospects to active traders. The following day, again, it essentially sidesteps until noon, when it makes a lukewarm attempt to reach the prior days' highs.

On a daily or weekly chart, peak reversals can roil through time in a volatile manner, a spewing skyward in jagged spikes, then crumbling just as fast. It makes sense. The rambunctious bulls don't want to admit the party is over. In a last-ditch effort, they bully the bears by driving prices higher (think "short squeeze"), before they take the pipe and tumble off the price cliff into a downtrend. (Turn back to Figure 6–4 to review how INTC's top-reversal battle between bulls and bears caused ulcers in its investors in the year 2000.)

> **Hot Tip:** Both bases and rollover phases ultimately sidestep through their patterns in a price range. Both are responsible for reversing the prior trend. But while a base can form in a relatively quiet manner in a narrow range, a top reversal, or rollover, may develop explosive price swings before it succumbs to a downtrend. Warning to position and swing traders: stay clear of rollover or top-reversal phases.

And when the bloodthirsty bears, who are loaded for bull, finally gain control, they push price to a lower low, the top reversal pattern is complete, and the stock rolls into a downtrend.

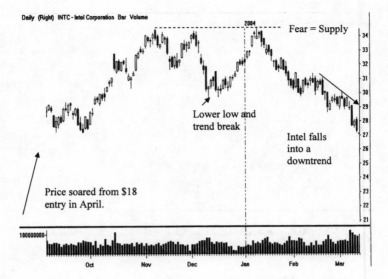

Figure 6–8. On this daily chart of Intel Corp. (INTC), which continues the chart in Figure 6–6, you can see how the uptrend from April got "tuckered out" in November. By mid-December, INTC slid south to a lower low, breaking its uptrend. Then, to keep things interesting and cause sharp pain to the gluttonous short-sellers, buyers stepped in, and INTC surged back to its November/Demember highs. At that point, the bulls jammed their wallets back into their pockets. INTC fell fast and hard on distribution, passing prior lows. This top-reversal pattern was volatile, indeed.

The definition of a downtrend is: *price making lower highs and lower lows.*

In a downtrend, highs are the most important component to the trend continuation. While a stock can chug through one or two successive lows that remain fairly equal price-levels, if it makes a higher high than the prior one, and follows it with a higher low, the downtrend is broken.

Figure 6–9 shows the continuing daily chart of Intel and illustrates how the stock fell into a grisly downtrend.

As mentioned before, downtrends by their nature will give you a bumpier ride down than uptrends will give you on the trip up. (When we ride on roller coasters, we don't yell as loud riding *up* the track as we do hurtling *down*.) Most times, fear pushes prices down three times faster than greed carries them up.

When sellers have exhausted their supply, and fear dissipates, the downtrend bottoms out (trough). Buyers start to nibble, and price unwinds into a sideways mode. When a higher low and higher high form, the downtrend is broken and a new base begins.

Check Figure 6–9 again, to see Intel's happy ending. The stock bottomed in

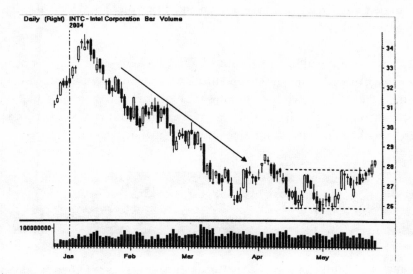

Figure 6–9. After its showcase uptrend in 2003, Intel Corp. (INTC) retraced a portion of that move up by the midpoint of 2004. Note on this daily chart the series of lower highs and lower lows. Now it appears that the semiconductor giant is trying to formulate a base, then break into an uptrend.

early May, clambered to a slightly higher high, and held a higher low, starting a new base.

Buddy Up to Your Friend, the Trend

If you've been an active participant in the financial markets, you've heard "The trend is your friend" a zillion times. That statement is true, because you need a *trending* market to capture consistent profits. As mentioned before, markets that jitterbug sideways offer few trading opportunities, because the range between the highs and lows is narrow and unpredictable.

Your goal as a trader is to jump on—and stay on—the right side of a trend. To help you do that, we'll take a quick look at the technique for drawing trendlines.

A trendline is a slanted line drawn between two or more points on a chart. We draw trendlines for these reasons:

- to define price action

- to determine support or resistance (buying or selling) price zones

- to determine the strength of a trend and/or predict possible weakening or reversal

To draw an uptrend line, locate a stock that's broken out of a base or consolidation area, moved to the upside, and made at least two higher lows. Start at the first higher low above the base, or consolidation low. Draw the line under the trend and connect it with the next pivot low. When you can connect three or more lows, the trend line is considered to be a "major trend line."

> **Hot Tip: When price breaks a major trend line, look for two consecutive closes below the trend line for confirmation. (This does not mean that you lower your protective stop if the price drops through it.)**

Figure 6–10 displays a *weekly* chart of Lam Research Corporation (LRCX). The long-term trend line connects the lows of the trend. The semiconductor stock shot out of its base in early 2003 and never looked back. It soared from $11 to almost $36, tripling in value during those ten months.

Figure 6–11 shows a *daily* chart of LRCX, and the initial uptrend. You can see the trend line connecting the first three lows. The subsequent low in August broke that trend line.

Figure 6–10. On this weekly chart of Lam Research Corp. (LRCX) you can see how we connected the lows of the uptrend to draw an uptrend line. We started with the first low after the lowest low of the bottom reversal pattern, then extended it through INTC's "swan song" in the first months of 2004. This is a major trend line, since it touches four pivot lows. (Three touches signify a "major" trend line.)

Daily (Right) LRCX - Lam Research Corporation Bar Volume

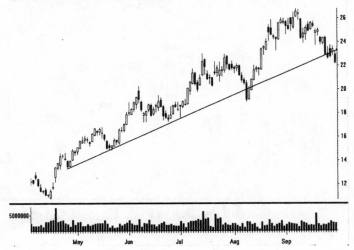

Figure 6–11. This daily chart of Lam Research Corp. (LRCX) shows a close-up of a section of the weekly price action during the semiconductor's uptrend. Note the major uptrend line drawn on this daily chart, connecting three lows. LRCX stumbled the last part of July and the first week in August. Still, the price did not make a lower low, so the uptrend remained in force. When LRCX establishes a new pivot low, we'll adjust the trend line slope.

Keep in mind, though, the August low was still higher than the prior low in June. The *trend line* was broken, and not necessarily the trend. (As just mentioned, LRCX continued up to January highs of $35.50.) The uptrend itself is only broken when the price makes a *lower low.*

As long as the trend remains intact, a trend line break tells you to connect the new low with the next higher low, and those that follow. Draw new trend lines and adjust them as the angle of the trend changes.

> Hot Tip: When the price pattern falls below an uptrend line, many times that trend line, which acted as support (buying pressure), will now act as resistance (selling pressure). If the price slid in a downtrend, but popped up above the trend line, the line *may* act as future support, although this happens more rarely than the support-to-resistance example.

As the trend matures, pay attention to the slope of the angle. The varying grade tells a story. When the slope of the angle drifts into a more shallow incline—especially after an extended uptrend—it signals the trend may be tiring.

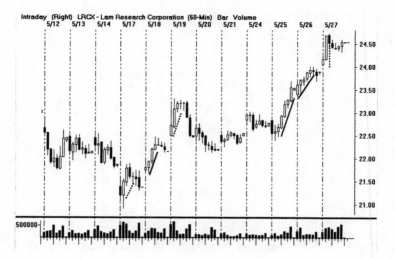

Figure 6–12. This intraday 60-minute chart of Lam Research Corp. (LRCX) illustrates how prices create uptrends on an intraday basis. The solid lines indicate days where uptrends maintained orderly patterns for most of the day, and the price closed near the high of the day. These moves offer the best opportunities to swing and day traders. The dotted lines indicate days in which LRCX's price rose during morning hours, presenting good intraday trading scenarios. The afternoon hours, however, took back a portion of the gains. Many days, you will find that morning hours in the market trend nicely, but the afternoons drift sideways, or retrace earlier gains.

That's important information if you are watching a daily chart and have open positions with swing or core trades. A flattening slope warns you to tighten your protective stop and/or take some profits off the table.

Now, study Figure 6–12, which displays an hourly chart of LRCX. We've taken trend lines to an intraday basis. This chart shows twelve days of price history, with each candle representing sixty minutes.

Out of the twelve days shown, three days exhibited solid uptrends that lasted through the trading day. These are marked with solid trend lines. Three more days could have been traded intraday, but they sold off in the afternoon (dotted lines). The remaining days basically chopped sideways. Scalpers might have sliced some quick gains from those moves.

Figure 6–13 shows a five-minute chart of LRCX. As you can see, this tech stock cooperates nicely when it comes to rising in orderly uptrends, on all time frames. The stock drew a dandy intraday trend, touching the same trend line five times during trading hours.

Figures 6–10 through 6–13 displayed uptrends on four different time frames. Profits could be taken from these trends in trades that lasted from five months to

Figure 6–13. Not to be outdone by the longer-term uptrends, this 5-minute chart of Lam Research Corp. (LRCX) illustrates that orderly, predictable uptrends also take place in the very short term. Note how this trend line touched five lows. If you check back to the 60-minute chart on Figure 6–12, you can locate May 25 (5/25), the day shown here. Notice on that chart how every hourly candle, except for the initial one, closed at, or near, its high. That indicates price strength. It doesn't get any better than that for swing and active traders!

five minutes. It depends on which time frame you trade, as to which of these trends are important to your style of trading.

Next, let's move to downtrend lines. This time, we draw the trend line on top of the price pattern. To draw one, find a stock that's falling in the context of a downtrend; it's fallen down from a top-reversal pattern and experienced at least two lower highs. Find the top-reversal high. Then connect the first lower high below the top-reversal high to the second lower high. Extend the trend line to forecast potential future direction.

The weekly chart of Forest Laboratories, Inc. (FRX) shown in Figure 6–14 portrays this pharmaceutical company hurtling through a top-reversal pattern in early 2004. In March, it capitulated into an intermediate-term downtrend that hasn't repaired itself as yet.

On Figure 6–15, this daily chart of FRX now shows the details of that downtrend. Interestingly enough, the downtrend line *has* been broken. Since FRX has managed to rise to the former rally high, though, we have to wait and see if it can make a higher low. If FRX makes a U-turn here and collapses below the $58 lows just established, the downtrend remains in place.

Figure 6–16 displays an hourly chart of FRX. The downtrends drawn on the chart handed dandy profits to swing and intraday traders who sold this stock

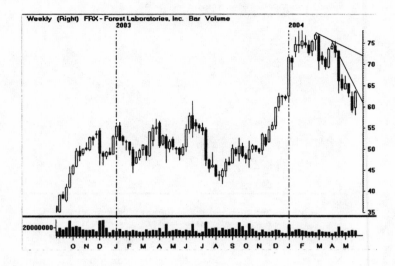

Figure 6–14. This weekly chart exhibits Forest Laboratories, Inc. (FRX) as it grinds through a top reversal and distribution pattern in early 2004. Then the drug maker rolled off its price cliff with the help of drooling bears. A quick rally in March offered a quick jolt of hope to bulls, but panic took over and drove the price south, nearly returning it to earlier 2003 highs.

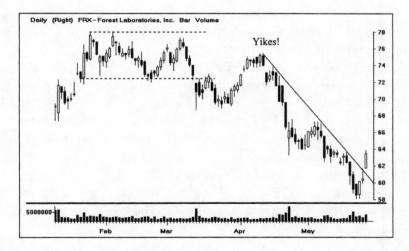

Figure 6–15. On this daily chart of Forest Laboratories Inc. (FRX), you can see in more detail how the top reversal pattern stretched to three highs in the $78 area before sliding south, rallying in a last heroic effort, then succumbing to fear and outright panic. The trend line starts at the first high below the top reversal highs, then slants down over the tops of FRX's rally highs. On the "hard right edge" of the chart, you can see how FRX broke the downtrend line. If price rallies to new highs and a higher low, the downtrend, at least for the moment, will have concluded.

Figure 6–16. Once again, we swoop in for a close-up of daily action. On this hourly chart of Forest Laboratories Inc. (FRX) you can see price action more easily. Note the downtrend lines drawn over the highs of the legs-down. If you are a swing trader, you will probably use daily and hourly charts as your primary focus.

short. Notice how the stock fell from May 19 to May 24, from $64 to $58. Then, it reversed on May 24 and flew back up to $64. Hope nobody traded on the wrong side of those moves, either down or up!

Figure 6–17 focuses a microscopic lens on FRX. It reveals the last two days of the downtrend shown on the hourly chart in Figure 6–16, but now the price action is on a five-minute chart. In both cases, poor FRX gapped up (opened higher than the prior day's closing price) at the open, then tumbled into free fall until eleven a.m. What a sweet pattern for daytraders.

From this basic discussion on trends, remember that the longer a trend is in place, the more powerful it is *and* the more likely it is to continue in the direction it's going.

Monthly and weekly trends are stronger than daily or intraday trends. Trends on a sixty-minute chart are more forceful than those on a five-minute chart. After all, you can wheel a Volkswagen into a U-turn a heck of a lot easier than you can a Mack truck.

When I scan for swing trades, I use daily charts. If I find a setup I like, I flip to a weekly chart to get a reality check. As you can see by comparing daily and weekly charts above, they look quite different from each other. While a stock may be experiencing a long-term uptrend (say, a year or so), the intermediate-term trend (multiple months or weeks) may be down.

When I make swing trades or position trades to the long side, I want a stock

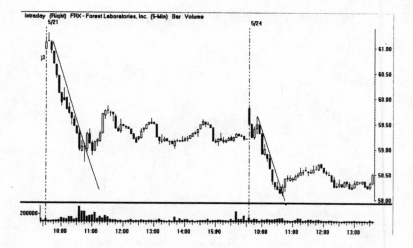

Figure 6–17. On this 5-minute chart of Forest Laboratories, Inc. (FRX), you can see how mini-downtrends tumble hard and fast on an intraday basis. In both instances, FRX gapped open to the upside (opened higher than the prior day's closing price), then fell like a brick tied to a rock until 11 a.m. Generally, you will find the morning hours tend to offer more clear-cut trends than do afternoon hours. And as stated and restated, orderly trending action is where we make our money.

that's in an uptrend, or at least breaking out of a base, on a weekly chart. That way, the primary pressure is buying pressure. If I'm entering short trades, I check weekly charts to make sure the primary pressure is selling pressure. In other words, the stock is in a downtrend.

> **Hot Tip:** Swing traders, beware! If you sit glued to your computer screen all day and watch a 5-minute chart of your trade (or worse, a Level II screen), you're likely to micromanage your trade, abandon your plan, and exit at the wrong time.

It follows that if you are a day trader with an upside bias for the day, you buy positions in stocks or other trading vehicles rising in uptrends on daily charts. If your opening bias is negative, sell short stocks intraday that are in downtrends on daily charts.

Otherwise, you are swimming against the tide. And hey, trading can be exciting enough without fighting the major currents.

Rapid-Fire Overview: Support and Resistance

We've talked about greed and fear, and how they propel markets by fueling demand and supply. Now we'll add the final dynamic duo to those teams: support and resistance.

Simply put: Support = Buyers.

Resistance = Sellers

The complete equations:

Greed = demand = support (buyers)

Fear = supply = resistance (sellers)

On a chart of any time frame, support levels reside below the current trading price and represent potential buyers. Resistance levels hover above the trading price and signify potential sellers.

You will locate support and resistance levels on charts at:

- Prior price levels

- Trend lines

- Channel lines

- Moving averages

- Fibonacci retracement levels

- Pivot lines

We'll talk briefly about support and resistance using price levels, trend lines, and channel lines in the text that follows. Moving averages, Fibonacci levels, and pivot lines will be discussed in upcoming chapters.

Figure 6–18 illustrates a daily chart of Johnson & Johnson (JNJ). It shows basic, horizontal trendlines drawn to indicate support and resistance price levels. Note how JNJ rose from its December lows at $49 to February highs of $55. Then, in March, this multinational pharmaceutical company fell right back down to December lows of $49, which was price support.

Support means buyers are willing to support the price by purchasing the stock at that level. And they did. The more days clustered in this time frame, the more potential support (buyers) JNJ's price had when it fell down to that March level.

If JNJ had not found support in March, when it fell to the $49 price level, we check the chart for the next level of support below $49. That tells us where that downtrend might hesitate next, or even reverse—if demand is strong enough.

Now look at JNJ's return to the $55 level in May. Since JNJ reversed at the $55 level before, in February, we look for traders to take profits there in May. Prevailing logic "JNJ couldn't move over $55 in February, and it might not be able to

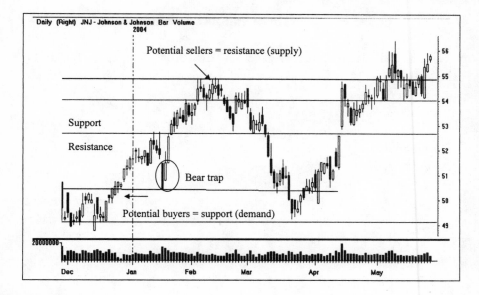

Figure 6–18. On this daily chart of Johnson & Johnson (JNJ), note how the price churned sideways in late 2003, establishing a firm line of potential support (buyers) when the price rose above those levels. (Had the price fallen below that consolidation, that area would then represent resistance, or sellers.) Price did, indeed, go on to drop sharply in mid-January, and return to support areas. On cue, buyers stepped in so quickly that the rapid fall and recovery created a bear trap. Notice how pattern evolution causes price levels to change from support to resistance.

now." Or, "I bought this doggone stock at $55, and it immediately tanked. Now that it's back to where I bought it, I'm going to sell it, and at least get out even."

That's why we call that $55 area "resistance," as potential sellers lurk there to dump their shares of stock, or supply, onto the market. Naturally, if that supply (selling pressure) overcame the demand (buying pressure) at $55, the fear would goad sellers to abandon their stock at decreasing prices.

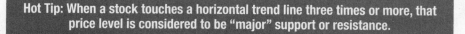

Hot Tip: When a stock touches a horizontal trend line three times or more, that price level is considered to be "major" support or resistance.

Here's one of the most important concepts of support and resistance: When a stock moves up, through old resistance levels, that level becomes support. As a stock falls through old support areas, that old support becomes future resistance, when the stock tries to rise back through it.

Imagine that you are in a three-story house, standing in a room on the first floor. You look up and note the ceiling overhead. Think of the ceiling as resistance, as your barrier to a higher level.

Next, you climb the stairs and stand in a second-floor room. You have penetrated the "barrier." What was the ceiling when you stood on the first floor now forms the floor you stand on. It "supports" you.

If you climb the stairway to the third floor, you will again rise through the resistance "barrier." And again, the floor you stand on (support) formed the ceiling (resistance) when you were on the second floor.

Finally, start back down the stairs. Symbolically, you are descending through your earlier "support." When you reach the second floor, you look up. Once again, the ceiling above presents a barrier.

Figure 6–19 shows a ten-minute chart of JNJ. Besides the horizontal support and resistance lines, dotted lines plot an uptrend line and the corresponding channel line.

Prices tend to move in channels. Because channel lines, like trend lines, act as support and resistance for trend movement, channel lines are useful tools for adding predictive power to a trend line.

To draw a channel line, simply draw an upward sloping line that connects at

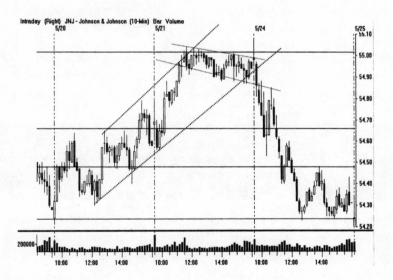

Figure 6–19. This 10-minute chart of Johnson & Johnson exhibits horizontal support and resistance lines, an uptrend line and corresponding channel line, and channel lines containing the mini top reversal pattern. We could have drawn many more lines on this chart, but the result would be confusing. You may want to draw a downtrend line for the last day, along with a corresponding channel line. You can probably find more support and resistance levels, as well.

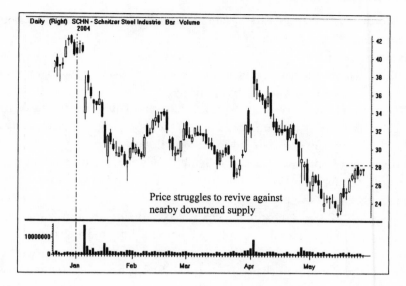

Figure 6–20. This daily chart of Schnitzer Steel Industries (SCHN) shows the progress of a hair-raising price ride. Prices have a hard time rallying to the upside when closely preceded by a vicious downtrend. When SCHN shot straight up in April with the help of several price gaps, short-covering no doubt influenced that froth-filled rally. The bulls who didn't recognize trouble signs got caught with their prices down.

least two swing highs of an uptrend, or one that connects at least two lows of a downtrend. Extend both the trend line and the channel line. When the price deviates from the channel, it tells you that it's gaining, or losing, momentum.

> **Hot Tip: When a stock falls sharply through a line of support, naturally, the bears rush in to punch it lower. If the bulls counter the bear attack, and the bears give up quickly, the stock bounces back up into its previous support area. This is called a "bear trap."**

Overhead price consolidation is not the only area where resistance lurks. Downtrends offer resistance, as well. Timewise, the closer resistance lies to current price action, the more power it has to hold the price down. The farther away resistance resides, the less power it has. That's why a stock that forms a two- or three-month base has better odds of breaking into a brawny uptrend than does a stock that merely chops through a base in a matter of days and struggles to make a "V-shaped" recovery.

Why? People have memories. Fresh resistance means fresh pain! Look at Figure 6–20 to understand this concept. On this daily chart, two sharp downtrends hammer Schnitzer Steel Industries (SCHN) down.

Say, your neighbor, Fred, can't read a chart, and doesn't know the definition of "downtrend." A cab driver tells him that China's building boom means that country is buying steel like crazy. Since Schnitzer Steel (SCHN) supplies metal to China, odds are the stock will make a moon shot—and soon. Fred immediately buys five hundred shares of SCHN.

Within days, however, Schnitzer slides into free fall. Poor Fred watches, slack-jawed. (From January 1 to the 29, SCHN lost nearly 50 percent of its value.)

After the downtrend slows, the embattled stock tries to poke its head up. It doesn't get far. Why? Any sign of price recovery is jumped on by supply, or "mad people" like Fred, trying to recoup a fraction of their losses. Notice how the February "dead cat bounce" didn't last long. The March rally bounced with even less enthusiasm.

In April—talk about alternating fear and greed!—SCHN rocketed straight up to nosebleed altitude. Then *whap!* It's Free Fall City all over again. Another bull trap extraordinaire! Now SCHN screeches past earlier lows to the 23 area. A lukewarm rally brings it back to resistance.

Again, fresh resistance in the form of a downtrend exudes more power to stifle a recovery than does "old," or faraway, resistance. Fresh memories of pain (lost money) are more potent than those tempered by time.

That's why the longer time a base takes to form and the farther away, time-wise, it travels from downtrend resistance, the more likely that an uptrend breaking out of it will have "legs," or firm support.

Finally, while we assign exact dollar amounts to support and resistance in order to define them, they are actually "zones."

Let's say that Fickle Freightways is trading at $33, and it has support on its daily chart at $32. And let's further establish that the $32 price support was established six months ago. When you consider all the global events influencing the stock market, the number of players who buy and sell each second, and the billions of dollars that pass through hands each day, can we *really* expect Fickle Freightways to slide down to $32.02, then 32.01, and tiptoe down to $32 even, ring a bell to alert us, and then settle complacently at that price for all to see? I don't think so! In the best-case scenario, Fickle will settle a fraction of a point to either side of $32.

Support and resistance zones are elastic. They stretch. This presents a challenge to traders, because many times, we use support and resistance numbers to enter a trade, establish protective stops and/or profit targets.

We've all placed stops under support, or consolidation areas, only to get "stopped-out" then morosely watch the stock recover and streak to higher prices without us.

Conversely, we all know what a deadly practice it is to play "drop the stop." That means when your protective stop is hit (long position), you move it lower.

Please don't use the excuse "Well, heck, support and resistance are elastic zones" to justify remaining in a losing trade.

Common sense and experience will help you target support and resistance areas. You'll soon learn, if you haven't already, how to pinpoint prices that will serve as appropriate entry, protective stop, and profit targets.

We'll be talking about support and resistance in one form or another for the remainder of this book. If you're not an expert on this subject now, you'll become one as you progress through the following chapters.

Chart Patterns: Psychological Maps

The price patterns that dance across our charts represent exciting maps of human behavior. And, because we humans operate the financial markets, it makes perfect sense that stocks, indices, and futures markets form patterns that appear over and over again. While no two patterns fit an exact or identical mold, the resemblance is strong enough for us to assign the patterns names and use them to predict possible price movement.

Two basic types of patterns produce price breakouts on all time frames: reversal patterns and continuation patterns.

Reversal patterns, quite simply, reverse trends. Continuation patterns provide the "rest stops" between the price legs that form the trend expansion.

Basic reversal patterns create formations at the trend tops (distribution stage) and trend bottoms (accumulation stage or base). They come with descriptive names, such as "double top," "double bottom," "head and shoulders," "saucer," and "cup with handle."

When you spot a reversal pattern in the making, you can use it for setup opportunities, risk management, and exit strategies.

Double Top

When you see it: All time frames

What it looks like: An "M"

What it is: A double top is a reversal pattern that can halt an uptrend and smack it into a downtrend.

If you want to see one whopper of a double top, look at a daily chart of the NASDAQ 100 in March 2000. Those dual tops signaled the top of an explosive bull market, especially for the technology sector.

A double top begins to form when a stock (or index) moving in an uptrend soars to a new high. It pulls back, then makes another run at that prior high. When it touches that price area (or close to it) for the second time, the bulls refuse to pay a higher price for the stock. They jam their hands in their pockets. (This is similar to the mountain-top analogy in chapter 5.)

What happens when people refuse to pay more for a stock? Those who hold the stock become anxious and sell.

> **Hot Tip:** Now and then you'll see a "triple top" formation. If a double top makes for a strong top-reversal pattern, a triple top delivers a real wallop to prices. That's because prices tried three times to make new highs, and three times traders, in effect, said "No." Message to bulls: "Three strikes and you're out!"

Now, the stock falls to the prior pullback support area. If the buyers who are hanging out at that support area refuse to hold the price up, supply overcomes demand and the stock dives. At that point, the double-top pattern is complete, and the uptrend reverses.

Figure 6–21 shows a daily chart of the S&P Retail index (RLX). As you can see, in two instances, when the RLX tried to make a new high, bulls refused to pay up, so bears drove the index lower.

Keep in mind that candles play an important role in double-top formations. When you see a stock approach a prior high, then produce a candle reversal pattern, such as a dark cloud cover or, in the case of the RLX's June double top, three shooting stars in a row (!), if you're long, take profits. Short sellers may want to start looking for setups.

Figure 6–22 displays a five-minute chart of Genentech, Inc. (DNA). While double-top formations form powerful trend-reversal patterns on daily and longer-term charts, they also broadcast a critical message to intraday traders: When a trading instrument can't make a higher high, it means no one is willing to pay a higher price for it. What's the next logical move? It's likely to slide south—at least in the short term.

> **Hot Tip:** When you see a stock form a double top as lunchtime approaches (11:30 a.m.–1:30 p.m., EST), tighten your stops on intraday long trades, or take profits.

Head and Shoulders
When you see it: All time frames, more prevalent on daily/weekly charts
What it looks like: Silhouette of a human's left shoulder, head, and right shoulder
What it is: A top-reversal pattern

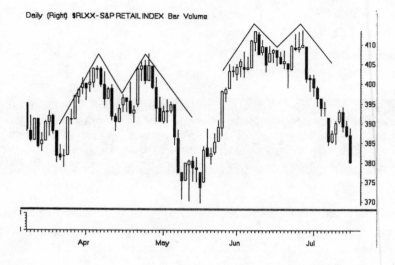

Figure 6–21. This daily chart of the Standard and Poor's Retail index (RLX), shows how powerful a double top can be. Whether it stops a short-term move up, as it did here, in April, and then again in June, or sends a bull market to its knees, a double top acts as a powerful reversal pattern.

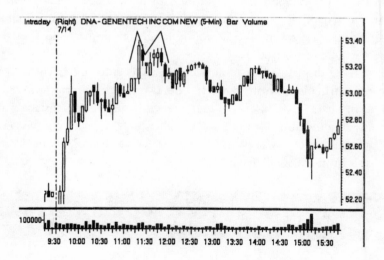

Figure 6–22. This 5-minute chart of Genentech, Inc. (DNA) illustrates how quickly a double top can form, and its near-term implications (lower prices). The biotech stock soared in a joy ride, tacking on a point+ from the opening bell to 11:30 a.m. EST. At noon, however, DNA couldn't push to a higher high. This signaled day traders holding long positions to take profits. Later in the day, at 2 p.m., DNA tried to push higher than its 12:30 high, but supply overwhelmed demand. Just remember, when a stock or other vehicle can't make a higher high, it will probably head lower, at least in the short term.

A head-and-shoulders top-reversal pattern is another powerful pattern that halts the progress of an uptrend and sends it lower.

> **Hot Tip: Occasionally, you'll see a shallow head-and-shoulders form that doesn't play out as a trend reversal. In this case, the formation fashions a continuation pattern.**

It forms when a stock in an uptrend rises to a new high on strong volume. The price soon pulls back, or retraces, completing what will be the left shoulder.

Now, the Johnnys-Late-to-the-Bull-Market (or uptrend) show up. They buy like crazy, pushing the price past resistance at the top of the left shoulder and up to yet a new high. This new high shapes the top of the head.

When these late bulls stop "paying up" for the overbought stock, anxiety creeps in. Price crumbles. (Yes, we're at the mountain top, again.) The stock drops down to the prior support area.

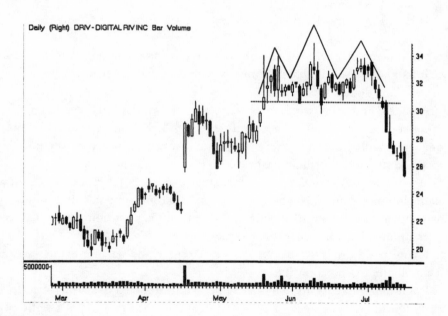

Figure 6–23. This daily chart of Digital River, Inc. (DRIV) displays the top-reversal pattern known as a "head and shoulders." Note how the stock soars in an uptrend, then forms the right shoulder on relatively strong volume. Euphoria pushes the stock to another new high (head), but the price falls back once again. Observe how the candle reversal pattern combination of a shooting star and dark cloud cover form the head. The stock consolidates in late June, then tries to push higher. When that run dissipates, bears attack poor DRIV and send it though the neckline (dotted line). The head-and-shoulders top reversal is complete, and the software and programming company careens to new lows.

The right shoulder develops as lukewarm momentum raises the price to form the right shoulder. Too weak to rise back to the top of the head, the price then drops back to support. If it falls through the "neckline" (see Figure 6–23), the pattern is complete. The uptrend is broken and the bears take control.

Figure 6–23 shows a mighty head-and-shoulders pattern in action on a daily chart of tech stock Digital River, Inc. (DRIV). You can see how the formation develops to create a distribution stage and powerful trend reversal. When you learn to identify this pattern, it warns you to take profits on long positions and prepare for a short setup.

To determine an approximate length of the first leg down of a head-and-shoulders reversal, measure the distance from the neckline to the top of the head. Then, subtract that measurement from the neckline.

Now, let's move on to bottom-reversal patterns.

Double Bottom
When you see it: All time frames
What it looks like: A "W"
What it is: An effective bottom-reversal pattern

Bottom-reversal patterns reverse downtrends into uptrends. The first one we'll look at is the "double bottom." As you can imagine, it forms the mirror image of the double top.

A double bottom unwinds in a base, or accumulation stage. Just as the second top on a double top means traders refuse to pay higher prices, the second bottom on a double bottom implies traders and investors intend to support the stock and stop it from falling lower.

When you see a double bottom forming, cover short positions. Watch for a favorable long setup when the retest (second bottom) unwinds. If it holds its lows and bounces on strong buying action, enter a long position and *immediately* enter a protective stop under the retest low price.

Figure 6–24 displays a daily chart of aerospace and defense firm Esterline Technologies Corporation (ESL).

From mid-February to mid-March, poor ESL tumbled like a rock tied to a brick. During the last week of March, it finally skidded to a low at $23. It rallied about 50 percent of the last move down, then, in mid-May, it slid back down to 22.50.

The double-bottom that ESL drew is interesting, in that the second bottom, or retest, revolved through a mini double-bottom of its own. Soon after, ESL completed the bigger pattern.

Figure 6–25 illustrates how double-bottom patterns appear on intraday time frames.

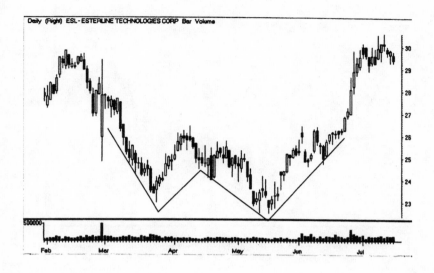

Figure 6–24. This daily chart of Esterline Technologies Corp. (ESL) illustrates a double bottom. And the second bottom developed its own "mini" double bottom. The aerospace and defense firm suffered from a downtrend. Toward the end of March, it fell to a nasty low of $23. It quickly shot higher by mid-April, then blew out the "weak hands" and tumbled back to $22.50 in May. Here's a great lesson in protective stops. ESL started up in mid-May, surely to the delight of the bulls. But note how it gapped down fast, scaring the jeepers out of long traders. It stubbornly held its lows, however, and quickly shot up to finish its double-bottom formation.

In this illustration, Applied Materials Inc., (AMAT) careens into an intraday downtrend, then rallies slightly before the day's close. The next morning finds the semiconductor giant with back-to-back (think "confusion") candles for the first twenty minutes after the bell. It then falls almost to the prior day's low.

If you had held a short day-trade in AMAT when it approached this low, you would have 1) tightened your protective stop, or 2) taken profits. While the retest of the prior day's low didn't *have* to hold, odds are it could (and did!). Remember, your primary goal in trading is to protect your capital.

> **Hot Tip:** While double bottoms appear regularly on all time frames, triple bottoms show up less frequently. If you see a triple bottom unwinding, prepare for a setup to the long side. This could turn into quite a buyers' party!

Reverse Head and Shoulders
When you see it: All time frames, more frequently on daily/weekly charts
What it looks like: An upside-down head and shoulders
What it is: A forceful bottom-reversal pattern

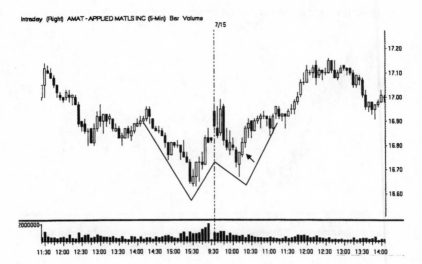

Figure 6–25. This 5-minute chart of Applied Materials, Inc. (AMAT) shows the giant semiconductor stock moving in an intraday downtrend. Just before the close, it rallied to prior intraday resistance. At the next day's open (vertical dotted line), AMAT gapped open slightly, experienced a volatile 20 minutes, then reversed to fall back to the prior day's low. Just before it reached those lows, however, it screeched into a U-turn. If you were short the stock for an intraday trade, this was the warning to cover your position. Minutes later, a bullish piercing pattern took it higher (arrow). When AMAT reached the prior resistance area (mid-point of the "W"), and then broke to the upside, the double-bottom pattern was complete.

A reverse head and shoulders halts a downtrend and sends the price into an uptrend. It operates similarly to the top-reversal pattern it reflects. When the price ultimately forms the right shoulder and climbs above resistance at the neckline, traders buy.

Figure 6–26 displays a daily chart of Alliant Techsystems Inc. (ATK) with dandy reverse head-and-shoulders pattern. Look at the dramatic gap up on October 30.

Although other news may have caused this multipoint leap, bottom-reversal patterns many times cause price gaps to the upside because of rampant short-covering. When "the shorts" cover their positions, they buy. When buyers join them and buy as well, it creates a buying frenzy that shoots a stock higher by several price levels.

Cup-with-a-Handle
When you see it: All time frames, more frequently on daily/weekly charts
What it looks like: The profile of a coffee cup and its handle
What it is: A methodical bottom-reversal pattern

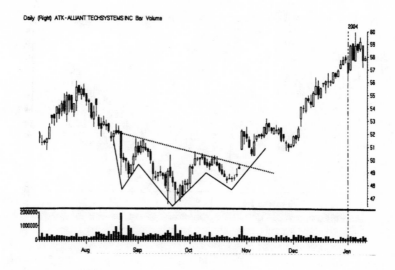

Daily (Right) ATK-ALLIANT TECHSYSTEMS INC Bar Volume

Figure 6–26. This daily chart of Alliant Techsystems, Inc. (ATK) shows how the aerospace and defense company reversed its downtrend by churning through a reverse head-and-shoulders pattern. Once the price breaks through the neckline to the upside, the pattern is complete and the downtrend is broken. In this case, when it formed the right shoulder, ATK gapped up multiple points and skipped right over any resistance it might have met at the neckline (dotted line).

William O'Neil of *Investor's Business Daily* named this pattern. You see it develop most often on the charts of blue-blooded, listed stocks that draw their patterns in an orderly manner.

The pattern forms in the accumulation, or basing stage of a trend. First, the price scoops out a cup. Then it hollows out a handle, dipping to a higher low.

When the price moves through resistance created by the top of the cup, it's a buy signal. The downtrend is broken and the bulls are in control.

Figure 6–27 shows a cup-with-a-handle reversal pattern on a daily chart of Lockheed Martin Corporation (LMT). You can see how this particular pattern played out in an organized trend reversal.

Note the morning-star candle reversal pattern on March 16. This pattern is fairly rare, so when it shows up, watch for a long setup.

Reverse cup-with-a-handle formations develop as top reversal patterns at the culmination of uptrends. As you can imagine, they are an upside-down version of the pattern.

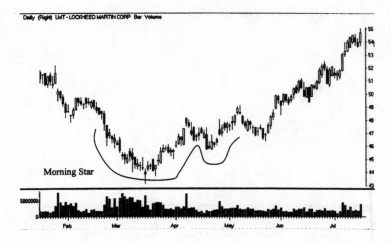

Figure 6–27. This daily chart of the Lockheed Martin Corp. (LMT) shows the giant aerospace company as its price hurtles through a downtrend until mid-March. Note increased volume on LMT's last leg down. *This is a clue that the downtrend may reverse,* as buyers step in to gradually absorb supply. LMT curves in a quick but orderly bottom into the first week of April, and completes the "cup" portion of the pattern. Note the morning-star candle reversal pattern on March 16. The stock dips down in April to form the "handle." It dips slightly again in May, and we see a second "handle" form. Soon after the second handle completes, the stock flies into a missile-borne uptrend.

> **Hot Tip:** The "saucer" reversal pattern is merely a shallow version of the cup-with-a-handle formation—without a handle. Stocks and their derivatives carve volatile patterns in today's market, and the gentle, serene saucer pattern shows up only on occasion.

Let's move on to a brief discussion of continuation patterns. If you've analyzed charts at all, you're already familiar with them.

Say you're watching the Daytona 500 car races. After a series of laps, each driver takes his race car off the course for a pit stop. During this time, team refuels the car, checks the engine, and replaces the tires. Soon the refreshed car and driver head back into the race.

Continuation patterns are pit stops for stocks. (*Stock car?* ☺ Oh, never mind.) *Characteristics:*

- These patterns form in the context of uptrends and downtrends

- They play out in patterns we call "flags," "pennants," and "triangles"

- We also refer to them simply as "pullbacks," "corrections," or "retracements"

> **Hot Tip:** Remember, stocks correct through *time* or *price*. We say that a stock that consolidates in a sideways pattern corrects through *time*. A stock that pulls back, or retraces in price, corrects through *price*.

What we use them for:

- Setup opportunities. (You may want to review basic setups in chapter 2.)

Basic Signals:

- A stock in an uptrend experiences an orderly continuation pattern. When the price breaks above resistance (continuation tops), *buy*.

- A stock in a downtrend churns through a continuation pattern. When the price begins to break below support (continuation bottoms), *sell short*.

What's important:

- The continuation pattern forms a tight, orderly move. Sloppy continuation patterns produce sloppy breakouts or breakdowns. And that means losses to us. Play only compact, orderly continuation patterns.

Let's roll out our buddy Lockheed Martin Corporation (LMT) once again. Figure 6–28 shows the same chart as Figure 6–27; this time, however, we've identified the continuation patterns in LMT's uptrend.

Ideally, you don't want a continuation pattern in an uptrend to continue for more than three weeks. A long, drawn-out continuation pattern goads impatient traders (who, us? *impatient?* ☺) to tend to look for greener pastures. So, if you jump into a continuation pattern early, in the hopes of catching the initial move up, jump back out if the pattern doesn't play out within a short time period.

Conversely, an old market saying states, "Never short a dull market." If you're watching a stock in a downtrend, and its continuation pattern keeps drifting sideways, *avoid shorting it early*. The bulls could rumble in and send the stock higher.

Figure 6–29 shows an intraday chart of the NASDAQ 100 E-mini contract.

The futures contract tumbles in an orderly downtrend on the day. You will use indicators on your charts—especially with the E-minis—to identify precision entries and exits. Still, your ability to recognize trends, trend reversals, and continuation patterns will confirm your entry, exit, and risk-management tactics.

One of the most important aspects of pattern recognition is your ability to understand the underlying human behavior. As your skill of interpreting the psychological moves that underpin market movement increases, so will your success as a trader.

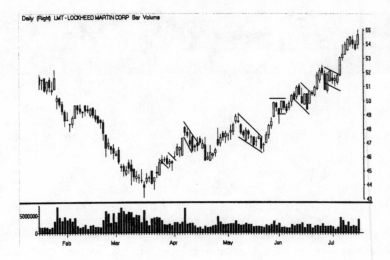

Figure 6–28. This time, we've identified the continuation patterns in Lockheed Martin's uptrend. The trick with continuation patterns is to let them play out. While many of us like to nibble early in the pattern to catch the initial breakout (or breakdown, in a downtrend), it's important to maintain a tight stop. Price patterns don't always behave as we think—or hope—they should. A safer plan is to wait for the stock to break out above resistance, or the tops of the continuation pattern, and then buy. Of course, we're going to add additional indicators to our charts to confirm buy and sell decisions.

(Please note: I did not isolate every continuation pattern on LMT's uptrend. Major continuation patterns are marked.)

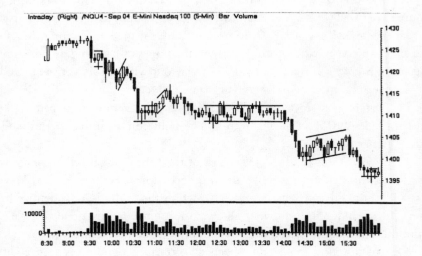

Figure 6–29. This display shows a 5-minute chart of the NASDAQ 100 E-minis, with continuation patterns identified. The minis cooperated nicely on this day, falling in an orderly downtrend and so creating opportunities for short traders.

Chapter 7 opens with an introduction to candlestick charting techniques written for this book by candle chart "guru," Steve Nison. Then we'll take a look at candle reversal patterns, the "voices" of volume, and the power of moving averages.

This has been a long chapter, and you've absorbed a lot of information. To find out what you've remembered, scan through the questions and answers that follow. That way, you'll reinforce prior knowledge and bring up new points you'll want to explore further.

Quiz

Questions

1. Give brief definitions of both fundamental and technical analysis.

2. Fear results in _____ (demand or supply?). Greed results in _____ (demand or supply?).

3. True or False: Optimism pushes a market higher and higher, then explodes into greed and euphoria. For a swing trade, that's the best time to buy a stock.

4. What is the definition of an uptrend? What is the definition of a downtrend?

5. True or False: When a market moves in a sideways pattern, or horizontal range, the odds of pulling consistent and sizeable trading profits are limited.

6. Which pattern is usually more volatile: 1) an accumulation or basing pattern, or 2) a distribution or top-reversal pattern?

7. When you can connect three or more (higher) lows on an uptrend, that trend is considered to be a _____ trend.

8. If a stock is falling in a downtrend on a daily chart, and the angle of the slope begins to flatten, does that mean the downtrend is gaining downward momentum? Or does the flattening angle indicate the downtrend may slow its descent?

9. Greed = _____ = _____. Fear = _____ = _____.

10. When a stock has fallen in a downtrend, is it easier for a stock to recover very soon after the downtrend's low has been established, or is it more likely the stock will recover its losses after it moves sideways for a period of time?

11. A head and shoulders is a _____ (top or bottom?) reversal pattern.

12. What is the function of a continuation pattern?

Answers

1. Fundamental analysis entails the process of studying a company's fundamental statistics, such as market share, quarterly earnings, and profit margins, to determine a value for its stock. Technical analysis is the process of analyzing a stock's historical price patterns in order to predict future price movement. Fundamental analysis serves traditional buy–and–hold investors. Technical analysis, with charts as its primary tool, is the choice of most traders.

2. Fear results in supply. Greed results in demand.

3. Please say "False!"

4. A stock or index is in an uptrend when the price rises in a series of higher highs and higher lows. A stock or index forms a downtrend when the price falls in a series of lower highs and lower lows.

5. True. Markets that trade in consolidations or horizontal trends give up little in the way of consistent or significant gains.

6. Distribution or top-reversal (rollover) patterns usually unwind in a more volatile fashion than basing patterns. Emotions are explosive because the stakes are high. Bulls want the uptrend to continue, bears want a downtrend to begin.

7. When you can connect three or more (higher) lows on an uptrend, that trend is considered to be a major trend. As well, when you connect three or more highs on a downtrend, the trend is also considered to be a major trend.

8. When the slope of a downtrend line begins to flatten, it warns that the downtrend could decelerate and even shift into basing mode.

9. Greed = demand = support (buyers). Fear = supply = resistance (sellers).

10. The farther away resistance is from a price pattern, the less power it has. The closer resistance remains to current price, the more power that resistance exudes.

11. Top.

12. A continuation pattern provides a "rest period" for stocks or other trading vehicles between legs-up of an uptrend, or legs-down of a downtrend.

CENTER POINT

Prosperity Is an Inside Job

Often people attempt to live their lives backwards. They try to have more things, or more money, in order to do more of what they want, so they will be happier. The way it actually works is the reverse. You must first be who you really are, then do what you need to do, in order to have what you want.
—Margaret Young

Do you know a wealthy person who is unhappy and worries over potentially losing what they have? On the other hand, do you know someone who lives on an average income yet glows with joy and prosperity?

True prosperity has little to do with material circumstances. It has everything to do with our attitude toward life.

In *True Prosperity*, Shakti Gawain writes, "Prosperity is an internal experience, not an external state, and it is an experience that is not tied to having a certain amount of money."

Acquire instant prosperity by enjoying what you have *right now*. Look around you. What resources do you have—material or talents—that you've ignored or forgotten about? Appreciate what you have, while you work toward what you want.

Here are three concepts that bring us true prosperity.

First, as Margaret Young's opening quote says, ". . . you must be who you really are." Self-awareness—knowing that you are a successful, prosperous person in progress—is key to manifesting wealth. Have you ever met a millionaire who stares at his (or her) feet and declares apologetically to the world what a failure he is? Doubtful.

Second, avoid focusing on lack. It places limits on your abundance. Such constant declarations as "I can't afford that," "There's too much month left at the end of the money," center your attention on scarcity. Instead, try paying your bills and buying groceries with a positive attitude—positive *feelings*—toward the money you *do* have. Positive energy expands; negative energy contracts.

Finally, ". . . do what you need to do to have what you want." Remember to look for prosperity in all areas of your life. Abundant health and rewarding relationships are just as worthy as financial goals. And while no level of income will guarantee feelings of prosperity, you can experience prosperity at almost any level of income.

Any way you look at it, prosperity is an inside job!

Triple Play: Candles, Volume, and Moving Averages

To me, the "tape" is the final arbiter of any investment decision. I have a cardinal rule: Never fight the tape!

—Martin Zweig

In this chapter, we're going to talk about three chart components that give you a terrific "bang for your buck": candlestick technology, volume signals, and moving averages. These three dynamic tools have made me money and added to my ability to stay in the game.

In fact, I know successful traders who, along with support-and-resistance price levels and trendlines/channel lines, use candle patterns, volume signals, and moving averages as their only decision support tools for entering and exiting trades.

Directly put, candlestick reversal patterns forecast a change or shift in supply and demand. Volume levels broadcast intensity of interest. Moving averages point to reliable support-and-resistance price zones. When that combined information points to either a buying or selling strategy, you have a basis for action that is strong and valid.

Candle Charts Shine Light on the Forces Underlying Price Behavior

As you know, the ability to identify upcoming price reversals represents one of the most important trading skills we can develop. Candle patterns offer a heads-up as to when those reversals are about to take place. If you don't use candlesticks on your charts now, you may want to give them a try. Candlestick charting techniques are easy to learn, and even rudimentary knowledge of how they work should add nicely to your bottom line.

Steve Nison, acknowledged expert of Japanese candlestick techniques, earns the credit for bringing this ancient and highly effective technique to the United States and Western Europe. Steve kindly agreed to contribute the introduction for candlestick charting techniques for this section. He writes:

Make use of your opportunities (Japanese proverb)

Steve Nison, president, *candlecharts.com*

You've probably heard of Japanese Candlesticks. They are trading techniques refined by generations of use in the Far East. As the first to reveal them to the Western world in the 1980s, I am flattered to see they are now available on almost every charting system.

The reasons candlesticks are "hot" is they visually offer a deep and powerful insight into who's winning the battle between the bulls and the bears.

As a longtime friend of Toni's, I know she harnesses the power of candlesticks as another weapon in her trading arsenal.

Here are some reasons why you may want to consider using candlesticks as part of your trading strategy:

Candle charts are easy to understand. Anyone, from the first-time chartist to the seasoned professional can easily use candle charts. This is because, as will be shown later, the data that is required to draw the candlestick chart is the same as that needed for the bar chart (high, low, open, and close).

Candlestick charting tools give you a jump on the competition. Candle charts not only show the trend of the move, as do bar charts, but also show the force underpinning the move. In addition, many of the candle signals are given in a few sessions, rather than the weeks often needed for a bar-chart signal. Thus, candle charts will help you enter and exit the market with better timing.

Candlestick charting tools will help preserve capital. In this volatile environment, capital preservation is just as important as capital accumulation. You will discover that the candles shine in helping you preserve capital since they often send out indications that a new high or low may not be sustained.

Candle charting techniques are easily joined with Western charting tools. Because candle charts use the same data as bar charts, it means that any of the technical analyses used with bar charts (such as retracements, trend lines, moving averages, stochastics, etc.) can be employed with candle charts. However, candle charts can send signals not available with bar charts.

Candlestick charts can be used in stocks, futures, and any market that has an open, high, low, and close. And they can be used in all time frames—from intraday to weekly.

How Candles Take Shape

A candle line (a single candle is sometimes referred to as a "line") is simply a bar, with the space between the bar's opening and closing price enclosed in a rectangle. We call the rectangle a "real body." When the high price of that candle extends above the opening or closing price, we call that line extension a "shadow." If the low of the candle extends below the opening or closing price, we also refer to that line as a "shadow." Some people call them "wicks" or "tails," but "shadow" is correct.

When the candle's closing price is higher than the opening price, we color the rectangle white, or clear. When the candle's closing price is below the opening price, we color the rectangle black. Many traders color-code their positive candles green and negative candles red. Since the graphics in this text are limited to black and white, we'll stay with white and black real bodies.

Figure 7–1 shows two candle lines. The "A" candle line is positive: the price closed higher than it opened. The "B" candle line is negative: the price closed lower than it opened.

Candle lines and patterns are valuable tools in that they illustrate prevailing market opinion. A long, white real body shows positive opinion, or high demand. An extended black real body forecasts negative opinion, or overwhelming supply.

> **Hot Tip:** You've surely heard the market axiom "Amateurs open the market, professionals close it." Japanese and Western technicians agree: the closing price represents the most important price of the day. Why? Because the closing price broadcasts the commitment level of those who are willing to hold positions overnight. If a stock closes on its highs, buyers are committed to holding. If it closes on its lows, commitment on the long side is weak.

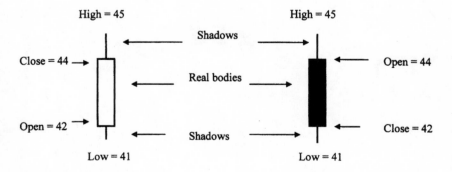

Figure 7–1. Candlestick Structure

Figure 7–2 exhibits a *doji*, along with two variations on this powerful candle line. You'll notice that doji (the plural of "doji" is "doji") have no real body. That's because doji open and close at, or very near, the same price.

A doji indicates indecision. When a price period opens, the bulls push it higher, then the bears push it lower. Still, neither gains control, and the price returns to its original beginning point.

In Figure 7–2, you'll also see the dragonfly doji. This doji represents positive opinion, because the price opens and closes on the high of the day, or period. Clearly, the bulls hold the reigns in this market.

The third candle line in Figure 7–2 reveals the dreaded gravestone doji. The descriptive Japanese term clearly portends impending doom. And it should! The candle opens and closes at the low of the day, or period. Even though the bulls manage to raise the price higher, the bears squelch the move up and trample the price down to close at its lows.

Important fact: Although they do both, doji mark top reversals more potently than they mark bottom reversals.

Also keep in mind that a doji *may* simply act as a pit stop for a price that's in the midst of a leg-up in an uptrend, or a move down in a downtrend.

Although doji act as powerful top-reversal candles (a doji's indecision message indicates anxiety is creeping in), practice patience and wait for confirmation from the follow-up candle that substantiates a reversal or price shift.

Figure 7–3 displays two variations on the doji theme. The first is a "spinning top." The spinning top can be either white or black. Shadows may extend above and/or below the real body, or not at all. As you can see, this candle line forms a "near doji," with the price closing very near to the open. Spinning tops also show a relatively even heat between the bulls and bears, or an undecided market mindset.

Figure 7–3 includes high–wave candles. A high–wave candle must display extreme shadows (relative to the normal price range) both above and below the

Figure 7–2.

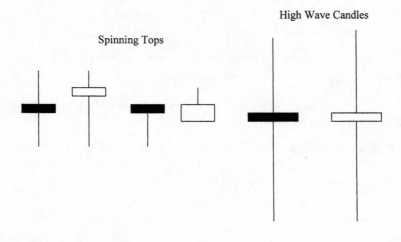

Figure 7–3.

narrow real body, which creates an extended price breadth. If doji and spinning tops suggest indecision, then high-wave candles broadcast downright havoc.

When we think through the price action that creates a high-wave candle, we understand. The price opens, and during the course of the trading day, the bulls push the price to a radical high. Bears take over and pound the price to an extreme low. By the end of the day, though, the tug o'war moves back to even. With no commitment maintained in either direction, the price returns to the starting point, to close near the open.

> **Hot Tip:** Look for high-wave candles on daily charts. They rarely appear on intraday charts, except during a volatile opening period. If the stock you are holding completes a high-wave candle on a daily chart, consider taking profits. The havoc and confusion that generates a high-wave candle usually continues, producing volatility and erratic price action.

Before we jump into candle reversal patterns themselves, here are some illuminating facts:

- Candle reversal patterns hold predictive value when they take shape at tops and bottoms of price or trend reversals. When a price pattern churns sideways, candles do not predict future moves.

- To confirm a candle pattern's message, wait for the subsequent candle to form. (You have to wait for confirmation with bar charts, as well.) If you don't have time to wait for the next candle to form, move to a smaller time frame, and obtain an earlier signal.

- To glean the most value from candle reversal patterns, use them in conjunction with Western technical indicators.

- Candle patterns confirm support and resistance areas, but they cannot predict future price targets.

- Generally speaking, candle patterns form and give signals on all time frames. Like most chart tools, the longer the time frame, the clearer and more powerful the patterns will be.

We're going to talk about candle reversal patterns throughout this book as decision support tools for trade entries and exits; the following illustrations will act as a reference guide.

Candle patterns form from one, two, or three candles. We'll look at single candle line reversal patterns first.

Figure 7–4 shows "northern" and "southern doji." Doji are powerful top- and bottom-reversal candles. Remember, doji appear more often, and with more force, as *top reversal* indicators.

Figure 7–5 exhibits bullish and bearish belt holds. The sumo wrestling term *yorikiri* provided the Japanese name for the belt hold patterns. *Yorikiri* means "pushing your opponent out of the ring while holding his belt." This vivid word-picture adds definition to these long-bodied, high-opinion candles that strong-arm a trend or retracement into a reversal at support and resistance areas.

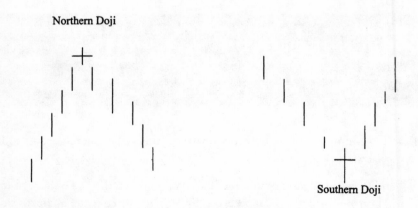

Figure 7–4. A *northern doji* appears at the top of an uptrend, or rally, and marks the reversal of that rally.

A *southern doji* appears at the bottom of a downtrend and marks the reversal of that trend.

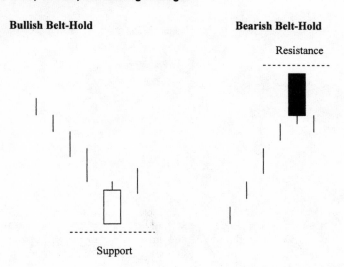

Bullish Belt-Hold   Bearish Belt-Hold

Resistance

Support

Figure 7–5. A *bullish belt hold* is a single candle line formed of a long, white real body. The candle opens at, or near, the low and closes at, or near, the high. When a bullish belt hold appears in a decline—especially when it opens on a former support area—it predicts a potential move up. In the context of an uptrend, the candle suggests a trend continuation.

A *bearish belt hold* is a single candle line formed from a long, black real body. The candle opens at or near, its highs, and closes at, or near, its lows. This candle is an especially powerful predictor to more downside action when it gaps open into prior resistance, and then falls. In the context of a downtrend, the candle forecasts a trend continuation.

Figure 7–6 exhibits three single candle reversal patterns: the hammer, hanging man, and shooting star. While the hammer acts as a bottom-reversal candle, the hanging man and shooting star both forecast top reversals, or price shifts.

Personally, I find the shooting star to be a very powerful top-reversal candle. When it appears on a daily chart, after an extended uptrend or rally that's moved sharply higher—especially into prior resistance—I take at least partial profits. Why? Although the bulls boosted the price higher, the bears shoved it lower and closed it at, or near, its lows. Note how the shooting star's structure resembles that of the gravestone doji; the shooting stars adds a real body.

Figure 7–7 displays two candle reversal patterns.

The first pattern in this illustration is the two-candle bullish piercing pattern, which is a bottom-reversal pattern.

The second pattern, the dark cloud cover, represents one of the most common—and most reliable—of candle reversal patterns. You'll see this configuration on all time frames. When you see a stock go ballistic and soar into overbought, overex-

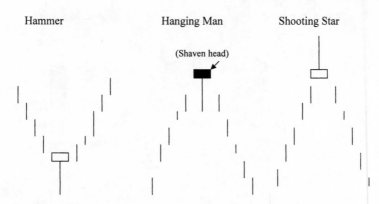

Figure 7–6. A *hammer* is a single reversal candle that appears at the bottom of a down-trend, or pivot low. The real body can be either white or black, and a lower shadow at least two times the length of the real body is preferred. The message: the hammer "hammers the price upwards."

A *hanging man* appears at the top of an uptrend or rally. Again, the real body can be white or black, and we prefer a lower shadow that's at least two times the length of the real body. Both the hammer and hanging man should have a "shaven head," which means that no shadow appears above the real body. The connotation of this candle's name, "hanging man," leaves no doubt as to future price direction.

A *shooting star* also appears at the top of an uptrend rally. The real body can be white or black. This time the shadow extends from the top of the real body, and it should be twice the height of the real body. None, or little shadow should extend below the real body. Since shooting stars streak across the night sky, the Japanese say this candle indicates darkness, or lower prices.

tended territory, then slow and reverse into a dark cloud cover pattern, pay attention! If you're long that stock, you'd be wise to grab at least partial profits.

> **Hot Tip: Dark cloud cover is the opposite formation to the bullish piercing pattern. There is no "bearish piercing pattern."**

Figure 7–8 displays bullish and bearish counterattack patterns. While the bullish counterattack pattern resembles the bullish piercing pattern, the counter-attack doesn't penetrate the preceding candle's real body. Ditto with the bearish counterattack, as compared to dark cloud cover. Still, counterattack patterns should be recognized and respected. Fervent opinion drove the pattern to the downside or upside, then opposite forces reversed that opinion.

Figure 7–9 shows two more potent candle reversal patterns, the bullish and bearish engulfing patterns. This is an interesting pattern, as the reversal candle

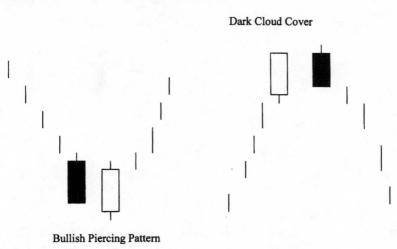

Figure 7–7. In a downtrend, the *bullish piercing pattern*—a long black candle—is followed by a candle that gaps lower but closes at, or near, its high. The strong white candle's real body should close more than halfway into the prior black candle's real body. The white candle "pierces" the downward price action and reverses it.

The opposite of the bullish piercing pattern is the *dark cloud cover*. The price is moving in a rally or uptrend. A white-bodied candle is followed by a candle that gaps open to the upside, but closes at, or near, its lows. The "dark cloud" candle should close more than halfway into the prior white candle's real body. The connotation of "dark cloud" spells gloom for the price.

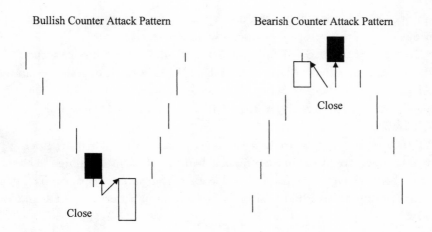

Figure 7–8. A *bullish counterattack* candle line takes place when a black candle in a downtrend or pullback is followed by a white candle that gaps lower at the open, and then closes unchanged from the black candle's low.

A *bearish counterattack* line occurs in a rally or uptrend. A white candle is followed by a candle that gaps higher, and then falls lower, but closes unchanged from the prior candle's close.

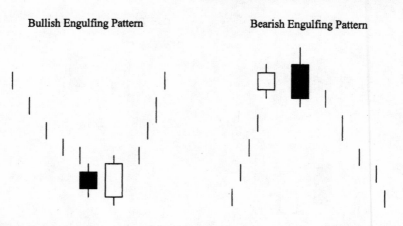

Bullish Engulfing Pattern   Bearish Engulfing Pattern

Figure 7–9. The *bullish engulfing pattern* occurs in the context of a downtrend or pull-back. A black candle is followed by a candle that gaps down at the open, then closes *above the prior candle's opening price*. The price action of the bottoming candle completely engulfs the candle preceding it. Supply reverts to demand, as the bulls wrest price control from the bears.

The *bearish engulfing pattern* takes place during a rally or uptrend. A white candle is followed by a candle that gaps open to the upside, then falls to close *below the white candle's opening price*. This time, the black candle's real body completely engulfs the white candle's real body. When a stock is overbought or overextended, and a bearish engulfing pattern forms, know that the stock may soon begin a steep slide south.

gaps open in the prevailing direction of the price move, then makes a fast and furious U-turn that reverses, or at least slows, the trend.

Does this pattern look familiar to you? It's the comparable pattern to the Western pattern called a "key-reversal day." When a stock experiences an uptrend, a key reversal occurs when the price gaps open to a new high, above the previous day's high. The price then falls hard and closes below the previous day's low.

If a stock is in a downtrend, a key reversal takes place when the stock gaps down to a new low, then finishes higher than the previous day's high. The difference between engulfing patterns and key-reversal patterns: Japanese use opening and closing prices as boundaries. Western reversal patterns use high and low prices.

> **Hot Tip:** Whether the pattern formed is a Japanese engulfing pattern or a Western key-reversal pattern, the wider the price range and the higher the volume, the stronger the chance that a trend reversal will follow through.

Bullish Harami Pattern   Bearish Harami Pattern

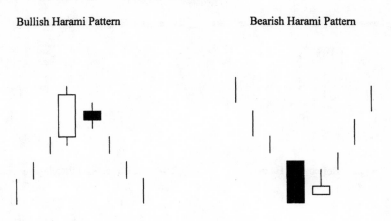

Figure 7–10. The *harami* is the opposite of the engulfing pattern.

The *bullish harami* is a top-reversal pattern. In an uptrend or rally, a white candle with a long, white real body is followed by a spinning top, either white or black.

The *bearish harami* forms a bottom-reversal pattern. Its appearance, the Japanese say, predicts that the decline is exhausting itself.

If either *harami* forms with a *doji* as the second candle, the pattern is called a "*harami* cross."

Figure 7–10 exhibits the bullish and bearish *harami*. In Japanese, *harami* means "mother and child."

Did you notice that this top- and bottom-reversal pattern forms as the opposite formation to the engulfing pattern? As a result, the *harami* is comparable to the Western "inside day." While the inside day requires that the highs and lows of the second bar stay within the highs and lows of the wider range topping or bottoming bar, the Japanese *harami* demands only that the second, or "baby," real body stay within the price confines of the prior, longer real body.

The *harami* has an advantage, because it demands that the second session's real body stay within the confines of the topping or bottoming candle's real body—even if the highs and lows of the "inside" real body stretch beyond those of the first. So, the *harami* may signal a reversal that the Western inside day may not.

Hot Tip: The *harami cross* forms with a doji for the second "inside" day. It is sometimes called a "petrifying" pattern. With a powerful doji for the second day, the pattern can "petrify" or stop the current trend, and thus act as a reversal agent.

Tweezers Top and Hanging Man   Tweezers Top and Dark Cloud Cover

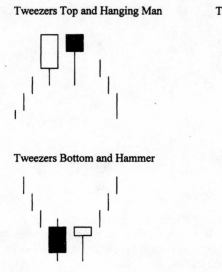

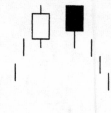

Tweezers Bottom and Hammer   Tweezers Bottom and Piercing Pattern

Figure 7–11. The candle pattern defined as *tweezers* occurs when two or more candles' lines have matching highs or lows. The ideal result occurs with the first session completing a long real body. The second session can have many variations. It's best, but not mandatory, when this candle completes with a small real body.

In this illustration, we're using single candles you are familiar with, to complete the pattern.

The *tweezers top* takes place in a rising market, when two or more consecutive highs match.

The *tweezers bottom* occurs in a falling market or downtrend, with two or more consecutive lows that match.

The resulting image is tweezer tongs that "pinch." The connotation: the tweezers are pinching the trend to a halt.

The last of the two-candle reversal patterns is shown in Figure 7–11. The pattern is called "tweezers." Essentially, tweezers appear in an uptrend or rally when two candles form with the same, or nearly the same, highs.

In a downtrend or pullback, when two candles appear side by side with identical lows, they act as tweezers to "pinch" the move down. Think of this pattern as a mini–double top. If the subsequent candle drops lower (uptrend), or climbs higher (downtrend), the tweezers have done their reversal work.

Figure 7–12 shines a light on a three-candle pattern known as the evening star. The unique aspect of this pattern is that the spinning top or doji that appears as the top or bottom reversal candle should gap away from the candlestick that precedes it *and* the candle that follows it. This leaves the "star" alone, and it is even referred to by some Western analysts as an island reversal.

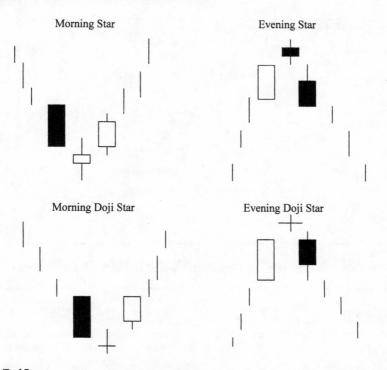

Figure 7–12. The *morning star* consists of a three-candle bottom-reversal pattern. In a downtrend or pullback, a candlestick with a long, black real body appears. Next, a spinning top (small real body of either color) appears, gapping down and away from the black real body. The third candle is white, and it gaps up from the bottoming spinning top. This leaves the spinning top by itself, as a "morning star." The connotation: a morning star appears just before the dawn—or just before the light (higher prices).

The *doji morning star* forms the same pattern, replacing the spinning top with the powerful *doji*.

The *evening star* forms a three-candle top-reversal pattern. In an uptrend or rally, a long, white candle appears. Then a spinning top appears, gapping up and keeping its real body above the white candle's real body. The third candle is black, and gaps down from the topping candle. Now the "evening star" hangs alone in the night sky, and suggests hours of darkness (lower prices) to come.

The *doji evening star* forms the same pattern as the morning star, but replaces the spinning top with the powerful top-reversal doji.

When you see this pattern occur, especially after an extended uptrend on a daily chart, you may want to take all or partial profits. If it forms as the second top to a double top, it may develop into a juicy setup for a short trade.

The last candle pattern is a window. A window compares equally with the Western term "gap." Keep in mind that windows, or gaps, act as support when a stock trades above them, and resistance when the price action trades below them. We'll talk more about gap strategies in upcoming chapters.

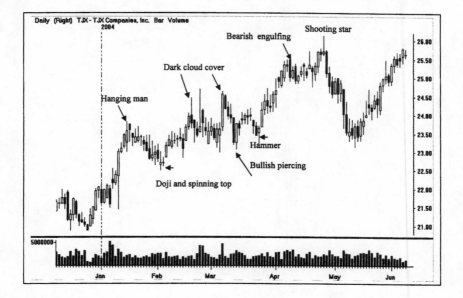

Figure 7–13. Several candle reversal patterns appear on this daily chart of TJX Companies, Inc. (TJX). You can see a hanging man and two examples of dark cloud cover. The second dark cloud cover in March doesn't show the dark cloud penetrating the long, white candle as much as we'd like to see, but it still brings forth a respectable price drop. Also note the shooting star that forms at the end of April. The ensuing reversal takes TJX back down to its March lows. More candle patterns occur on this chart, but see if you can identify them.

Figures 7–13 through 7–15 (pages 152–154) exhibit candle reversal patterns on daily, sixty-minute, and ten-minute charts. When you study these charts, you'll see how many times the patterns forecast future price action accurately.

The candlestick reversal patterns we've just discussed represent the most prevalent—and the most powerful—patterns I know of. We will refer to them throughout the remainder of this text.

You can study a full menu of candlestick patterns in Steve Nison's books, *Japanese Candlestick Charting Techniques, Beyond Candlesticks: More Japanese Charting Techniques Revealed*, and *The Candlestick Course*. Or go to Nison's Web site: *candlecharts.com*.

To obtain the most effective signal as mentioned before, please use candlestick techniques in conjunction with other indicators.

Speaking of other indicators, let's move ahead into a discussion of volume and its signals. Along with candlestick patterns, volume signals, when identified properly, can help you harvest bountiful profits!

Figure 7–14. On this hourly chart of TJX Companies, Inc. (TJX), you can see more reversal patterns. Dark cloud cover patterns announce three times that lower prices are ahead. After pullbacks, bullish piercing patterns help boost price upward. The shooting star appeared twice, warning of lower prices. Do you see what a powerful forecaster this lonely star can be? As with the prior chart, more patterns will emerge as you study it.

The Voices of Volume

We all know that the outcome of an event or situation depends directly upon the quality and quantity of human attention and enthusiasm it receives.

When we direct positive energy (greed) toward a stock or trading entity, it increases in value (demand). Replace that with negative energy (fear)—or even inattention—and it will decrease in value (supply). When positive and negative energy arrive in relatively equal amounts, they tend to offset each other. The market responds by trading in a horizontal range.

In its simplest form, volume spikes on a chart give the trader an instant message about the level of enthusiasm—or lack of it—directed to price movement of a stock or futures contract at any given moment. Take it to a slightly more sophisticated level, and exploding or imploding volume activity can alert us to trend reversals, confirm entry decisions, indicate the "health" of continuation patterns, and act as a dynamic decision-support tool for managing and exiting trades.

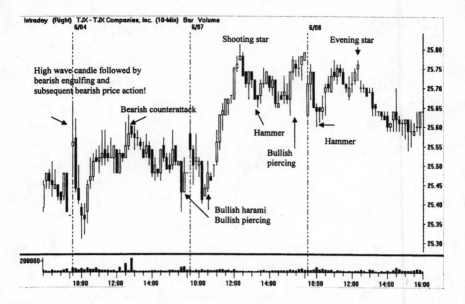

Figure 7–15. On this 10-minute chart of TJX Companies, Inc. (TJX), candle patterns forecast future price moves. I said in earlier text that high wave candles appear mostly on daily charts. One showed up, however, on this intraday chart. The next 10-minute candle is a bearish engulfing candle, and the stock fell for three more candles after that before a spinning top turned the trend back up. Notice how the shooting star halted the uptrend on the second day that started just after 10:00 a.m. EST and shot straight up until nearly 12:30 p.m. If you were day-trading TJX to the long side when the shooting star appeared, and *especially* when the dark cloud cover followed it, it warned you to take profits!

Volume as a Powerful Decision Support Tool

Most indicators used on charts are a derivative of price. For example, the MACD, RSI, and stochastics emerge from a statistical manipulation of price action.

Volume, however, acts as a variable independent of price. The information it broadcasts to us is unique, because it's separate from price action.

Here's what you need to remember about volume signals, on an overall basis:

- If the momentum and velocity of the volume cooperates with the price action—such as a breakout to the upside on strong volume—it tells us that the current movement is reliable. We say: Volume *confirms* price movement.

- If volume momentum *does not* match price movement, the *non-confirmation* alerts us that the implied price action may fail. Translation: Traders' enthusiasm doesn't match the pop up or down in price, so the outcome may turn into a bull or bear trap. For instance, a breakout to the upside on weak volume may skid right back to where it started, creating a trap for unhappy bulls.

The On-Balance Volume Indicator

The On-Balance Volume (OBV) is a single line that trends over your volume histogram, and it works as a reliable and trader-friendly indicator. Readily available on most charting packages, it also works well with candle charts, oscillators, and other charting tools.

Joe Granville originated On-Balance Volume. The indicator correlates volume to price change.

Again, displayed as a single line, the OBV moves over your volume spikes. As a running total, it rises when the coinciding bar or candle closes higher than the previous close. It falls when the security closes lower than the prior close.

The OBV moves in trends, accompanying price movement. So, if your stock is rising in an uptrend, the OBV will rise in concert with it. A stock falling in a downtrend will show its OBV tracing a downtrend, as well.

The OBV can precede price changes or reversals by displaying bullish or bearish divergences (divergence occurs when indicator and price head in opposite directions). That gives you a heads-up for entries and exits. The OBV's signals are particularly meaningful when they coincide with a price oscillator (MACD, stochastics, etc.) divergence.

From now on, most of the charts displayed in this book will show the OBV as an indicator.

The Voices of Volume—What Do They Tell You?

Let's look at how distinctive relationships between volume and price movement convey predictive signals as to future price action.

Please understand that these technical signals are not perfect "crystal balls." I don't know of one that is. (If I did, I'd be sunning on my yacht in the Mediterranean right now, sipping champagne. ☺)

More often than not, though, the warnings and confirmations volume signals display have made me—and saved me—money.

Volume precedes and/or accompanies price. When a stock moves up in the context of an uptrend (higher highs and higher lows), strong to average volume will

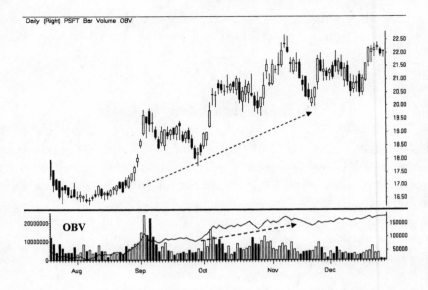

Daily (Right) PSFT Bar Volume OBV

Figure 7–16. On this daily chart of PeopleSoft, Inc. (PSFT), you can see how the stock shot up on high volume, then pulled back on lower volume. This is a healthy sign in an uptrend. The On-Balance Volume also (OBV) trended higher with PSFT's uptrend. When the software stock started to chop sideways in late November, it became more of a successful day-trading stock than a swing-trading stock. Note the evening star pattern in the first week of November. A window or gap down occurred two days later, and PSFT slid south, nearly to its previous low.

accompany it on most bars or candles. Keep in mind, however, that while *every* rising candle may not be fueled by high volume, the volume should maintain solid momentum.

Figure 7–16 shows PeopleSoft, Inc. (PSFT) breaking out of a base in mid-August. It soared higher in the following three legs, led by heavy volume (demand). In December, the price action and volume tapered off.

Volume message: If you were core- or position-trading (buy breakout of base and hold for duration of the uptrend) this stock, you'd take profits at the end of November or early December, when volume weakened and PSFT couldn't make a higher high. Swing traders (two-to-five-day hold) would have used price action, volume, and the OBV (along with moving averages and other indicators) to catch price swings from August to December. Day traders would trade PSFT to the long side while the trend was intact, especially during high-volume days when multiple points soared.

Low-to-average volume on pullback in uptrend = bullish. When a stock in an uptrend retraces in an orderly pullback, or consolidates in a horizontal continuation pattern, the volume should contract, as well. That shows that the stock is "resting" in a healthy manner. Traders and investors are holding, not folding. Figure 7–16 shows PSFT's volume contracting on the pullbacks or retracements in the mid–August to December uptrend. This volume expansion moves higher, and coupled with orderly contraction on consolidation or pullbacks, tells us the uptrend is healthy.

High volume on pullback in uptrend = bearish. When an uptrend is in progress, if you see strong, or stronger, volume on the pullback than occurred on the previous move up, it's a signal to pay attention. It indicates market participants are just as willing to sell it now, as they were to buy it earlier. The increased selling pressure will cause the stock to plunge—and fast!

Of course, in a downtrend, falling prices usually tumble on high volume, then rally or consolidate on low volume.

> **Hot Tip: Downtrends are usually more erratic and volatile than uptrends. So, know that if you are short a stock in a downtrend on a daily chart, you may be in for a *very* exciting ride. Monitor support areas, maintain your stop, and keep an eye on your plan. And don't let the trade get away from you.**

Figure 7–17 shows a daily chart of Texas Instruments, Inc. (TXN). Note how the change in volume leads the trend reversal starting in early November, when the stock soared into overbought territory and topped out.

Position traders surely took profits by mid-December, when TXN carved two lower highs and fell on high volume. Swing traders, who played the uptrend, waited for a rise into resistance and pullback on additional high volume to begin shorting a downtrend. Day traders, who grabbed long gains from TXN's muscular uptrend, may have taken advantage of the high-volume negative days to lock in profits on shorting opportunities.

By the end of December, TXN took a deep breath and flexed its muscles, soaring to a dazzling high in mid-January. Still, savvy traders knew that when the stock shot skyward, then careened down the steep price slope on *high* volume, the bull party was over.

New high on weak volume = bearish. As previously discussed, when a market continues to achieve new highs in an established uptrend, volume should maintain a healthy pace. So, when a market makes a new high on weak volume, it signals that the trend may be ready to shift or reverse.

Remember, volume measures and displays the momentum of excitement and enthusiasm of market participants. Escalating prices accompanied by weak volume shows a lack of enthusiasm. A lack of enthusiasm can lead to panic when it does not confirm a rising price—especially when it's a new high in an

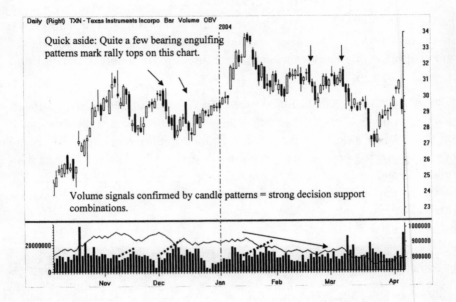

Figure 7–17. The volume signals ring loud and clear on this daily chart of Texas Instruments, Inc. (TXN). The dotted lines show how panicky volume levels told traders to exit long core positions in mid-November and December. The OBV started making lower lows in December. It moved into a trendless period in late December and January that Granville called "doubtful." He also said that these doubtful periods could break OBV trends. Note how this doubtful time was not impressed by TXN's rise to new highs in January. Of course, the low volume usually exhibited seasonally in December might have had something to do with that. In the late January cliff-fall from new highs, TXN's volume rose, indicating strong selling pressure.

overbought market. As indifference becomes evident, the rally soon becomes suspect. Fear sets in, and resulting supply takes the market south.

Figure 7–18 shows a daily chart of Priceline.com, Inc. (PCLN). This travel services stock climbed nicely to a high of $27.74 on April 12, retesting its highs of the previous week. By the end of that day, however, PCLN closed in a *doji* on relatively low volume. (Remember, *doji* form strong topping bars.) Swing traders who were long PCLN and were savvy enough to check their daily charts a few minutes before the market closed surely took partial or all profits off the table. Day traders who gravitate toward high-risk plays (PCLN is still in an uptrend) might have waited for a short setup the next morning.

> Hot Tip: Volume signals may sound as if they contradict each other. That's why it's imperative to combine them with candle patterns, moving averages, and other indicators to get an "all signals are go."

Soaring price + explosive volume = impending capitulation (bearish). The old saying "What goes up, must come down" is especially true in the financial markets. Stocks fueled by rampant euphoria that fly straight up to nosebleed territory, usually find their exhaustion (read: cliff fall) point soon after.

Look again at Figure 7–18. You'll see where PCLN shot to a new high on June 22. The stock flew up, then down, in a wide-range, three-point day. That bearish engulfing pattern coupled with climactic volume tells traders who hold long positions to tighten their stops or take profits.

"Hold it!" you reply. "Shouldn't I wait for the following candle to confirm the bearish engulfing pattern?"

You can. On the other hand, bearish engulfing patterns tell us that the psychology of the market turned negative at a potential top. When I see this pattern forming in an overbought stock, and I am long a position, I take at least *some* profits off the table to protect my gains. Result? I sleep better.

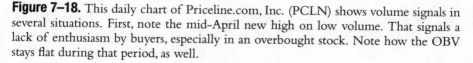

Figure 7–18. This daily chart of Priceline.com, Inc. (PCLN) shows volume signals in several situations. First, note the mid-April new high on low volume. That signals a lack of enthusiasm by buyers, especially in an overbought stock. Note how the OBV stays flat during that period, as well.

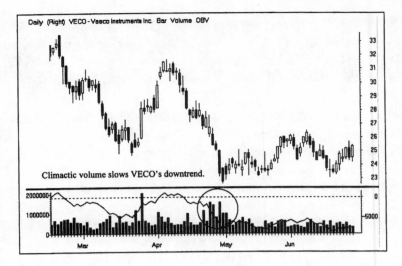

Figure 7–19. On this daily chart of Veeco Instruments, Inc. (VECO), you can see how the semiconductor's steep, 10-plus point slide came to a halt, when climactic volume slowed and finally halted its descent. In the last week in March, as well, an extreme volume spike pumped new life into the stock, at least for a couple of weeks. Caveat: use this signal in conjunction with other indicators. A single spike—especially—may cause a quick rally that may not last too long. A better idea: use this signal as a decision support tool for exiting short positions, rather than initiating long, "bottom-fishing" expeditions!

Climactic selling + high volume = impending low or "tradable bottom." When a market in a downtrend (lower highs and lower lows) experiences a low with climactic selling (high volume), it *may* result in the final low of that trend. The operative word here is "may." While a sharp volume increase in a crumbling stock points to an impending rally, the upside move may be short-lived. If you are a smart trader, when you bottom fish (and at all other times), you'll enter a protective stop order with your broker immediately after you enter a position.

This pattern is the mirror image of the soaring price with high-volume pattern. Obviously, the difference here is that the stock or market is in a downtrend, rather than an uptrend.

Figure 7–19 shows a daily chart of Veeco Instruments, Inc. (VECO), a semiconductor stock. This stock plummeted in April, from a high of $31.65 to a low of $22.62. Look at the climactic volume coming into it as it approached its lows. This volume warned short sellers to take cover.

By the end of April, the selling mania subsided. Poor VECO struggled up, licked its wounds, and is now churning through a basing mode. The extreme volume flushed out the majority of bears, at least for the time being. If VECO

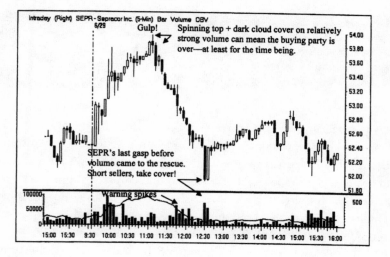

Figure 7–20. This 5-minute chart of Sepracor, Inc. (SEPR) shows clearly how volume precedes momentum. Volume carried the stock to an intraday high of nearly $54, and traders who entered at the open made a point and a half by 11 a.m. EST. Volume and candle signals warned traders with long positions to take profits shortly after that. SEPR tumbled hard for the next hour and a half, losing more than two points. Warnings in the form of increased volume spikes appeared by 11:45 a.m. The final drop ended in a complete reversal bar accompanied by extreme volume at 12:30 p.m. EST.

continues to etch out a base from here, long opportunities, both short-term and intermediate, may show up.

This signal works well for day trading, as well. Figure 7–20 shows a five-minute chart of Sepracor, Inc. (SEPR). Strong buying pressure hoisted this pharmaceutical company from its open at $52.39 to its intraday high of $53.95. Note that a spinning top marked the high. The next candle formed a dark cloud cover on strong volume, a sign that the intraday uptrend party had topped out. Follow SEPR's head-over-heels tumble down to its intraday low of $51.90. See when increased volume began to slow the stock's fall? If you were short this stock in a day trade, the volume signal warned you loud and clear: *Hey, take profits. The bulls are sneaking in the back gate!*

The overall message: when you're short a stock in a downtrend, and you see extreme volume coming into it (daily *or* intraday chart)—especially at a previous support area—think about taking profits or at least tightening your buy-to-cover stop. Extreme volume activity tells you that the stock or market may be ripe for a reversal.

Important low + strong, steady volume = bullish. Expanding volume that shoots a market upward from an important low signals that a tradable—or even a major—bottom may be in place.

> **Hot Tip: To spot an important low, watch for high volume as the stock moves down on a daily chart. Next, look for continued strong volume as the stock holds its lows and starts back up. One to two weeks of strong, steady volume that supports price can be a bullish signal.**

This is especially true on the retest of a previous low. On a daily chart, a stock may make an important low, rally higher, then slide back down to test the low. If the retest holds, many times the stock will then bounce up and off the second low and gap (skip several price levels) to the upside. A portion of the gap may be attributed to a "short squeeze" (shorts covering their positions by buying + bullish buying = the stock shoots up several price levels).

Figure 7–21 displays a daily chart of Amazon.com, Inc. (AMZN). Notice how AMZN made a low on May 10, which culminated in a *doji*. Subsequently, the dot.com retailer moved up, and then slid back down again, to retest the previous low—and ended in a *doji*, again. Two days later, prominent volume infused the stock, and AMZN shot up, forming a double bottom. Check the strong volume that drove it higher for the initial ten-point rocket shot.

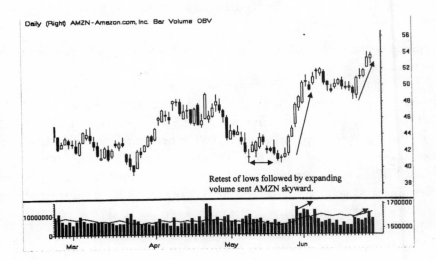

Figure 7–21. When a stock consolidates, as Amazon.com, Inc. (AMZN) is doing on this daily chart, watch for a retest of an important low, and a subsequent move up on high volume. This pattern can be explosive, as short covering can cause a "short squeeze" that drives prices high—fast! This can be utilized as either a swing or intraday trade setup. Just make sure your initial protective stop is no lower than the low of the retest. A stock that makes a failed breakout to the upside and then rolls over can slice through the lows and into a sharp fall.

Now, continue through the uptrend. Notice how the stock tapered off for a two-week pullback, then soared again on expanding volume.

Volume's Final Word

Strong price trends—short- or long-term—break out, rest, then continue when price and volume expand and contract together. When volume diverges from price, price will, at some point, follow volume's lead.

Volume signals and the OBV work well with candle signals, moving averages, and oscillators to direct you to high-probability setups and entries.

Once you enter a trade, volume signals act as a money-management tool by alerting you to a possible future trend change or reversal.

As you've surmised by now, no matter which time frame or market you trade, volume delivers high-quality messages and acts as a special forecaster of future price action.

Moving Averages: What They Are, How They Make You Money

Moving averages are like your favorite uncle: easygoing, dependable, and yet straightforward and to the point. Like volume, they are a "let's stay in the real world" indicator.

We calculate a moving average as a line indicator that displays the average value of a stock or index during a given time period. On daily charts, 20- (or 21-), 40-, 50-, and 200-day moving averages are popular. The 20- or 21-day line makes sense, because there are about 21 days in a trading month. Institutions favor 50-day and 200-day moving averages. With about 250 trading days in the year, the 200-day, or 39-week, moving average acts as a reliable long-term measurement of a stock or market's health.

Moving average lines act as support and resistance on all time frames. When a stock trades above a moving average, the average acts as potential support. When the stock trades below the line, the average represents potential resistance.

Important point: When a stock rises in an uptrend, *rising* moving averages below the price action offer strong potential support. When a stock collapses in a downtrend, *falling* moving averages over the price act as impending, head-smacking resistance.

> **Hot Tip:** Moving averages that shuffle sideways in horizontal lines don't hold the support/resistance power that rising and falling moving average lines exert.

As with most indicators, the longer the time frame, the more powerful moving average support and resistance becomes. For example, a 50-day moving average exerts more force as support than does the 10-period moving average on a 10-minute chart. Why? Because more time and more price information is used to calculate the *50-day* moving average versus the *10-period* moving average on a 10-minute chart, where a total of 100 minutes price action are used to calculate the moving average.

> **Please note:** When you see a notation, such as "the 20-*day* moving average," or "the 50-day moving average," we are referring to a moving indicator on a chart with a *daily* time frame. A 10-, 20-, or 39-*week* moving average, for example, applies to moving averages on weekly chart. When the reference is to "the 20-*period*" or the "200-*period*" moving averages, for example, we're talking about moving averages on *intraday* charts. Examples of intraday chart time frames are 5-minute, 10-minute, 15-minute, or hourly.

It follows that when a stock drops below its *50*-day moving average and closes below it, the move is potentially more catastrophic than if the stock slips below its *10*- or *20*-day moving average.

To calculate a simple 20-day moving average: Take the closing price of the last 20 days and add them. Divide the total by 20. Your answer is today's moving average. Tomorrow, drop the first (oldest) day of the series, and add tomorrow's closing price. Again, add the closing prices and divide the sum by 20. Then connect today's and tomorrow's prices with a line, and *voilà!* That's your moving average. Before computers became common tools, market technicians calculated moving averages by hand. Can you imagine? Better them than us!

Get to know how moving averages operate. As well as acting as support and resistance lines on your charts, they are smoothing devices in many indicators and oscillators, including the MACD, the stochastics, and ADX.

Here is a list of time periods we assign to moving averages (MAs), from short-term to long-term. Depending on whether a price pattern is trading above or below the MA, it indicates whether the stock is moving in a short-term, intermediate, or long-term trend.

- Very short term = five to 15 days

- Short term = 16 to 25 days

- Minor Intermediate = 26 to 49 days

- Intermediate = 50 to 100 days

- Long term = 100 to 200 days

Earlier, we stated that a short-term trend reverses more easily than a long-term trend. When you identify these moving averages on a chart, you can see more easily which trends have been in force for the short term, and which have grown more mature.

> **Hot Tip: Traders also use words "fast" and "slow" to describe moving averages. "Fast moving averages" refer to short-term, such as 10-day or period MAs. Slow MAs signify lines calculated with longer time frames, such as the 50- to 200-day periods.**

Several different types of moving averages include simple, exponential, weighted, and triangular. The most popular types for our trading needs are the simple and exponential moving averages.

We've already calculated a simple moving average. An exponential moving average involves a more complicated formula that uses percentages to place more weight on recent prices. Translation: Exponential moving averages show more sensitivity to current price action.

Ideally, a moving average would trace a straight line under a stock's lows in an uptrend, or slant down and touch each lower high in a stock's downtrend. But, as we know too well, stocks march to the beat of their own, individual drummers. They don't step through their uptrends or downtrends with precise and even steps, over precise and equal time periods.

Wouldn't it be great if you and I had enough time to change our moving average time periods to fit each stock's price fluctuation tendencies? Then we could see that Bitty Broadband waltzes nicely up the 40-day moving average, while Persnickety Power Cell prefers the tightrope of an 18-day line.

The real world, however, demands we move swiftly. So we use moving average time periods that seem the most dependable, and give accurate signals. On weekly charts, I use the 10-, 20-, and 39-week simple moving averages. Those closely equal the 50-, 100-, and 200-day moving averages on daily charts. (Since there are five trading days in a week, to change a weekly moving average to a comparable daily moving average, multiply the weekly number by five.)

On daily charts, I use a 10-, 20-, 50-, and 200-day simple moving averages. Figures 7–22 and 7–23 show weekly and daily charts with those moving averages plotted.

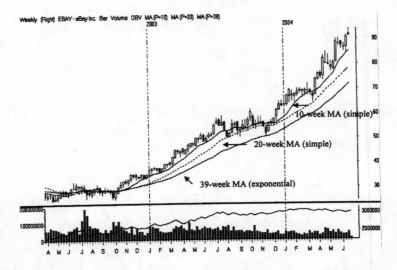

Figure 7–22. This weekly chart of eBay, Inc. (EBAY) shows the Internet stock climbing in a dandy uptrend. The moving averages rise underneath the price pattern, with the 10-, 20-, and 39-week lines rising in symmetrical support. Notice how EBAY uses each moving average as support at one time or another during the two years displayed.

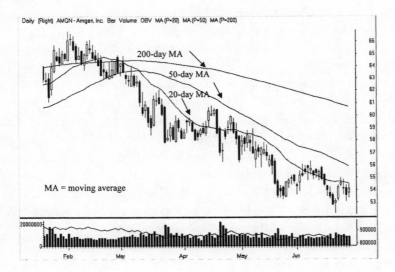

Figure 7–23. This daily chart of Amgen, Inc. (AMGN) shows the 20-, 50-, and 200-day simple moving averages. Because AMGN is tumbling in a downtrend, the moving averages head down over the top of the price pattern. The moving averages are layered from the slowest, which is the 200-day MA, down to the fastest, the 20-day MA. Note how the moving averages lay on top of the price pattern like a hot, wet blanket. The 50-day MA, in particular, acts as resistance to AMGN's weak rallies. (As mentioned in the chapter text, I use a 10-day MA on my charts.) For the sake of easier viewing, the 10-day MA does not appear on this chart.

On my 60-minute, or hourly, charts, I use a 65-period and a 135-period simple moving averages. Where did I unearth those odd numbers?

When I'm looking for setups on daily charts for swing and day trades, I want to see a close-up version of the daily chart with the two fastest moving averages intact. So, I switch to my 60-minute chart plotted with the 65- and 135-period MAs. The 65-period moving average tracks the same path on the 60-minute chart that the 10-day moving average tracks on the daily chart. There are six and one-half hours in a trading day. To convert the 10-day MA to appear on a 60-minute chart, multiply 10 (days) times 6.50 = 65. To convert the 20-day moving average to a 60-minute chart, multiply 20 (days) times 6.50 = 135.

Figure 7–24 shows a 60-minute chart of the QQQQ, the NASDAQ 100 index tracking stock. Note how the 10- and 20-day MAs inserted into the hourly time frame give you a realistic view of what's going on in the larger picture.

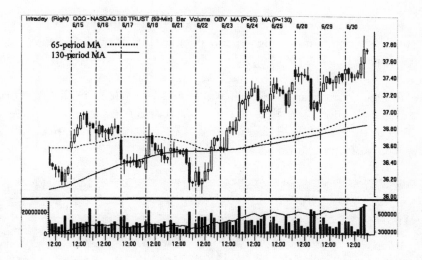

Figure 7–24. On this hourly chart of the QQQQ, or tracking stock for the NASDAQ 100 Index, note how the stock gapped open on 6/15, then drifted down to retest its 6/14 low on 6/22. Then the "cubes," as we sometimes call it, shot up once again over its major short-term moving averages. Note the strong, steady volume on the breakout day and the two days that followed. Also note how the OBV started rising on 6/22, another bullish signal. In addition, on this chart, you can see how the 10-day moving average on a daily chart transferred into the 65-period MA, and the 20-day MA transferred into the 130-period MA. When you see moving averages come together and move sideways, as they did on this chart, the price pattern will have consolidated, as well. When the price pattern starts up (or down), the faster moving average will start up (or down) first, as it will always stay closer to the price action. Remember, moving averages are lagging, trend-following indicators.

Since I don't enter stocks to the long side unless they are trading above their 20-day MA, the 60-minute chart with the 65- and 130-period moving averages allows me to watch a setup forming—or trade evolving—on an intraday time frame, but keep the 20-day MA in focus.

On time frames smaller than hourly, I usually overlay the 20- and 200-period simple moving averages. I prefer to keep my intraday charts extremely simple. Candle patterns, volume and the OBV, a couple of moving averages, and perhaps stochastics contribute plenty of information for profitable day-trading strategies. Figure 7–25 displays a 5-minute chart of the QQQQ. This chart moves in for a close-up of the last day shown in the 60-minute chart in Figure 7–24.

Please use whichever moving averages work best for your style. A friend of mine, who day-trades successfully, swears by the 13-period moving average on a *15*-minute chart. The 21-, 30-, 35-, 40-, and 100-day moving averages are popular on daily charts. The bottom line: Traders find that short-term moving averages suit their needs, as these lines match their time frames. Investors gravitate to long-term moving averages, as the short-term holds no interest for them.

You'll be a happier trader if you keep your charts simple by limiting your indicators. Three to four moving averages on a daily chart provide plenty of support and resistance information. Try a selection that includes a "fast" MA, such as the ten-, 12-, or 13-period. Then add a short-term MA, perhaps 21, or 21-day. You may want to include an intermediate MA, such as the 50-day. Finally, plot a "slow" or long-term line, in either a 100 or 200-day line.

Two or three moving averages, such as the 10, 20 and 200 period, will also offer plenty of information on an intraday chart.

> **Hot Tip: Institutions watch the 50-day and 200-day moving averages on daily charts. That's a good reason to keep those MAs on *your* daily charts. When you see a market mover, such as a Dow component, retrace to the 50-day MA and then begin to bounce on strong volume, institutions might be nibbling on the stock. If the setup meets your criteria, you may choose to join them!**

The Bottom Line on Moving Averages, and How They Help Yours

- Moving averages help keep you on the right side of the trend you are trading. (Believe it or not, that's easier said than done!) For example, when a price pattern trades above a 20-day moving average, it may be in a short-term uptrend. When it trades above the 20-day and 50-day MAs, and the 20-day MA is rising above the 50-day MA, the stock may be in a stronger,

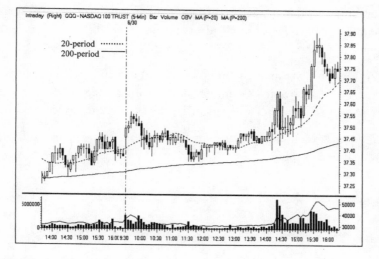

Intraday (Right) QQQ-NASDAQ 100 TRUST (5-Min) Bar Volume OBV MA (P=20) MA (P=200) 6/30

20-period ·········
200-period ————

Figure 7–25. On this five-minute chart of the QQQQ, you can see a close-up of the price action that took place during the last day of the hourly chart in Figure 7–23. The 20-period MA and 200-period MA moving averages are all I use on intraday charts, (as mentioned, I use 65-period and 130-period MAs on hourly chart) although you may want to plot additional moving averages. Note how the 20-period MA hugs the price pattern, while the slower 200-MA trades below.

Do you see the huge volume that came into the Qs at about 2:15 p.m. EST? This was due to the announcement of ¼ point interest rate hike by the FOMC (Federal Open Market Committee). Despite the hike, rates are still low as of this writing, and the U.S. economy appears to be in good shape. You can tell by the Qs' sharp rise, the NASDAQ approved of the Fed's decision.

more mature uptrend. Conversely, if a stock trades under its 50-day MA and its 20-day MA, and the 50-day MA rides above the 20-day MA, the stock is probably falling in a downtrend.

- Moving averages act as magnets to price. When prices trade too high or too far below a major moving average, such as a 20-day MA, we say they are "overextended." It's only a matter of time before they pull back to that line, or the MA catches up to the price moves.

- When a stock sails into an uptrend, and a faster-moving average crosses up and above a slower-moving average—such as the 20-day MA moves up and over the 50-day MA—this is a bullish signal that's referred to as a "golden cross." On the flip side, if a faster-moving average falls and crosses down over a slower-moving average, this is a bearish signal. Investors many times use moving average crossovers as pure buy and sell signals. Although crossover signals are usually too late for traders—we jump onto trend reversals early—they still make great confirmations that a trend is in place.

- Combine moving average information with candle reversal patterns and
  volume signals to locate high-quality setups. For swing or day trades to the
  long side, locate:

  —A stock rising in an early (not too mature) uptrend on a daily chart, trad-
    ing slightly above its 20- and 50-day moving averages (above the 20-day
    MA is mandatory, for my personal criteria regarding swing trades).

  —The stock is pulling back to—or consolidating into—price and/or mov-
    ing average support.

Figure 7–26. This daily chart of Hyperion Solutions Corp. (HYSL) shows the software developer rising out of a base in late January, promoted by an extreme gap up.
Note the MA crossover at that time. The 20-day MA moved sharply above the 200-
and 50-day MAs, producing two bullish crossovers in a few days' time. During the
volatile uptrend that followed, HYSL moved through several legs-up that offered great
swing- and day-trading opportunities. Two good ones: 1) Toward the end of February,
HYSL retested its prior low with a *doji* that came close to its rising 50-day MA. The
next candle was a bullish piercing candle that broke higher on strong volume and was
accompanied by a rising OBV. Swing traders bought when the bullish piercing candle
shot above the high of the *doji*, or possibly waited until the close, when the candle
punctured the 20-day MA. 2) HYSL consolidated in a range from mid-May until
mid-June. During the last few days of the consolidation, you can see increasing volume in the stock, and the 20-day MA rises underneath the price pattern and starts
back up. The OBV coincides. On June 16, HYSL breaks to the upside shooting over
its 50-day MA on strong volume. Both swing and day traders entered as the stock rose
on the volume's momentum. Each candle for that day, and the next three, closed near
their highs, a bullish sign. Finally, take note of the occasions HYSL traded high above
its 20-day MA, reaching overextended territory. Each time, it reversed and returned to
its "magnets." During mid-May, the stock traded at a multipoint discount to its 20-day
MA. In this case, it retested previous lows, then climbed back into an uptrend.

—The stock begins to move higher *on strong volume* and the OBV rises in an uptrend.

Figure 7–26 gives you a good picture of how MAs work as trend identifiers, how crossovers confirm trend movement. It also shows a great swing and day-trading setup, and how candles, volume, and moving averages work together as indicators.

> **Hot Tip: If you're interested in keeping up with four-year market/business cycles, plot a simple 200-week moving average on your weekly chart. This MA tracks nearly four years of data, so it helps you gain perspective on long-term price movement.**

For swing or day trades to sell short, reverse the criteria:

- A stock falling in a downtrend on a daily chart, trading below its 50- and 20-day moving averages (layered in that order). The stock is rallying to— or consolidating into—price and/or moving average resistance.

- The OBV is heading south.

- The stock starts to fall on strong volume

Figure 7–27 shows a chart of metals-mining and manufacturing giant Phelps Dodge Corporation (PD). The setup for a short sell for both swing and day trades is a beauty, with a double top, a moving average crossover above the second top, plus long black candle lines predicting PD's "look out below" fall.

Now you can see how candles, volume signals, and moving averages work together to serve up great trading opportunities, both long and short.

In chapter 8, we're going to run through a selection of overbought-oversold oscillators. They add the final team member to the lineup of chart tools.

First, though, you'll want to glance over the quiz. We covered a lot of material in this chapter, and unless you're a highly experienced trader, you may want to review some important points.

Figure 7–27. On this daily chart of Phelps Dodge Corp. (PD), you can see how the copper mining and engineered products conglomerate retested its mid-March high during the first week in April. Note how the OBV made a lower high on PD's second high, despite the fact that the price rose to a near-matching high price. Shortly after the second high failed to make a higher high, PD tumbled, diving under its 20- and 50-day MAs. At the same time, the 20-day MA crossed below the 50-day MA, a bearish sign. The entry day for a short swing or day trade is on the long black candle that plunges below the moving average crossover. Volume is not ultra-strong on this candle—and that's okay. While stocks should have increased volume on breakouts to the upside, they can fall fast and hard on medium- to low-volume days, when buyers flee.

Quiz

Questions

1. Does a candle line that completes its formation with a long real body display indecision or strong opinion?

2. The candle line that opens and closes near the same price is called a a) *doji*, b) a high wave candle, or c) a dark cloud cover.

3. Are *doji* and spinning stops more proficient at predicting top reversal or bottom reversal patterns?

4. True or false: Volume is a derivative of price.

5. Explain briefly why a stock moving higher an uptrend should show high volume on the legs–up and reduced volume when it pulls back or consolidates.

6. You're long a stock in a day trade that's going wildly vertical on a five-minute chart. Suddenly, extreme volume carries the stock even higher. Do you hold or fold?

7. You're watching your short position on a five-minute chart. As it dives lower, you smile with satisfaction. Within a half–point of the next support level, you notice increased volume coming into each five-minute candle. Do you add shares to your short position, or close the trade?

8. Moving averages act as _____ and _____ to a price pattern.

9. True or false: A 50-day moving average is faster than a 10-day moving average.

10. True or false: When you are scanning for a long swing trade setup, you find the best trades occur when the candle pattern, volume and OBV, and the moving averages all agree on a "buy" signal.

Answers

1. A candle that completes its formation with a long real body displays strong opinion.

2. *Doji.*

3. *Doji* and spinning tops exert more power in halting uptrends than they do in downtrends.

4. False. Volume displays the total number of shares, or contracts, traded in a designated time period. Simple volume information does not reveal price.

5. A stock moving higher an uptrend should display increased volume on the legs–up, to indicate that enthusiasm for the stock continues to attract buyers. In contrast, the stock should show reduced volume when it pulls back or consolidates; that demonstrates that traders are holding the stock, and not selling to the same degree that they bought it on the legs–up.

6. When you're long a stock in a day trade that shoots skyward on an in-traday chart, and an extreme volume dose propels it even higher, take

partial or all profits. The climactic volume spike forecasts that the price may reverse—and soon!

7. When you're short a stock, and in the context of an extended leg-down you suddenly see volume arrive in big busloads, tighten your stop or take profits. The added volume could mean that buyers are gobbling up supply and the stock will soon reverse or at least end its slide south.

8. Depending upon whether the stock is trading above or below its major moving averages, the indicators act as *support* and *resistance* to a price pattern.

9. False. A 50-day moving average is "slower" than a 10-day moving average. A 50-day moving average includes more closing price information than does a 10-day moving average, so it makes sense that it would move more slowly and trade farther away from the price pattern.

10. True. When scanning for a setup and when entering a trade on any time frame, you have the best odds of a successful trade when the candle pattern, volume/OBV, and moving averages all agree on a "buy" or "sell" signal.

CENTER POINT

Your Personal Uptrend: Take the Path of Least Resistance

The average bottom-of-the-ladder person is potentially as creative as the top executive who sits in the big office. The problem is that the person on the bottom of the ladder doesn't trust his own brilliance and doesn't, therefore, believe in his own ideas.

—Rev. Robert Schuller

As traders and technicians, we know that a stock or an index rising in a healthy uptrend gains value. We also know that the less resistance it meets along the way, the easier it is for that stock or index to soar.

Wouldn't it be interesting to chart the "sectors" of our lives? We could look at areas including career, relationships, health and fitness, finance, and spirituality, and see which are in "uptrends," which are static or consolidating, and which are meeting with "resistance."

While events in the outside world present themselves as resistance to our personal uptrends, much of the resistance we encounter is self-inflicted! We can get proactive and eliminate these resistance zones with a little work and dedication.

First resistance zone: our thoughts. Thoughts are the most powerful force on earth. When you think "I can't do that," or "everyone knows more than I do," you're placing resistance in your own path.

Second resistance zone: our words. Words communicate how we feel about ourselves and our lives. You can wear an Armani suit and $500 shoes, but if you continually apologize for your actions and berate yourself in front of others, that self-inflicted "resistance" slows down your personal uptrend.

Third resistance zone: our actions. When we go through life as *reactive*, rather than *pro*active, we let (invite!) other people make our decisions. We cooperate rather than compete. We let environment, people, and circumstances dictate our progress. Instead, let's dictate—create—the environment and circumstances that lead to success.

The more "resistance" we eliminate from our thoughts, words, and actions, the easier it will be to keep making personal "higher highs."

Add Up a Setup

Bull markets are born on skepticism, mature on optimism, and die on euphoria.
—Sir John Templeton
(Founder, Templeton Funds)

Turn your television to a financial channel, and chances are a puckered-browed pundit will be spouting his or her take on the future direction of the stock market.

After clearing his throat and knitting his eyebrows to alert the audience to the brain-busting magnitude of his pending revelations, said guru begins:

"Harrumph, ahem (snort). At Crystal Ball Brokerage, we project the stock market will edge upward in the near term. If, however, the market shifts into a horizontal mode and takes a more conservative approach, it is clearly contemplating geopolitical tensions, some of which we integrated into our earlier forecast. Of course, if Wall Street embeds current interest rates as part of the fiscal outlook, and apparent overvaluation of benchmark indices warrants further contraction, we suspect the market may (snort), ahem, retrace somewhat here."

In between throat-clearing, what our expert *really* said was that the markets will either move up, sideways, or down. Got it, thanks. That's all the markets *can* do.

Here's another example of market fortune-telling by a guru who is so sure of himself he doesn't bother to hedge his statements. At a financial conference in Chicago, I overheard a speaker tell his audience (with a straight face!), "I *always* know where the market is going next."

Baloney.

No one knows which direction our financial markets will head in the next five years, five months, or five minutes. At least our throat-clearing television expert had the sense to leave himself safe exits.

It's literally our business as traders to make *educated guesses* as to the market's near-term direction. We know that unexpected global events mushroom without warning. And we are aware that, to a larger or lesser degree, they incite reactions in financial markets—around the world, around the clock, from heartbeat to heartbeat.

Underneath those events, though, we humans proceed with our usual patterns. Our collective behavior bubbles and churns from day to day, and from week to week, in patterns similar enough that we can measure our actions on charts.

This chapter offers more insight on market movement; it explores momentum indicators, namely the MACD, stochastics, and the ADX with Plus and Minus Directional Indicators. We'll also look at Fibonacci retracement levels. These tools will help you anticipate price behavior and add an extra punch to your buy/sell decisions.

When an orchestra plays a musical piece, each member of the orchestra plays a slightly different rendition, depending on his or her instrument. Still, the blended sounds of the instruments create a single song.

In a football game, each offensive team member is assigned a different responsibility, whether as blocking, passing, or receiving. Yet the members work together on a single game and share the identical purpose—to move the ball closer to the goal post.

Whatever you trade—stocks, E-minis, or another financial product—your objective is to target setups gleaned from a convergence of signals. Price (and its relationship to support and resistance), candle patterns, volume signals, moving averages and momentum indicators should separately—and together—point to a "buy" or a "sell" signal.

The more indicators agree to the same signal, the higher the probability the setup will evolve into a profitable trade.

What do you do when signals are mixed? Example: A stock's price is falling in a downtrend (negative), but it's bouncing off of its rising two hundred-day moving average (positive), but it's doing so on low volume and lower OBV (negative), but the stochastics indicator is hooking up from the oversold zone in a potential bullish divergence (positive).

Action: Look for greener pastures. Diving into a position with those contradictory signals would be akin to driving a car with two flat tires.

As a winning trader, you'll shun murky setups. You'll choose high-quality opportunities, where all systems read "go."

Now, before we move into momentum indicators, here are three quick reminders.

First, please remember to keep your charts simple. Again, when you identify price action and its primary trend, then evaluate candle patterns, volume and OBV signals, moving averages, and a momentum indicator or oscillator—two at the most—you should have *plenty* of input for entries and exits.

Second, when we refer to oscillators, it's a general description. The MACD, stochastics, and ADX are called "oscillators" simply because they vacillate—or oscillate—between oversold and overbought numerical boundaries.

Third, here's a brief refresher explanation on the meaning of "divergence":

- A bullish divergence takes place when a momentum indicator moves up, yet price remains flat or drifts down.

- A bearish divergence occurs when a momentum indicator heads down, yet the price consolidates or rises higher.

- In each case, the indicator "diverges"—or moves in a different direction—from the price. The divergence alerts you that the price may soon follow the indicator's direction.

The MACD—How It Boosts Your Buy/Sell Decisions

The MACD (traders call it the *"mack-dee"*), i.e., the "moving average convergence divergence," is a technical chart tool developed by renowned technician Gerald Appel. Traders and investors use this dual-line chart component as decision support for entry and exits.

What It Is

The MACD is a trend-following indicator. It consists of two lines on your chart; the MACD line and the signal line. Your software will plot them in a panel above or below the price pattern.

The MACD lines oscillate together to the top of the scale, which represents the overbought zone, down to the bottom of the scale, which signifies the oversold zone. Some software uses values that range from +100 to −100. Others use round numbers. Zero acts as the MACD's median line.

Remember how, in chapter 7, we talked about "fast" and "slow" moving averages? Here's another example of those terms in action.

The MACD line represents the "fast" line. It's calculated by subtracting the difference between the twelve- and twenty-six-period exponential moving averages (EMAs).

The signal line represents the "slow" line. It's actually a nine-period EMA of the MACD.

(Before you paw through your desk drawer to find your calculator, know that most charting software includes the MACD on its studies.)

As a generality, when the MACD line rides above the signal line, the price is in an uptrend and you'll concentrate on long positions. When the MACD line travels below the signal line, the price is probably falling in a downtrend. You'll stay short and bearish.

Why We Use It

We add the MACD indicator to our charts because it acts as a reliable trend-following indicator. It helps us trade on the right side of the trend. We combine its signals with other chart signals to confirm entries, support risk-management, and validate exits.

MACD Buy and Sell Signals

The MACD displays buy/sell signals when:

- It reaches oversold (buy signal) or overbought (sell signal) conditions

- The MACD line crosses above (buy signal), or below (sell signal), the signal line; these are known as *crossovers*

- The lines diverge from price (divergence) action

> **Hot Tip: Although this signal usually appears late for short-term traders, investors like to buy when the MACD line crosses above the zero line; they sell when the MACD crosses below the zero line.**

Most traders prefer to use the two-line MACD on weekly, daily, and hourly charts. On shorter, intraday time frames, a MACD histogram, minus the signal line, issues fairly reliable momentum signals. Experiment with your software and find the approach that best suits your trading style.

MACD Quirks

Moving average information fuels this indicator. Just as moving averages lose much of their predictive power when they shuffle sideways in a nontrending market, the MACD loses effectiveness in horizontal markets. Bottom line: Use the MACD's signals in uptrending or downtrending markets.

Overbought/oversold signals: When you see the MACD pull away from the signal line in a sharp move, pay attention. The increasing spread between the two lines announces that the stock is probably heading into overextended territory either to the upside or to the downside. Result: sooner or later, it will correct to find equilibrium.

Speed of signal: The MACD was designed as a trend-*following* indicator. It gives slower trend-reversal signals than many of its buddies, such as the stochastics oscillator. That's why you won't see as many dramatic bullish or bearish di-

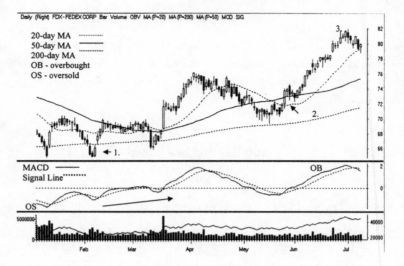

Figure 8–1. This daily chart of the FedEx Corporation (FDX) shows how the MACD and its signal line hint at upcoming price movements of the global air courier. Note that the MACD line is solid, while its signal line is dotted. Remember, your goal as a trader is to find setups where the price action, candle pattern, volume and OBV, moving averages, and momentum indicator all line up in a buy *or* sell signal.

1. During the first week in February, FDX skidded down to test the prior January low, then held firm. Note the increased volume as FDX slides to the retest price at $64.90, then reverses. On February 6, the reversal day, candle pattern: bullish piercing pattern. Volume: strong + bullish OBV divergence. Moving averages: price trading under 20-, 50-, 200-day MAs (bearish, but customary with a double-bottom pattern). MACD—bullish: hooks up in higher low than previous January low. The price retested the same price as former low, but the MACD made a HIGHER low. That signals a powerful trend change may occur.
2. FDX dips to 50-day MA ($69), which is also price support from January to March. On May 24, the MACD makes a bullish crossover, and FDX soars into a two-month moonshot.
3. On July 1, FDX makes an all-time high. The high shoots it into overextended territory. The day ends in a dark cloud cover. Three days later, the MACD gives a sell signal, and the stock falters. Traders with longs positions take profits.

vergences with this indicator as you will with more volatile momentum tools.

Figure 8–1 displays a daily chart of the FedEx Corporation (FDX) with the MACD indicator inserted in the panel above the volume and OBV.

Note how the indicator climbs in its own bullish uptrend, making two higher lows in February and March. Both dips resulted in MACD crossovers. First, the MACD crossed below the signal line—a bearish signal that indicated the current move up had ended. Then, it hooked back up, a bullish signal that the uptrend had regained momentum.

An extremely bullish divergence took place with the February retest of the January low. Although FDX's price returned in February to the previous low, the MACD *made a higher low*. That signaled a potentially powerful trend change.

Also note where FDX soared into overbought territory in April and early July; a MACD crossover to the downside followed. (The MACD indicated the stock fell to oversold status in early January.) When the MACD issued both the April and July signals, the stock was overextended (trading high above its twenty-day MA) and made new highs on low volume. All of these warning signs point to a sell—or take profits—signal.

Again, the MACD indicator gives great signals on longer-term time frames. Most active traders find it less helpful on intraday charts. But for those who want to try it for day trading, check out Figure 8–2.

Figure 8–2 shows a three-day, ten-minute chart of WalMart Stores, Inc. (WMT), with the MACD line (minus the signal line) in histogram form. The histogram shows WMT slicing through the median, or zero line, on the second day (7/12). As the day unwinds, the rising histogram tells you that WalMart's momentum is building, and it stays strong into the close.

On the third day, the giant retailer takes off. Even though the price stays strong for the afternoon, the histogram tapers off. If you'd jumped out of a long

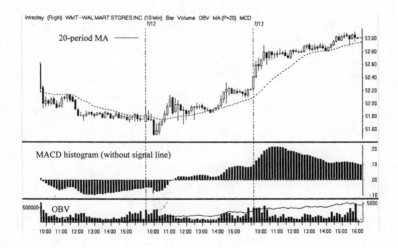

Figure 8–2. This 10-minute chart of WalMart Stores, Inc. (WMT) illustrates how the MACD looks as a histogram on a short-term, intraday chart. Technically speaking, when the histogram crosses up and over the zero line (on all time frames) it signals that momentum to the upside is accelerating. Note how momentum rises on the middle day (7/12), then soars the next morning. Still, the MACD's momentum decelerates during the afternoon, while WalMart's price stays strong. Although the MACD is a great indicator, most traders agree that it gives better signals on longer term (daily and longer) time frames.

trade early, you would have left money on the table. That's why you'll want to investigate other indicators for intraday trading.

The Stochastics Oscillator—How It Helps You Profit

For now, we'll take the MACD off our charts and plug in the stochastics oscillator.

This popular guy hops up and down faster than the MACD. In fact, you won't find many investors who have even heard his name. If you met him in a singles bar, you'd peg him as "the sensitive type." Let a stock frown, or breathe funny, and its stochastic indicator shows dejection by hooking down. On the flip side, when a stock flashes a smile, it sends stochastics soaring.

It is known as a.: the stochastic indicator
                    b.: stochastics (traders understand this)

What It Is

Like the MACD, the stochastics (pronounced *stow-kas'-ticks*) indicator runs as a two-line oscillator. The lines are plotted as the %K line, which is the main line, and the %D line, which is a moving average of %K. Values range from 0 (oversold) to 100 percent (overbought), with 50 representing the median line.

Most charting software offers the option of "fast" or "slow" stochastics. (That means the %K is smoothed with a value of one for fast stochastics, and a value of three for slow stochastics. The %D line is a moving average of the %K, with a common default of three periods. My default for slow stochastics: %K = fourteen periods, with an internal slowing period of three periods. The %D period = three. (Do these numbers make you want to toss this book through a window? Leave your software set to its current defaults and read on.)

For all trading time frames, I prefer slow stochastics. If you haven't used this indicator before, experiment with fast, then slow stochastics on your charts. Then decide which appeals to your trading style.

As you study the indicator, keep in mind the reasoning behind the formula. Stochastics tells us where a security's price closed *relative to its highs* over a designated time period.

As a stock escalates in an uptrend, the many bars or candles close near their highs. That pushes the stochastics lines higher.

When the trend and its bulls get tuckered out, and buying enthusiasm wanes, even if prices inch up or start to consolidate, *closing* prices begin to slide toward their lows. (Reminder: The closing price is the most important price of the period, or day.)

Stochastics "sees" the sinking closing prices. It alerts you by hooking the %K line down and crossing below the %D line in a sell signal. The sell signal may simply warn of a pullback, or it could mean the bull's party is over for a while.

On the other hand, a downtrend in motion develops with many bars or candles closing at or near their lows.

When the bears finally tire, bulls sneak in the back gate and start to graze and buy. Even if price makes a new low, bullish grazing causes *closing* prices to edge up. Again, the stochastics indicator detects price closing nearer, or at, its highs. This time, the %K comes from under the %D, crosses it to the upside, and shouts a buy signal.

We consider stochastics to be oversold when the lines drop below twenty, and overbought when they cross above eighty.

Why We Use It

The stochastics indicator broadcasts reliable signals on all time frames. It tells us when a stock is overbought or oversold. That helps fine-tune entries, exits, and risk tactics.

Say you bought a stock in a swing trade several points ago. It's soared past your profit target, and you're scratching your head, wondering if you should sell it. If one glance at the stock's daily chart tells you the stock is overextended and stochastics are bumping their linear heads on the overbought ceiling—tighten your protective stop, or sell.

Or, say, you're short a stock, and it's approaching a strong support area. Stochastics had wallowed in the oversold zone beneath twenty, but now it hooks up in a bullish divergence. Again, you'll want to tighten your stop or take profits.

Stochastics displays bullish or bearish divergences early enough that we can prepare for a potential trend reversal and profit from it.

Like all indicators, we combine stochastics signals with other indicators to obtain the optimum signal. Please don't buy a stock—swing trade, day trade, or any other time frame—based solely on stochastics. Use it as a decision-support tool with candle patterns, volume, moving averages, and other indicators of your choice.

Stochastics Buy and Sell Signals

You can interpret the stochastic oscillator many ways, but for now we'll stick to the most popular and straightforward methods.

- Buy when the oscillator lines skid into oversold territory below twenty, then hook up. Sell when the lines climb into the overbought zone above eighty, then hook down.

- Buy when the %K rises about the %D line. Sell when the %K descends below the %D line.

- Buy bullish divergences that occur when prices move sideways or drift lower, yet stochastics move higher. Sell bearish divergences when prices move sideways or higher, yet stochastics head lower.

An additional signal given by stochastics occurs when an extended %K line moves back to the %D line, doesn't touch it, and then reverses back into its previous direction. This indicates that the trend is continuing. We call this pattern a "stochastic pop."

Figure 8–3 shows a daily chart of the QQQQ, the NASDAQ 100 tracking stock.

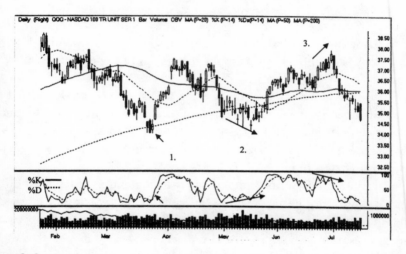

Figure 8–3. On this daily chart of the QQQQ the NASDAQ 100 index tracking stock, you can see how the stochastics oscillator stretches like a rubber band to overbought boundaries at the top of the scale (100), then plunges to oversold territory at the bottom (0). Like most oscillators, this indicator gives the best signals when it reaches extremes.

1. Notice the bullish divergence on March 24, when %K bottoms out at oversold extremes, then hooks up just before price scoots higher. Day traders anticipate long intraday opportunities.
2. During the first two weeks of May, the QQQQ bounces all over the map (no swing trades here, please), yet stochastics made two higher lows—a bullish divergence and sign. The OBV also starts to rise. Short sellers—take cover. Buyers anticipate a reversal to the upside.
3. On June 30, the QQQQ makes a new relative high, but stochastic lines dive south, unimpressed by the price action. Long-swing traders, take profits. Short sellers—get ready to party. Price soon follows stochastics' dissipating momentum and skids toward prior lows.

During the time period shown, the QQQQ bounces up and down in a range between about $34 and $38. Its stochastics oscillator moves even faster. It soars to overbought heights, then crashes to oversold levels with the vigor of a coffee-loving rabbit on a trampoline.

On March 22 through 24, note how the QQQQ gapped down, then danced precariously for three days on the 200-day MA tightrope. Just below, stochastics applauded and gave the stock a bullish divergence by hooking up.

Would I buy the QQQQ and hold it overnight on the strength of that bullish sign? No way, Jose. It's legally still in a downtrend. I *might* day trade it to the long side on March 24. Alternately, if I were holding a short position, that divergence tells me in a loud voice to cover my position.

Now, move to the last high the Qs made near the hard right edge of the chart, on June 30. For openers, the OBV had been snoring in a sideways slumber for some time. When the QQQQ made a relative new high, the OBV barely yawned. Then it went back to sleep. (Bearish sign.)

Look at the trio of zingy highs made by stochastics. Most important, though, notice how the stochastics pop that correlates to the new price high *is lower than the prior stochastics high*. This bearish divergence between the indicator, and the price tells you that danger is brewing.

As further confirmation that the QQQQ might be in trouble, if you travel back to the last week in May, stochastics soared at that time to a reading of 100 percent. On June 30, they barely touched 91.

Figure 8–4 shows a five-minute chart of Lam Research Corporation. (LRCX). The chart displays terrific examples of how indicators can work together on an intraday basis to give clear signals that point to high–quality setups and profitable outcomes.

Stochastic Quirks

Just like every other chart tool, stochastics exhibits quirky characteristics.

Stochastics lines can fly into their overbought or oversold zones fast and furiously. Then, they can bump and grind along the top or bottom of these zones for long periods of time. Please take that quirk into consideration when you factor stochastics signals into your decisions.

> **Hot Tip: A stock breaking out of a base can display overbought stochastics within a few days and continue that signal for an extended period of time. If you're planning a core or position trade, you may choose to ignore the stochastics signal. Look to factors such as support and resistance, trendlines, moving averages, etc., to indicate a buy signal.**

Figure 8–4. This 5-minute chart of Lam Research Corp. (LRCX) shows how the stochastics oscillator combined with a simple 20-period MA and volume/OBV signals to offer timely and ultimately profitable information for intraday trades. LRCX essentially trades sideways for the morning hours, hopping up and down over its 20-period MA, with light volume, and sidestepping OBV and stochastics. The semiconductor stock "woke up" at 11:30 a.m. EST.

1. Minutes before, three strong volume spikes appeared, and stochastics crossed up in a bullish divergence (price consolidated). Savvy traders started nibbling on long positions, establishing tight protective stops under the consolidation "ledge." Low-risk traders waited for the breakout—an alternative and equally good choice. At 11:25 a.m. EST, LRCX broke out. It rose in a sweet, hourlong, one-point run.

2. At the top, price and indicators signaled considerately to day traders that the leg up was over. The overextended stock (on an intraday basis) formed a topping candle—a shooting star. Stochastics called out a bearish divergence, heading lower. OBV soon followed. Traders with long positions had plenty of warning to take profits.

3. At around 3:00 p.m. EST, LRCX started higher once again. Stochastics made a quick divergence, but wise traders would have noticed that the OBV remained unconvinced and shrugged off the move.

Bear in mind that when the %K flies away from the %D in a zany move up or down, the stock is making a radical move, too. Take caution with entries when this happens, as—at some point—the %K and %D *will* kiss and make up. When that happens, price momentum will dissipate.

The degree and length of time that the widened %K and %D spread maintains momentum depends on the trading habits of the stock. Look left, meaning, analyze the stock's previous price and oscillator history to judge how elastic its price and oscillator has been in the past. If you are holding a position during this period, maintain a trailing protective stop so you keep your profits.

ADX (Average Directional Movement Index) with Plus (+DI) and Minus (−DI) Directional Indicators— What They Are, How They Send Signals

Doesn't this sound like a gadget that ought to be glued onto the nose of an airplane? It actually refers to a valuable series of momentum filters developed by Welles Wilder, called the directional movement system.

We're going to explore three lines, or indicators, from the system, the Plus Directional Indicator (+DI), the Minus Directional Indicator (−DI), and the Average Directional Movement Index (ADX).

The lines give clear and sensitive signals as to whether a stock is trending—or not. More important, the lines send early—and reliable—reversal signals. To traders, that's important information for entries, exits, and risk management.

What It Is

There's a lot of talk these days about "true range." This is especially true with E-mini traders, where identifying true range can help forecast immediate direction. If you're a fan of true range, you'll be an extra happy camper with this section. Directional movement indicators integrate true-range information into their signals.

First, we'll look at the fourteen-day (or period on an intraday chart) +DI (Plus Directional Indicator) and the fourteen-day (or period) −DI (Minus Directional Indicator). When you plot these indicators on a single scale, they move in *opposite* directions. Their opposing actions alert us to these basic signals:

- Buy when the +DI rises above the −DI

- Sell when the +DI crosses down and heads below the −DI

Each of these lines measures the current period's (we'll call it "today") range, compared to the previous period's (referred to as "yesterday") range.

Here's a simplified example of true range: Yesterday, Bitty Broadband ranged from a low of $51 to a high of $53. Today, Bitty traded in a range from a low of $51.50 to a high of $53.50. A *positive directional movement* occurred, because the today's high surpassed yesterday's high. Plus, today's low exceeds yesterday's low. Result: +DI moves up.

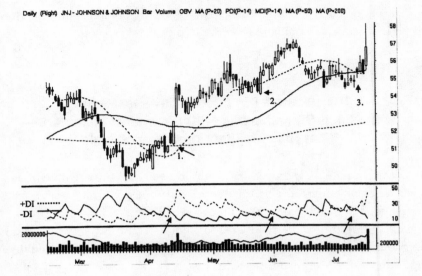

Figure 8–5. On this daily chart of Johnson & Johnson (JNJ), you can see how the +DI and the −DI move in opposite directions. When price comes down, as it did at the end of February and half of March, the −DI moved *up*. The +DI faltered and moved *down*.

1. JNJ began a V-shaped recovery that climbed over the 200-day MA, in mid-April. The +DI crossed to the upside. Then, it held its ground above the −DI until the third week in May. At the same time, the drug giant's stock consolidated along the 20-day MA.
2. When JNJ's price popped out of the continuation pattern, or bull flag, at the end of May, the +DI crossed up and over the −DI again, but this time with less enthusiasm. It's interesting how JNJ made a two-point run, then cratered fast. The two-point run took about three weeks to develop, and three *days* to disintegrate and return to old support.
3. For much of June and early July, JNJ roiled in a congestion pattern. As it unwound, however, traders with a keen eye for the +DI, saw the indicator line cross to the upside. Extreme volume sent the pharmaceutical stock in a 2½, point run, but it "came in" (retraced) by the closing bell.

If the reverse takes place, with today's low falling below yesterday's low, and today's high dropping below yesterday's high, a *minus directional movement* occurs Result: +DI moves down.

Why do you care? Because a stock that enlarges its high/low range, either to the upside or downside, may be building energy for an explosive price move.

Figure 8–5 shows the +DI and the −DI in action on a daily chart of pharmaceutical manufacturer, Johnson & Johnson (JNJ). You can see how the two lines alternate directions, depending on price action.

Note how the directional indicators gave traders a heads–up each time JNJ prepared to take off on a joy ride.

The downside to using only the +DI and –DI without a smoothing line is that you'll likely receive too many signals. That leads to getting "whipsawed," as well as overtrading.

To avoid that, we'll add the ADX. The ADX line records the difference between the +DI and the –DI in the form of an exponential moving indicator. Again, I use a standard default of fourteen periods.

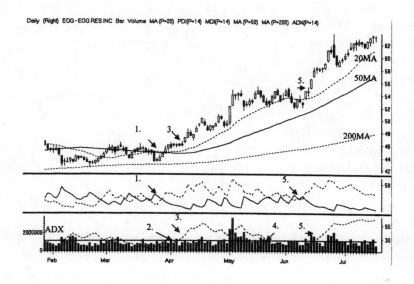

Figure 8–6. This daily chart of EOG Resources, Inc. (EOG) shows the energy stock breaking out of a near-perfect base (orderly + tight price range) on the last day of March.

1. You can see how on March 29, the +DI (dotted line) crosses up and over the –DI (solid line). The next day, price rises over its 20-day and 50-day MAs. Two bullish alerts have appeared. Still, the ADX remains below 30, so we wait and watch.
2. On April 5, the ADX (volume panel) rises over 30. Volume remains average to strong. Moving averages fan out in perfect layering for a long position, with the 20-day MA layered above the 50-day MA, and the 50 above the 200-day MA. Long position and swing traders start nibbling while the stock continues to consolidate.
3. On April 8, EOG initiates an uptrend with a final break out of its base. The ADX and +DI move up in concert.
4. The ADX stays above the 30 benchmark until May 19, when the long-term consolidation takes it lower. Swing traders would have played the price swings until the ADX fell below 30, signaling a nontrending market.
5. The signals repeat themselves again in June, when EOG makes another 10-point moonshot.

The ADX moves on a scale that ranges from 0 to 100. When the ADX breaks up and above 30, it signals a trend in motion.

This is the part that makes traders go slack-jawed. *An ADX that rises over 30 may be signaling the birth of an uptrend* or *a downtrend.*

With most other indicators, up means buy. Down means sell. Not this time. Again, when the ADX rises above 30, you will see either an uptrend *or* a down-trend developing. If the line falls below 30, it signals "no trend, so no trade."

You may prefer to add the ADX to the same scale that displays the +DI and –DI. That system works well on software that allows you to color-code the different lines. (I code the +DI green, the –DI red, and the ADX blue.)

Because of the black-and-white graphics in this text, however, the ADX will replace the OBV on the charts that follow (and where indicated in future chapters). That way, you can clearly see its line action in comparison to the Plus and Minus DIs.

Figure 8–6 displays a chart of EOG Resources, Inc. (EOG). Note how crossovers by the +DI and the –DI go unnoticed by the ADX from February through March; it stays beneath the 30 signal line during those two months. This keeps traders from buying (or selling) too soon.

When EOG pops out of its base on April 8, traders have prepared for the breakout for two to three days, because of the earlier +DI crossover above the –DI.

Also, take note of the perfect layering of the moving averages. Remember, when you buy a stock, the averages should layer as support under the stock, from the fastest to the slowest. As you work with ADX and directional indicators, you'll notice how smoothly they work together with moving averages.

Figure 8–7 shows a five-minute chart of Winnebago Industries, Inc. (WGO). You can see clearly how the ADX and the +DI and –DI signaled two short day-trade entries—one at about 10:00 a.m. and one at about 2:00 p.m. EST.

Although you can see a shorting opportunity fifteen-twenty minutes into the open, where the price rolled over, the ADX nixed it. Why? Because during that time period, the price moved up, and then reversed. The ADX, in effect, said, "That's not a trend."

When the trades set up, in both cases the –DI crossed above the +DI first, giving us a heads-up that a short setup might be forming. Ten minutes later, the ADX crossed above 30, sounding a sell-short signal.

Can you nibble during the time spread between the DI's crossover and the ADX breaks 30? It's your call. If you see the ADX spiking in a sharp angle, soon after the crossover, and you're convinced it's going to break through the 30 *soon*, go ahead. Too, those who have the ADX on the same panel as the DIs will see the ADX cross the weak (falling) DI as additional input.

As a general rule, when the ADX peaks or begins to correct, the DI's begin

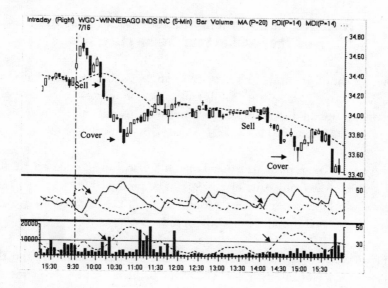

Figure 8–7. On this 5-minute chart of Winnebago Industries, Inc. (WGO), you see how the recreational vehicle manufacturer offered two delicious short trades for active traders. The arrows show the price entries and the indicator signals. In both cases, I would have entered shortly after the DI crossover took place, as the ADX approached the 30 signal line. You need an uptick to enter a trade short (stocks), so entering a falling stock can take time and finesse. When you see the ADX peak and the DI lines lessen their spread, cover your position to protect your profits.

to narrow their spread. When you see that occurring, tighten your stop and plan to close your trade.

ADX with +DI –DI Buy and Sell Signals

- Buy (bullish) when ADX slices above 30 and moves higher in concert with +DI; –DI heads south.

- Sell (bearish) when ADX breaks above 30 and spikes higher, along with the –DI; +DI falls lower.

ADX with +DI and –DI Quirks

When the ADX wanders below 30 and slides under both DI signals, and the DIs weave around each other with jumbled signals, the market is too trendless to trade.

On the flip side, when the ADX soars above both the +DI and the –DI, the market is experiencing extreme volatility.

Fibonacci Retracement Studies—What They Are, How They Add to Your Trading Decisions

We owe a debt of gratitude to Leonardo Pisano, a twelfth-century Italian mathematician, who often answered to his nickname, Fibonacci.

Fibonacci was an important mathematician of his day, and wrote several texts on the subject. In one of his books, *Liber abaci*, he poses this problem:

> A certain man put a pair of rabbits in a place surrounded on all sides by a wall. How many pairs of rabbits can be produced from that pair in a year if it is supposed that every month each pair begets a new pair, which from the second month on becomes productive?

The answer led to the introduction of the Fibonacci numbers and the Fibonacci sequence of numbers, for which the mathematician is best remembered today.

In the sequence, each successive number equals the sum of the two previous numbers: 1, 1, 2, 3, 5, 8, 13, 21, 34, 55, 89, and so forth.

Any of these numbers equals approximately 1.618 times the preceding number. And any number equals approximately 0.618 times the subsequent number.

Studies of these proportions led to the discovery that they coincide with those of a wide range of earthly inhabitants, including nautilus shells, butterflies, and the human body.

How do we connect the Fibonacci sequence to trading? Easily and with success!

The four popular Fibonacci studies we overlay on charts include retracements, arcs, fans, and time zones.

For now, we'll focus on the most popular study, Fibonacci retracement levels. Many charting software programs include this tool.

What They Are

Fibonacci retracement levels act as support and resistance levels. When you've identified a high and a low on any time frame, you can apply "Fibs," as traders have nicknamed these lines, to gauge possible support and support areas within those boundaries.

Fibonacci retracement levels are measure-gauged at 38.2 percent, 50 percent, and 61.8 percent.

If a stock or other instrument is trading below the retracement line(s), the line acts as potential resistance. If the stock trades above the line(s), the lines act as potential support.

To see how this indicator works, draw an uptrend, or downtrend line, on a chart, connecting a major peak and trough. Activate your charting software's Fibonacci retracement option. Start at the bottom of the trend line and drag your cursor to the top of the trend. You'll see five horizontal lines, representing 0.0 percent, then 38.2, 50, 61.8, and 100 percent stretch the length of the entire move, or trend. Some chart programs include a 23.6-percent line.

Figure 8–8 shows a daily chart of the Dow Jones Industrial Average. We measured from the peak to the trough of a downtrend, then stretched Fibonacci retracement from the top to the bottom. As the subsequent rally played out, it used the retracement lines as resistance in near-perfect form.

Figure 8–9 displays a five-minute chart of the S&P 500 E-mini contract. This time we measured an intraday uptrend, from the low of the trend, to the high. Our goal was to gauge possible retracement support levels.

As it turned out, short sellers who entered as the contract rolled over the top of the intraday trend did well. The retracement of the uptrend tumbled in a wa-

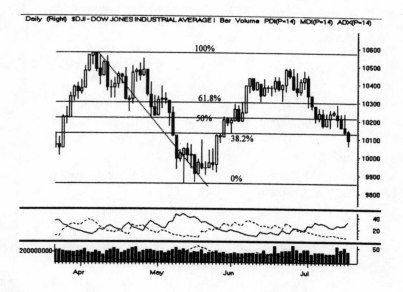

Figure 8–8. On this daily chart of the Dow Jones Industrial Average, we plotted a short-term downtrend from its peak in April at 10,570 to its May trough, which bottomed at 9,852. The subsequent rally found a day's resistance at the 38.2 percent level marked by Fibonacci lines. The next rally stopped at the 50 percent line. The next leg-up drew back-to-back candles held down by the 61.8 percent line. The new uptrend could not make it to the 100 percent retracement line, and subsequently slid south. It's intriguing how these retracement lines produce such accurate readings.

Intraday (Right) /ESU4 - Sep 04 E-Mini S&P 500 (5-Min) Bar Volume PDI(P=14) MDI(P=14) ADX(P=14)

Figure 8–9. On this 5-minute chart of the E-mini S&P 500 contract, we measured an intraday uptrend from its trough, or low, to its peak, or high. (Check out that shooting star at the top of the uptrend, followed by a bearish engulfing candle. That's bearish.) After we measure the trend, which happened to halt precisely at an early-morning high, we watched it retrace. The move down corrected nearly 100 percent of the move up. As you can see, along the way the retracement quickly sliced below potential support furnished by the lines, then used those lines as resistance. The ignored support showed how feeble the correction really was.

terfall pattern, cutting through Fibonacci support lines like a knife through warm butter.

You can pick any high and any low to measure retracement levels in between. If you apply Fib lines to a number of nearby highs and lows, you'll find they concentrate in certain areas. We designate those areas as Fibonacci "clusters," and they may offer extra-strong support or resistance.

Why We Use Them

After an important price move, or trend, the price usually retraces a portion, or all, of the original distance. In this process, they often use Fibonacci retracement levels as support and resistance. The retracement lines work well on all time frames.

"Fib lines" are very popular with futures traders. Stock traders draw on retracements, as well.

We usually don't use the lines as definite buy or sell signals. Their value emerges when the retracement lines converge with other forms of support and resistance, such as trend lines, pivots, or moving averages. Then the lines strengthen your buy or sell decisions.

Example: Say your stock traveled in an uptrend, and is now retracing to the 38.2-percent area. If it hesitates there, and the ADX and directional indicators give a buy signal, along with strong volume and perhaps a bullish piercing candle, you've got enough information to enter a high-probability long trade.

Besides gauging potential zones in a trend retracement, you can determine the strength of a move depending on how quickly, and at what angle, a price moves through retracement zones.

> **Hot Tip:** Traders use Fib lines to measure support and resistance areas in gaps. One method: Stretch the lines from the closing price of the gap to the opening price. You can gauge potential support or resistance areas if traders try to close the gap.

Since so many traders use Fibonacci retracement levels for guidance, some support/resistance action may be a self-fulfilling prophecy. Still, it's positively uncanny how many times a stock in an uptrend will pull back to a Fibonacci level, then bounce. Or a stock in a downtrend will rebound to a Fibonacci level, then begin its fall anew.

That said, I have to issue the standard warning. No indicator (or guru!) can predict future price movement with absolute accuracy. When your stock or E-mini approaches a Fibonacci retracement level, there's no guarantee it's going to halt there and bounce. It could just as easily slice right through it.

Indicators—no matter what flavor they come in—are just that. They *indicate*. Please don't use them as an excuse to stay in a losing position.

> **Hot Tip:** Stocks often retrace about 50 percent of their last major move up (or down). When the stock you're holding corrects more than 50 percent, it may be weaker, or stronger, than you anticipated. Consider downsizing share size or taking early profits.

The indicators listed in this chapter are among my favorites. Many, many more are available for you to explore. Selections of these are explained on my Web site, *toniturner.com*.

In the chapters that follow, we're going to take the chart components discussed and apply them to setups, entries, and exits on stocks, ETFs, E-minis, and other products.

Before you read on, though, please glance at the quiz. Review is a great way to solidify knowledge.

Quiz

Questions

1. When referring to a momentum indicator and price, what does the term "divergence mean"?

2. Is the MACD a *trend-leading* or *trend-following* indicator?

3. Give an example of a MACD buy signal.

4. What is the underlying reasoning behind the stochastics oscillator?

5. True or false: No matter how overbought a market becomes, the stochastics oscillator continues to emit clear, trend-advancing signals.

6. What overall signals do the ADX with Plus and Minus DI give us?

7. True or false: If you jump into a long trade every time the +DI crosses above the –DI, you're likely to get whipsawed.

8. The ADX gives a long or short entry signal when it breaks above _____.

9. Give the first five numbers in the Fibonacci sequence. How do they relate to each other?

10. What are the main Fibonacci retracement percentages?

Answers

1. In the relationship between a momentum indicator and price, a divergence takes place when the indicator makes a move, or series of moves, that depart from the patterns of the price. So, when a price makes a higher high, yet the indicator falls lower, the two entities "diverge." This is a warning signal called a "bearish divergence." It indicates that the price will soon follow the direction of the indicator. When an indicator

moves higher, while price shifts sideways or even lower, it's called a "bullish divergence." Once again, the indicator alerts us to the possibility of price following the indicator's lead.

2. The MACD is a *trend-following* indicator.

3. One buy signal given by the MACD occurs when both lines dip into the panels oversold territory. Then the MACD line crosses up and over the signal line.

4. The underlying reasoning behind stochastics is that a stock or other trading instrument in an uptrend will continue to close near its highs until the trend weakens. At that time, closing prices begin to drop nearer to their lows. Stochastics "sees" that shift in momentum, by crossing the %K line below the %D line. In the context of a downtrend, the reverse situation takes place.

5. False. One drawback to the stochastics is that a stock's price action can register an overbought or oversold signal very quickly. If the stock continues to rise without many pullbacks, or fall with shallow rallies, the indicator "glues itself" to the top or bottom of its scale and can stay there for an extended period.

6. Overall, the ADX with Plus and Minus DI tell us whether a stock is trending or not. The lines also send early reversal signals.

7. True. If you jump into a long trade every time the +DI crosses above the –DI, you're likely to get whipsawed—big time!

8. The ADX gives a long or short entry signal when it breaks above 30.

9. The first five numbers in the Fibonacci sequence are 1, 1, 2, 3, and 5. Each successive number equals the sum of the two previous numbers: 1 + 1 = 2; 1 + 2 = 3; 2 + 3 = 5, and so forth. Each one of these numbers equals approximately 1.618 times the preceding number, and approximately 0.618 times the subsequent number.

10. The main Fibonacci retracement percentages range from 0 to 38.2, 50, 61.8, and 100 percentage.

CENTER POINT

Practice Makes *Im*perfect

I cannot give you a formula for success, but I can give you a formula for failure: Try to please everybody.

—Herbert Swope

Does your inner critic constantly harp on your shortcomings? Do you set near-unattainable goals for yourself, and then berate yourself when you can't achieve them? Or do you believe that you have to accomplish everything perfectly to be accepted by others?

If you've answered "yes" to any or all of these questions, chances are you've acquired a character trait called "perfectionism."

Dr. Brett Steenbarger says, "Most achievement-oriented, successful individuals are perfectionists."

While it may act as a driving force, perfectionism is also a less-than-gentle master that, in many cases, can slow down personal growth and development. The perfectionist part of us focuses on flaws and perceived failures. In turn, that negative and misdirected energy depletes our resources.

How can we lighten up our perfectionistic tendencies?

First, gently tell your inner critic to take a hike! Next, flip negative self-talk to positive. Instead of, "I'm so stupid, I forgot my glasses again," try, "Hmm, I'm going to buy a spare pair of glasses and leave them in the car."

Instead of setting achievement-oriented goals, establish reasonable goals that are process-oriented. Then focus on enjoying the process. You'll achieve more—faster.

Finally, as Herbert Swope stated in the quote above, recognize that your efforts to please everyone will lead to failure. Talk about an impossible task!

Instead, focus on self-acceptance. Healthy self-acceptance—like true prosperity—is an "inside job." When you believe in yourself—warts and all—you'll find anxiety lifting. Plus, it sends a message to yourself, and to others: "I may not be perfect, but I'm one fantastic work in progress!"

CHAPTER NINE

Hold that Position!

Long-Term Trading Tactics

*In the market environment, you have to make the rules to the game and then
have the discipline to abide by these rules, even though the market moves in ways
that will constantly tempt you into believing you don't need to follow your rules
this* time.

—Mark Douglas, in
The Disciplined Trader[i]

For all you "kick back, feet-on-the-desk" traders out there, position trading represents a relaxed method of taking gains from the market.

The technique consists of buying (or selling short) a stock position at the birth of a new trend. Assuming the stock cooperates and gallops into the trend with enthusiasm, you ride the stock through its price trend, until it shows signs of reversing. Profit objective: multiple points.

The time period for which you hold the position optimally stretches from weeks to months. Operative theory: the longer the trend survives, and the longer you hold the trade, the more money you'll make. When the trend deteriorates—or *shows signs* of deteriorating—you'll take your proceeds and bow out.

Unlike investors, who ride positions to profits and then back down to a loss, you'll grab your gains right before the party ends and the neighbors call the cops. ☺

Position trading demands far less monitoring than do swing and day trading. We can also refer to it as "short-term investing." It's definitely an approach investors would do well to understand.

---

[i]Douglas, Mark, *The Disciplined Trader* (NJ, NY Institute of Finance, 1990), p. 65.

Focus on Position Trades—Strategies

The overall market environment will influence many of your core, or position trades. In muscular, trending markets you may want to use the "big picture" or top-down methodology. When sideways environments prevail, you can seek out stocks that ignore the market's range-bound symphony, and instead, dance to the strains of their own music.

Basic position or core trading strategies:

- Buy a stock initiating an uptrend that moves in tandem with the Dow, S&P 500 Index, or the NASDAQ 100; use the index as a guideline for stock direction. (In bear markets, you would sell short a stock dropping from a top reversal that moves with a larger index, and use the index as a guideline for stock direction.)

- Buy a leading component of a major index, such as bank, biotech, oil services, software, etc. Use the index, plus a benchmark index, such as the S&P 500, as a guideline for stock direction. (When bearish, you sell short a lagging component of a weak index, then use the group index and benchmark as guidelines.)

- In a bear market environment, commodities stocks such as oil, gold, copper, lumber, and energy may go their separate ways. Target a commodity index that suits your comfort level (these indices can be volatile), such as the XAU—the Gold and Silver Index, or the XOI—the Amex Oil Index. Ideally, the index is breaking out of a base, or recently drew a higher low above its base, showing signs of rising into an uptrend. Then, take a core trade in a stock that tracks the index. For example, at the moment, Amerada Hess Corporation (AHC) moves hand-in-glove with the XOI.

- Using the bottom-up strategy, buy a stock initiating an uptrend (or sell short a stock dropping into a downtrend). Concentrate on the stock's progress, and except for radical movements, ignore the rest of the market.

> **Hot Tip: Rising oil costs are a sign of inflation, and inflation can be negative for the stock market. That's one reason equities may fall when oil stocks soar.**

Figure 9–1 shows a daily chart of Nextel Communications, Inc. (NXTL). As you can see, the telecom stock provided a delicious core trade. The telecom stock hopped out of a quick summer consolidation (August 29, price $18.50), to waltz sweetly up its twenty-day MA for the next four months. By the time it

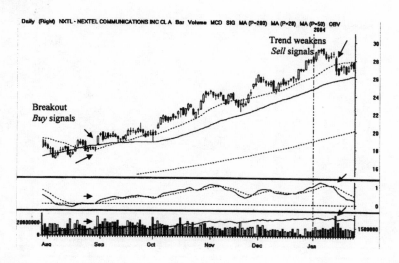

Figure 9–1. On this daily chart of Nextel Communications, Inc. (NXTL), you can see how the stock broke out of a brief consolidation area on August 29. Buy signal: the stock made two consolidation lows on August 14, then again, on August 25. On August 28, the MACD rose off the zero line in a quick bullish divergence. On August 29, NXTL gapped open 40 cents to $18.48 on strong volume. Without stopping to fill that price gap, the telecom stock then stepped up the 20-day MA, until it topped out at $29.34 on January 8. Soon after, the price broke down, the MACD hooked down in a sell signal, and volume rose as the stock fell. Position traders closed long positions. Those who entered at the August breakout and rode the stock to its highs made a sweet profit, indeed!

reached its top in January ($29.37), it tacked on more than a 30-percent profit. We would have taken profits during the first week of January.

Had you followed a daily chart of the XTC, or the North American Telecommunications Index, in which NXTL is a component, you'd find it rose in a gentle uptrend from August through January. That's good supportive information. Figure 9–2 shows a daily chart of the XTC during the same time period.

Okay, back to Figure 9–1. While you can easily see where NXTL broke out of the August continuation, how do you know to exit the trade on, or before, the first week in January?

Two clues: first, notice how the telecom stock took off in the last week of December, jumping up in a steeper angle. Whenever a stock uses a relatively fast (20-day) moving average as a trampoline, then flies high above it for a relatively long period—in this case, two weeks—gravity *will* jerk on the stock's leash, sooner or later.

Second, evaluate the late-December MACD. The MACD line took off from

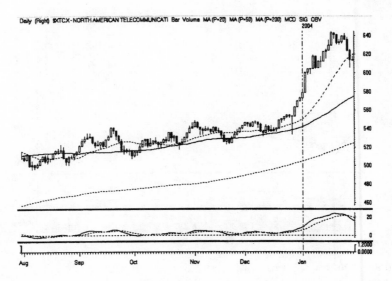

Daily (Right) $XTCX-NORTH AMERICAN TELECOMMUNICATI Bar Volume MA(P-20) MA(P-50) MA(P-200) MCD SIG OBV

Figure 9–2. This daily chart of the North American Telecommunications index (XTC) represents the industry group in which our core trade, Nextel Communications Inc. (NXTL), is a component. Note how the XTC shuffled through a shallow uptrend from August to mid-December, then soared to moonshot highs in mid-January. The steep angle up forecasts an oncoming catastrophic fall. And odds were good NXTL would "come in" with the XTC. This is an example of how you can monitor the index where your core trade stock resides, for additional risk-management information.

its signal line at a steeper angle—widening the spread radically. This broadening spread alerts you to a zealous price move, as well.

Were you in a *swing* trade experiencing this scenario, you would tighten your trailing stop.

As a position trader, you may want to locate prior resistance by flipping to a weekly or monthly chart. If you make it a habit to check longer-term charts before you enter core trades, especially, you'll have a clearer picture of your target stock's health.

Figure 9–3 shows a weekly chart of NXTL. The last time NXTL traded at $30 occurred when it churned through a volatile, three-month consolidation period in early 2001. And, yes, that resistance—nearly three years prior—can definitely bop NXTL on the head at this point.

How does old resistance maintain its power? In this case, that early 2001 congestion (volatile consolidation) range tells us plenty of folks bought NXTL then, at about $30. And since the telecom stock tanked in an ugly downtrend right after that, I'll betcha my duck slippers, a good portion of those investors still own the stock. Their reaction: "After three years of tanking, this stupid

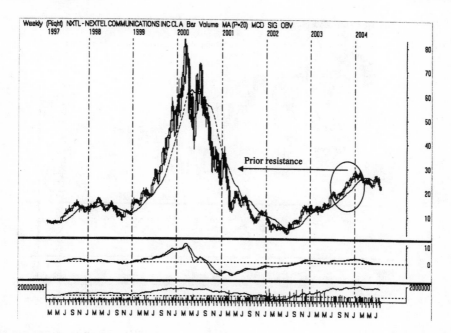

Figure 9–3. On this weekly chart of Nextel Communications, Inc. (NXTL), you can see how the stock formed resistance in late 2000 to early 2001, which would surely impact our trade in early 2004. Our core trade took place in the circled segment. When you target a core trade setup, it's always a good idea to check long-term charts for prior support and resistance.

stock finally climbed back to the price where I bought it. Now I'll sell it, while I can at least get out even." That supply turns into resistance.

Figure 9–4 shows Bed Bath & Beyond, Inc. (BBBY) as it roils through a volatile downtrend.

Why didn't I insert a calm, drip-by-price-drip downtrend and point to a single short entry and exit? Unless we're in the throes of a bear market, tidy, well-behaved downtrends are rare critters.

Since downtrends usually evolve with more unpredictability than uptrends (fear creates more unpredictable price action than greed) it's easier to get stopped out in a downtrend. As with all trades, remember to establish a protective stop immediately after you enter.

In Figure 9–4, you can see where BBBY sidestepped in a horizontal trend since the beginning of the year, weakened in March. When the retailer fell below all three of its major moving averages (20, 50, 200), created a MACD sell (MACD line hooked below signal line and both dove below zero), and sent the OBV south, it presented a short opportunity for swing and core traders.

On March 31, BBBY closed in a doji evening star. These bearish stars appear

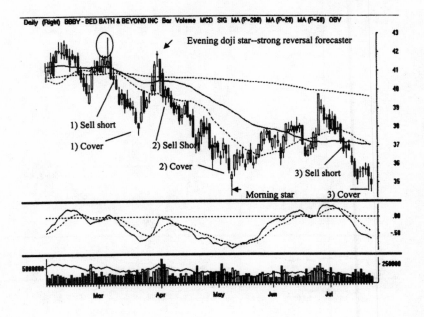

Figure 9–4. This daily chart of Bed Bath & Beyond, Inc. (BBBY) shows three position trade opportunities in 1) March, 2) April–May, and 3) July. BBBY topped out in February, and in early March lacked the buying energy to climb to a higher high. A clue that price might drop more appeared in the March 5 candle: the intraday's price rose to the prior high, but the bears pounded it lower (circled). That created a mini-double top and a long upper shadow confirming strong selling pressure. We sold short each position trade after BBBY rallied, then reversed and fell below its 50-day and 20-day MAs. Just as I hesitate to *buy* a stock that's trading at a discount to its 20-day MA, I do not *sell* stocks short for swing or core trades that trade above their 20-day MA. This rule helps minimize risk.

rarely—so if you happen to be long when they show up, please remember they can act as powerful top-reversal patterns.

The two subsequent candles (April 1 and 2) slid down with long black real bodies, confirming the star's potent presence.

When poor BBBY fell below its twenty-day MA, traders sold short. (Many traders sold short earlier. However, one of my rules for swing and core trades: sell short only when stock trades below twenty-day MA.)

> **Hot Tip: There is an old market saying: "Down is faster." Since fear provokes more emotion than greed does, short positions can produce profits (and losses!) faster than long positions. Many expert traders would rather sell short than enter a long position.**

The stock continued to move south until May 10—about a five-point fall. Check out the candle that created a "billboard" for a possible shift in trend: On May 10, a bullish morning star candle reversal pattern appeared.

The next day, the OBV turned up, and the MACD hooked back up as well. For shorts, it's profit-taking time.

Long Position Trades—The Setup and Buying Criteria

As mentioned, when entering a position trade to the long side, you buy the target stock as it breaks over the tops or horizontal resistance lineout of a base on strong volume. (Unless otherwise indicated, all examples refer to daily chart activity.)

I prefer to enter position trades in a stock that's consolidating in an orderly base with the twenty-day, fifty-day, and two-hundred-day moving averages tracking horizontally, along with the price pattern. If the stock recently fell in a downtrend, these moving averages may line up with the two-hundred-day MA, slightly over the fifty-day and twenty-day MAs. The lines will realign themselves in the proper order twenty, fifty, and two-hundred) when (if) the stock breaks into an uptrend.

Here's a list of buying criteria for a core trade. You can apply the criteria to the strategies in the previous section. Please add or alter this list to suit your personal long-term trading style.

- Locate a stock in a basing, or accumulation, pattern. Optimally, its twenty-day, fifty-day, and two-hundred-day moving averages chug sideways along with orderly price action.

- Price begins to rise from the base on a strong, positive candle that closes at, or near, its high. The twenty-day MA starts to rise.

- Volume on the move up is strong; OBV is moving higher.

- The stock moves above its twenty-day, fifty-day, and two-hundred-day moving averages (in this case, in that order).

- The MACD has crossed or is crossing above its signal line.

- Risk-reward analysis: one part risk to at least three parts reward.

> **Hot Tip:** When you first enter a core or position trade, take a partial position. That lowers risk during the uptrend's "birthing" period. Add shares to it when the stock confirms a bona fide uptrend by scooting above the base and etching a higher low and higher high.

Figure 9–5 shows a daily chart of Transocean, Inc. (RIG). Previously, the oil services stock had fallen in a downtrend. Now, it has traveled through an orderly four-month base. Its twenty, fifty, and two-hundred-day moving averages ambled along with it.

For additional information, Figure 9–6 displays a daily chart of the OSX.X, the Oil Services Index. Note how RIG moves in concert with the OSX. RIG moves along with it. That means if the OSX takes a huge dive—or spikes higher—odds are RIG will do the same.

Now, check back to the chart of RIG. The most recent day shown on the chart, December 4, is the entry day for the trade. On that day, price action, volume, the MACD, and the OBV all agreed. RIG shot through its moving averages and closed on the high price of the day—a bullish sign.

The risk-reward analysis looks good: approximately one part risk to five parts reward. It was calculated from these prices that entry-$20.80, protective stop-$19.65, and "temporary" potential reward-$26.

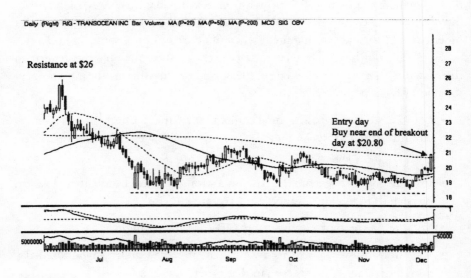

Figure 9–5. This daily chart of Transocean, Inc. (RIG) shows an orderly base formation that can provide strong core trade opportunities. Note how RIG's price tightened into a methodical sideways pattern during the last week of October and November, holding its lows. The base looks ripe for a break to the upside. The breakout day was December 4. The entry occurred just before the close, as the stock closed at the high of the day on strong momentum. Had the stock risen to its highs, then fallen back to an intraday midpoint or lower, we would *not* have taken the trade. We would have waited for a more promising breakout day. But RIG closed on its highs on strong volume, creating a long white candle (positive opinion). The MACD hooked up and rose over its zero line—a buy signal—and the OBV was rising. All signs pointed to a high-quality setup and entry.

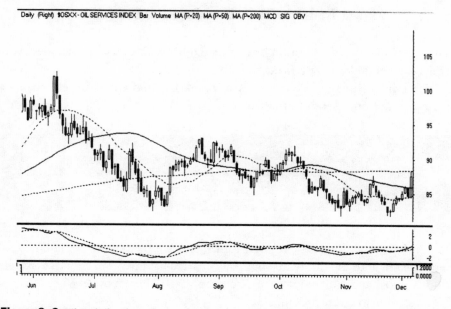

Daily (Right) †OSXX - OIL SERVICES INDEX Bar Volume MA (P-20) MA (P-50) MA (P-200) MCD SIG OBV

Figure 9–6. This daily chart shows the Oil Services Index (OSX). When you compare it with the chart of Transocean, Inc. RIG, you can see how RIG, a component of this index, moves neatly in tandem with it. Since major moves in the OSX can forecast a major move in RIG, the index provides a dandy guideline.

The prices resulted from this analysis:

On Figure 9–5, RIG etched a prior high in June, at $26. That number may provide the first area of potential resistance, or supply, and provides a temporary reward point. The reward is labeled "temporary" because your objective is to stay in the trade beyond the first leg-up. We commit to the position *as long as it stays healthy*.

An obvious place for the initial protective stop, or initial risk, is at the low of the entry day. The December 4 low was 19.75, so the initial stop is set at $19.65.

Since we'll buy five hundred shares near the end of the trading day, at $20.80, we'll adjust the stop higher the following morning.

> **Hot Tip: Avoid entering long position trades where the two-hundred-day moving average slopes down over the tops of price pattern. This average exerts muscular resistance. It can halt a stock in its tracks and take you out of a core trade early on.**

From Trader to Risk Manager—the Long Side

Once you've entered a position or core trade—as with every other trade—you convert from trader to risk manager.

After all, buying a stock is easy. Knowing when and where to sell separates the crash-and-burn set from the winners.

> **Hot Tip:** Here's a good plug for checking weekly charts. Had you flipped to a weekly chart of Transocean, Inc. (RIG), you would have seen the mega-bullish *quadruple* bottom it drew during the year prior to our entry. Those patterns are much easier to see on weekly charts.

Once your stock makes two higher lows, connect them with a trendline. Extend the line into the future on your daily chart. That gives you an idea as to the stock's initial angle of momentum. You can draw a line above the tops of the highs, as well, to create a channel.

Trailing stop choices for position trades:

- When the stock breaks the initial trend line (although the uptrend itself may not break down), exit the trade. (Depending on the angle of the initial trend, this tactic can stop the trade out fairly early in the trend.)

- When the stock makes two consecutive closes below the twenty-day MA, exit the trade (my favorite trailing stop strategy). Use common sense: If catastrophic news hits the markets, jump out sooner.

- Place a trailing stop $0.10 to $0.25 below successive pivot low; adjust the stop higher as each higher low or continuation pattern completes.

- When the stock makes a lower low (uptrend is broken), exit the trade. Period.

Now, check Figure 9–7, which shows the path of our RIG position trade. Wooo-hooo! Life is good!

We exited on March 10, at $29, because:

- Simply put, mission accomplished. If you held this stock through the soaring, multiple-month uptrend, you realized gains equal over 30 percent.

- Technicals: RIG experienced a mature uptrend and just shot into nosebleed territory. Now, on March 10, it's breaking its twenty-day MA and its trendline.

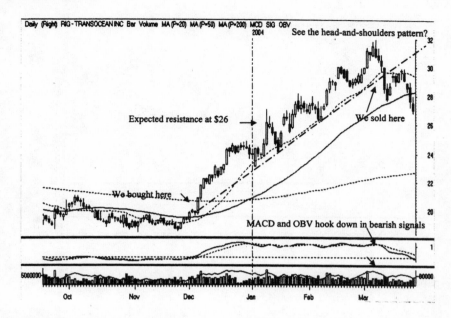

Figure 9–7. The daily chart shows how the position trade in Transocean Inc. (RIG) played out. Note how the stock zoomed out of its base, then went ballistic. We drew a trend line as soon as the stock made a pivot low, in January. The MACD lines soared along with the December price movement. Warning: December volume subsides with most stocks. That will cause the OBV to fall, as it calculates low volume as "disinterest." If you used the "two consecutive closes under the 20-day MA" as your stop criterion, you closed the trade or stayed in the trade until its final gasp on March 11. We closed the trade a day earlier, on March 10 (see long, black candle), at $29, with a gain of over 30 percent. Common sense, combined with other technical signals, indicates the stock is ready to roll over. It's time to "get, while the gettin's good."

- MACD hooking down from overbought zone.

- OBV agrees with MACD and points down.

- OSX.X shows definate weakness, diving through its twenty-day MA earlier on March 10. This helps confirm profit-taking on RIG.

Here's a hint for an earlier exit: In January and February, note how RIG walked up its initial trendline and twenty-day MA, as though they were tightropes. When the trend matured, it suddenly took off like a rocket. In fact, its next pullback in late February didn't touch either line. That type of ballistic price action in a mature uptrend tells you that euphoric Johnnys-come-lately (dumb money) just hitched a ride.

On all time frames, when those Johnnys show up, it's a perfect time to show

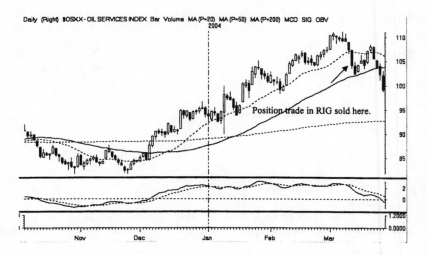

Figure 9–8. This daily chart of the OSX again shows how the index acts as a reliable guideline to RIG's price progress. The falling action of the OSX confirms the decision to take profits on RIG. Note how price action into March finalized a head-and-shoulders top-reversal pattern, indicating lower prices to come.

your generosity. Sell them your stock. Then, slip out the back door before the squawlin' and bawlin' begins!

> **Hot Tip: You may want to target "the generals" for your core trades, or refer to them as drivers of market action. These are single-equity movers and shakers, such as GE, Microsoft, Intel, Cisco Systems, Ebay, Xilinx, Citigroup, and IBM.**

Short Position Trades—The Setup and Selling Short Criteria

When you take a core position on the short side, your objective is to profit multiple points from a stock experiencing a downtrend.

Your objective with this trade may be speculation, or hedging (offset risk) a long portfolio against losses. While you cannot be long *and* short the same equity in the same account (your broker won't allow it), you can hedge long positions by selling short comparable equities, or stock indexes such as the DIA, SPY, or QQQQ.

To enter a short position that you intend to hold for weeks, look for a stock that's traveled through an uptrend and is now grinding through a top-reversal pattern on a daily chart. The top-reversal pattern could be one we've mentioned in chapter 6, such as head and shoulders, or double or triple top. Or the stock can churn through its misery by drawing a plain-vanilla top reversal.

For the *safest* short entry, watch the stock weaken and drop through the pattern's support area. To avoid getting caught in a bear trap, give it at least two days of closes under the 20-day and 50-day moving averages.

Or watch it skid to its first low, then revive into a "throwback rally." This means the price 1) falls though support, 2) reverses and pops up to previous resistance, and 3) fails. When the stock snaps back up to prior resistance, but cannot penetrate it, odds are the price is really out of steam. The failure day is your entry day.

Once you've established your position—or a partial position, if you're scaling in—place your initial protective stop.

Here's a list of basic shorting criteria for core trades. Add or alter the list to suit your style.

- Locate an equity that's formed a top reversal, or distribution pattern

- Price breaks below pattern support lines and its 20-day and 50-day moving averages; the averages lay on top of the price pattern in that order

- Price closes below averages for two days.

- Price falls below averages, rallies, then fails again, indicating weakness

- Volume increases on the failure (entry) day (not absolutely necessary, but helpful); OBV points lower

- The MACD hooks down below its signal line

- Risk-reward analysis: one part risk to at least three parts initial reward

> **Hot Tip:** Say you sell short a crumbling stock. Later in the day, it suddenly turns happy. It bounces off its lows, and by the closing bell, it trades near its daily high. Check prior support areas *fast,* and if necessary, exercise early damage control by covering part of your position. Nothing spells stress like waking up to your short position in gap-up mode!

Whether you use the bottom-up or top-down method, most of us pay at least passing attention to market environment when we enter short position trades.

Here's an example: Say, the NASDAQ danced through an uptrend for the past several months and currently looks "toppy."

And, say, a technology index, such as the Semiconductor Index (SOX), stayed in

Figure 9–9. This daily chart exhibits the price action of Intel Corp. (INTC), as it agitates through a triple top-reversal pattern. The "three strikes and you're out" model tells us that INTC is exhausted—at least for the present.

lockstep with the NASDAQ's uptrend. Now, though, the SOX has run through what appears to be a top-reversal pattern; it displays signs of exhaustion.

Move to the SOX components to find a stock that looks as weak as—or weaker than—the index, and is in the process of forming a high-probability setup.

Figure 9–9 displays a daily chart of Intel Corporation (INTC) as it sets up for a short position. The semiconductor giant doubled its price (not shown) in 2003, moving from a low of 14.88 to a high of $34.50. You can see the stock shooting to its highs in November and early December.

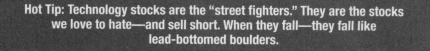

Hot Tip: Technology stocks are the "street fighters." They are the stocks we love to hate—and sell short. When they fall—they fall like lead-bottomed boulders.

Check out the MACD. You can see how INTC's *price* white-knuckled it to its second high in December—*but the MACD formed a much lower high.* This bearish divergence alerted all savvy bulls to tighten stops, or take profits.

After selling off after the December high, INTC made one more "run for the roses." On January 9, the tech stock touched $34.60 on strong volume. The

Figure 9–10. This daily chart of the Philadelphia [Stock Exchange] Semiconductor Index (SOX), referred to by traders as "the Sox," displays the aggregate movement of the biggest semiconductor companies. Intel Corp. (INTC), our target stock for a short core trade, represents a component of the SOX, and many times moves nearly "in sync" with this index. Whenever I trade a semiconductor stock—and whatever the time frame—I always keep an eye on the SOX.

new high was short-lived, though, and it finished the day in a bearish shooting star pattern.

Two days later, on January 13, INTC closed in a bearish engulfing candle on much higher volume. That candle rang a final alarm to all bulls: *If you're long, you're wrong.*

For added decision support, verify action in the Philadelphia Semiconductor Index (SOX.X) shown in Figure 9–10. INTC is a major component of the SOX. You can see how the SOX matched INTC's muscular uptrend in 2003. In January, it formed a mini doubled-top, then gave back its monthly gains in a hurry.

Figure 9–11 exhibits a chart of the NASDAQ 100 index (NDX). Since INTC is also a weighty component of the NASDAQ 100 index, we'll also keep an eye on this index for guidance. While the index is still legally in an uptrend, it's moved down sharply. The MACD issued a sell signal as the NDX corrected.

Okay . . . back to the INTC setup on Figure 9–9. The stock has struggled through a six-day consolidation and continuation pattern, complete with a half-hearted, one-day (white candle) "rally" that failed.

Risk-reward analysis shows nearby potential support from December lows, at around $31.00. We'll tread lightly here and enter with a small starting position. While all signals point to lower prices for the stock, we'll still manage our initial risk tightly.

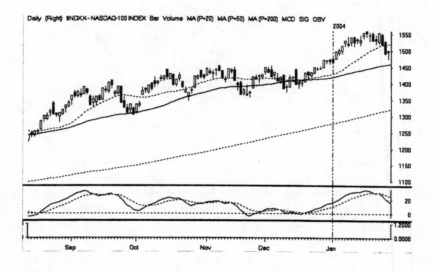

Figure 9–11. This is a daily chart of the NDX, or the NASDAQ 100 Index. When you trade a technology stock—especially a large-cap that rises and falls with the NAS-DAQ—you'll want to keep an eye on this index or its partner, the NASDAQ Composite (COMPX). Of course, no matter what the broader market direction, a few stocks always wander away on their own, usually on stock-specific news. This chart indicates the tech-heavy index rose in a gently angled uptrend for the final months of 2003. January brought a spurt of buying for the first half, then gave back most of the month's gains during the second half. If you compare it to the chart of Intel Corp. (INTC) and the chart of the SOX, you'll notice the SOX and INTC are weaker than the NDX.

January 28, the most recent day on the chart's hard right edge, is our entry day. When the price breaks below the present consolidation support of $31.60, we sell short a small position, just one hundred shares. We place an initial stop at $32.25, just over the high of the entry day and the fifty-day moving average. Tomorrow, when (if) the price breaks below our entry price, we'll pull our stop down to break even.

From Trader to Risk Manager—the Short Side

Plan: If all goes well and INTC sinks through the December consolidation $29.70 lows, we'll add the remaining four hundred shares to our position.

Assuming INTC craters in an ugly downtrend (beautiful to us!), we'll also

Figure 9–12. This daily chart of Intel Corp. (INTC) shows how the core trade to the short side played out. The falling 20-day MA acted as potent resistance to the semiconductor stock. Toward the middle of March, note the rising volume coming into the stock. When that occurs in a mature downtrend, it signifies a reversal may lurk in the offing. By the following week, the MACD showed signs of bottoming out. The price also stretched down as far below the 20-MA as it had in the past. Time to cash out!

initiate the trailing stop that takes us out with two consecutive closes above the 20-day moving average.

Figure 9–12 shows the outcome of this trade. INTC broke to the downside. And while we didn't get stopped out early, the ride had its hairy moments. The break-even $31.60 stop, established on the second day of trade, felt the hot air of an oncoming white candle fake-out on February 3. Since the stock clearly suffered anemia at that point, we held firm.

On February 23, INTC sunk through the December lows. As planned, four hundred shares were added to the position.

When Will the Trend End?

On March 24, we cashed into cover our position at $26.25. Time in the trade: eight weeks.

Exit logic:

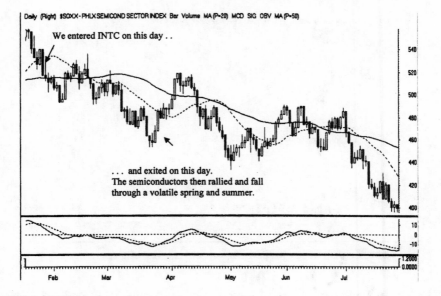

Daly (Right) $SOXX-PHLX SEMICOND SECTOR INDEX Bar Volume MA (P=20) MCD SIG OBV MA (P=50)

Figure 9–13. This daily chart of the Semiconductor Index confirms our decision to exit our INTC short core trade. The SOX shows signs of recovering—at least temporarily. As you can see, it recovered, then fell into another volatile series of short-term rallies and downtrends for the spring and summer months.

- A glance at a weekly chart showed INTC had support from the previous July at $25

- On March 24, the MACD started to hook up from overbought territory into a buy signal

- The same day's price action extends far below the 20-day moving average

- March 24 itself whipped into a positive mood with increased volume

- The SOX, displayed in Figure 9–13, also shows signs of recovery

Profit on this trade (not including commissions): $1,635. Sweet!

In trending markets, many traders—myself included—like to manage risk by devoting a portion of their account to core trades, and the remainder to swing trades.

Chapter 10 delves into swing trading setups and strategies that apply to both long and short positions. See you there!

Quiz

Questions

1. What is the objective of entering a position, or core trade, either long or short?

2. In bearish market environments, why would you look to selected commodities indexes, such as the gold and silver index (XAU) and the Oil index (XOI), for a position trade to the long side?

3. True or false: You can apply the 1) top-down, or 2) bottom-up trading style to position trades.

4. Briefly describe the basic setup for both long and short core trades.

5. True or false: Since core trades can last a long time, it's best to buy your entire position as soon as your target stock breaks out of its base.

6. Describe two stop-loss tactics applicable to core trades.

7. Why do you check long-term charts, such as weekly or monthly, to manage risk in core trades?

Answers

1. The objective of entering a core trade is to buy (or sell) in the early stages of an uptrend (or downtrend), and to hold the position until that trend weakens or shows signs of reversing.

2. When the broader markets turn bearish, selected commodities indexes, such as the gold and silver index (XAU) and the oil index (XOI), often move up. When you see these indices jump out of troughs, or basing modes, check major index stock components for potential core positions to the long side.

3. True.

4. The basic setup for a long core trade: Buy a stock breaking out of an orderly base on strong volume. Basic setup for a short core trade: Sell short a stock breaking down from a top-reversal or distribution pattern.

5. False. One tactic for entering core trades is to "scale in." That means you buy one-third to one-half your intended position at the breakout level,

then add the remaining shares when the stock heads up from its first higher low.

6. Two stop-loss tactics applicable to core trades are 1) when the stock makes two consecutive closes below the twenty-day MA, exit the trade, and 2) when the stock makes a lower low (uptrend is broken), exit the trade immediately.

7. Many times old support and resistance, which could be a year or two distant from current price action, still have the power to exert buying or selling pressure. Take a moment before you enter position or swing trades to analyze the big picture!

CENTER POINT

How Are Your Thoughts "Charged"?

Our life is what our thoughts make it.

—Marcus Aurelius

Thoughts are the most powerful force on earth. If you glance around right now, you see your desk, the chair you sit in, the walls of your office—even the body you live in. All started with a thought, or series of thoughts, that led to materialization.

Our thoughts act as a compelling energy force that creates and acts upon the world around us. They produce a positive or negative effect, depending on the energy with which we "charge" them.

Let's expand that concept to Newton's law of attraction, which theorizes upon the force that attracts and binds atoms together, exerts a pull on celestial bodies, and even maintains them in constant orbit.

When we apply that natural law, or principle, to our thoughts, we realize that the kind of thought energy we exude attracts like energy back to us. Negatively charged thoughts draw—indeed, invite!—negative situations into our lives.

Positively charged thoughts (which turn into words and actions) become magnets to bring positive people and circumstances into our experience.

Studies show the happiest and most successful people automatically re-circuit the "charge" of negative situations. They rethink challenges they encounter and transform them into growth opportunities, like rungs on a ladder.

Here are two actions you can take to "recircuit" your thoughts.

First, spend a day monitoring your thoughts, ideas, and opinions. As they surface, conduct a quick assessment of their energy content: Are they positively or negatively charged? You might be surprised.

Then, each morning, take a moment to decide *how* you want to "charge" your thoughts for the day. Negatively charged thoughts attract negative results. Positively charged thoughts create positive results. You decide!

Swing Trading Strategies

A good trader has to have three things: a chronic inability to accept things at face value, to feel continuously unsettled, and to have humility.
— Michael Steinhardt

Why has swing trading gained such popularity?

First, this style of trading, in which you hold a position for two to five days, puts you in the market when the "gettin's good," and sets you on the sidelines when price action turns skittish.

As well, since the "old days" (late 1990s) of twenty- and thirty-point swings live only in our memories, many day traders have crossed over into swing trading tactics, opting to stay in trades for days (rather than hours) in order to reap multiple points.

Active investors use swing trading to limit exposure in the markets when times become dicey.

Finally, this approach appeals to many folks who don't have the time to trade on an intraday basis, but who want to grab money-making opportunities as they crop up.

In the text that follows, we'll look at three setups to the long side: the "Double Got 'Em," the "Moving Average Leapfrog," and the "Stealthy Sidewinder." For the short side, we'll explore the "Moving Average Hot Blanket."

Since swing-trading setups often result in the best day-trading setups, I'm going to point out day-trading opportunities when they appear. The trades will progress through multiple time frames on daily, sixty-minute, and fifteen-minute charts.

(To review earlier overview of swing trading, check chapter 2.)

Swing Trading Objectives

As you know, swing trading is the trading style that profits by taking the "sweet spots" out of the price swings that carry a stock higher in an uptrend, or lower in a downtrend.

Ideally, consecutive daily bars, each culminating with higher lows and higher highs, form a single upswing. Successive bars that finalize with lower highs and lower lows produce a downswing. Your goal is to enter, and then hold the trade as long as the stock moves with positive, or negative (short), momentum.

Once price exhibits reversal or correction signals, it gives you the signal to close the trade.

With this style of trading, you can refer primarily to daily charts. Strictly speaking, that's all you need to swing-trade successfully. If, however, you have access to intraday charts (for example, sixty-minute and fifteen-minute charts), you can fine-tune your entries, risk management, and exits, with added precision.

> **Hot Tip: Why does technical analysis still work?**
> **Although time marches on, human reaction (think "fear and greed")**
> **to news and price action stays the same.**

Figure 10–1 shows a daily chart of Lennar Corporation (LEN) as it sails upward in a fairly orderly uptrend. You can see swing trading opportunities to the long side that yielded multiple-point profits on multiple-day holds.

Figure 10–2 displays a daily chart of Hutchinson Technology, Inc. (HTCH), as it tumbles in a downtrend. Several swing trades to the short side followed through, bearing multipoint profits.

Now, let's trade!

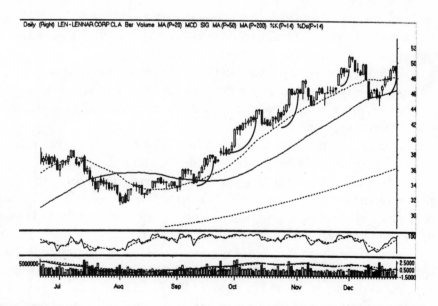

Figure 10–1. This daily chart of Lennar Corp. (LEN) shows four opportunities for long swing trades in the homebuilding stock's uptrend. Many of the entry days for the swing trade setups provided good day-trading prospects, as well.

Figure 10–2. This daily chart of Hutchinson Technology, Inc. (HTCH) displays five short swing-trading opportunities. As with Lennar Corp. (LEN) in Figure 10–1, the entry days in these short swing trades offered intraday trading possibilities.

The Double Got 'Em—Background

The pretrade price action for this trade begins when the bears push a market through a downtrend, and chase it to a momentum low.

When it can stretch no lower, tentative bulls nudge it to a reaction high. The wearying bears harass it back to the prior low.

In this important valley, the bulls and bears start their pivotal battle.

If enough brawny bulls arrive on the retest battlefield and hold their ground, the exhausted bears' second shot at driving the stock below the initial low—give or take a few cents—will flop.

Once the bad-tempered beasts exhaust their selling power, the bulls take the price by the horns. Now they can carry it higher, with little resistance.

The dynamic that infuses this trade with "zowie!" potential is the short squeeze. If demand overcomes supply at the retest levels, the short sellers (bears) go berserk and cover their positions. With the shorts covering (bears buying) *and* the bulls buying, price can streak higher *fast.*

As you can see, this trade profits from the second low in the pattern that develops as a double-bottom pattern. (Review: a double bottom forms when a stock churns through a base and completes a W-shaped formation.) Figure 10–3 illustrates the pattern, two variations on the setups—A and B—and correlating buy signals.

For optimum swing-trade entries, please allow eight days to pass, minimum,

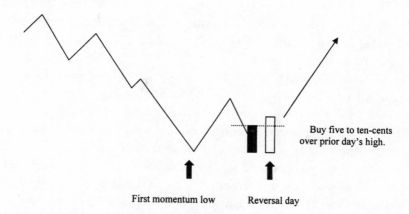

Buy five to ten-cents
over prior day's high.

First momentum low   Reversal day

Figure 10–3. Double Got 'Em—Setup A The buy signal arrives when the positive-reversal day shoots higher than the high price of last negative day of the retest move. An example of this will be shown in our sample trade using Verizon Communications. (Trade follows.)

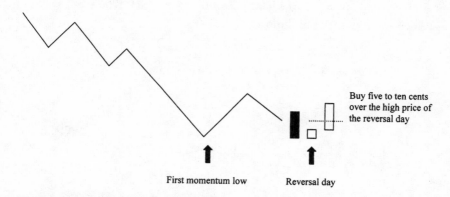

Buy five to ten cents
over the high price of
the reversal day

First momentum low   Reversal day

Figure 10–3. Double Got 'Em—Setup B Setup B issues a buy signal when the reversal day stays in a small intraday range. The entry day should move higher than the reversal day's high. When it does, buy when price moves 5 to 10 cents above that high.

between the first momentum low and the retest and reversal/entry day. Why? Because a reversal day that emerges sooner may not accumulate enough "pressure in the cooker" to fuel a reliable breakout.

Once you enter, the potential short squeeze explodes the price higher, resulting in a rocket style, two-to-three day swing trade. Remember, depending on the individual volatility of the stock, the swing trade entry day can produce a great day-trading opportunity, as well.

Please understand that the "Double Got 'Em" is a countertrend trading technique that demands patience and steely discipline. You'll need patience to wait for the proper amount of time to lapse between lows.

Before we go on, let me explain a point. You will notice that this setup calls for a buy signal that usually occurs while a stock is trading below the 20-day moving average on a daily chart.

You probably remember, as well, that I don't enter a long position unless it's trading over its 20-day moving average on a daily chart.

When I trade this setup, however, I make an exception to that rule. The "Double Got 'Em" represents a "bottom fishing" setup, and I consider the possible reward opportunity great enough to offset the risk.

Once in the trade, ironclad discipline is essential, especially when you set your initial stop-loss. As a countertrend trade; this is an aggressive technique. If you buy a position on the entry day, and the market makes a sudden U-turn to the downside, *you absolutely, positively* must *exit before the stock breaks the lows of the retest.* If the stock's price dives below the retest zone (and the initial low), it's likely to crash hard and fast to new lows.

Figure 10–4 shows a daily chart of Verizon Communications (VZ). The most recent day on the chart's hard right edge is June 21. The stock is retesting a momentum low made on June 1.

Figure 10–4. This daily chart of Verizon Communications (VZ) definitely shows the telecom in a world of hurt. Traders with a keen eye, though, will monitor the stock for a potential reversal and double-bottom setup. Stochastics is oversold and hooking up as the stock retests its prior low on June 1 of $34.25. Today's candle (most recent) closed at $34.13. If the stock reverses to the upside tomorrow, we'll buy for a long swing trade when it closes above today's high, $34.85. (To keep the chart simple, I plotted only the 20-day moving average.) If VZ opens positively and market internals agree, day traders may see long opportunities.

Please note: As you remember, in chapter 9, I used the MACD and its signal line as a momentum indicator on position trades. In looking for swing trades, I want a more sensitive indicator, so in upcoming daily, sixty-minute, and fifteen-minute charts, I swapped the MACD for the stochastic indicator. The OBV remains the same.

VZ looks ripe for a reversal. As traders, we choose to anticipate a reversal rather than react after it's too late. We'll plan a trade, then enter if our criteria are met.

Double Got 'Em Setup and Strategy:

The following lists the setup and entry criteria for the "Double Got 'Em" swing trade.

- Stock (or ETF) has experienced a downtrend on a daily chart. Bears have driven it to a new low. (VZ made a relative new low on June 1.)

- Price rebounds. Then, no less than eight days later, price retests the low. ("Today," July 21, VZ retests the June 1 low of $34.25.)

- When (if) the stock holds its lows and reverses, we'll buy when it reverses and trades a few cents above the high of the retest day. (VZ's June 1 high is $34.80.)

- Once in, the initial protective stop will be established just under low price of entry day, or under strong support zone on sixty-minute chart.

- Initial profit target: prior high. (VZ shows prior resistance on July 1 high at $36.60.)

Figure 10–5 shows the reversal and entry day, July 22. VZ held its lows and shot up to trade above the July 21 high, meeting our criterion.

Action:

- We bought five hundred shares at $34.90, $0.05 above July 21 high.

- The initial protective stop was set at $34.30, just under strong support levels on the sixty-minute chart. (If you don't have access to intraday charts, set your initial stop a few cents under the entry day's low.)

- With a profit target of $36.60, the risk–reward ratio is 1:3+.

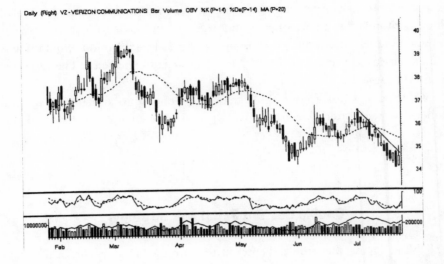

Figure 10–5. This daily chart of Verizon Communications (VZ) shows the following day's price action. The stock held its lows successfully and provided an entry day for a swing trade. Volume was healthy, stochastics crossed into a buy signal, and OBV hooked up. We bought at $34.90, 5 cents over the prior day's high. The initial stop, which will be adjusted higher tomorrow, is now set just under support identified on the 60-minute chart (see Figure 10–6), at $34.30. Profit target: $36.60. Initial risk-reward ratio: 1:3+.

Figure 10–6 shows a sixty-minute chart of VZ and our entry and initial stop placement.

You can see how VZ shot up during the first three hours of trading on the entry day, July 22. With such favorable price action, are you wondering why we didn't enter the trade earlier?

Answer: if you have access to intraday charts, you *can* enter the trade earlier. Make sure the price is shooting higher on strong volume and market internals are in your corner. Stay aware, though, of the possibility that the stock may meet resistance at the prior day's high—and fail to overcome it before the closing bell. That's a negative alarm.

Now, check Figure 10–7, which displays a fifteen-minute chart of VZ for the same time period. Again, you can see the swing trade entry on July 22.

Day traders could have capitalized on VZ's early bounce. Risk-averse traders would have waited until the stock consolidated, then climbed above its twenty-period MA at about 10:30 a.m. EST. When it shot up on rising volume at 10:30, traders could have entered by $34.60 and taken a quick ride to the intra-day high of $35.05.

Exit alerts for this intraday trade fifteen-minute chart:

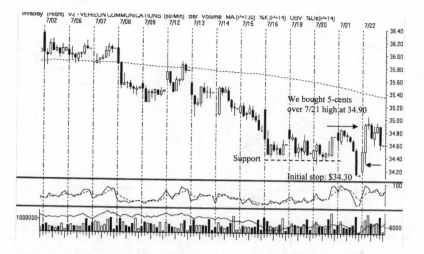

Figure 10–6. This 60-minute chart of Verizon Communications (VZ) shows the swing trade entry. Note the relatively light volume on the negative day before, June 21, as compared to the strong and steady volume that came into the telecom stock early on the entry day, June 22. On that day, swing traders would wait until the stock trades over the prior day's high to enter. If you choose to buy earlier in the day, you would keep an eye on the prior day's high to see how the stock handled it. The moving average shown is the 130-period moving average (on this 60-minute chart), which plots the same line relative to price as the 20-day moving average does on the daily chart.

- At 11:15, after climbing for forty-five minutes, VZ is overextended on an intraday basis.

- Three white candles formed the leg-up. The third candle materialized in a small real body (indecision). The following candle completed a dark cloud cover on increased volume (selling pressure).

- Stochastics has hooked over and down.

- Lunchtime doldrums lurk in the offing.

VZ closed on July 22 at $34.60.

On Friday, July 23, VZ gapped open to $35.23. The robust volume on the gap open told active traders *not* to fade (in this case, sell short) the gap.

As the stock moved higher, we raised our protective stop to $34.95. Now, if the stop is hit, the position will close a few dollars higher than break-even, including commissions. The stock closes at $35.32.

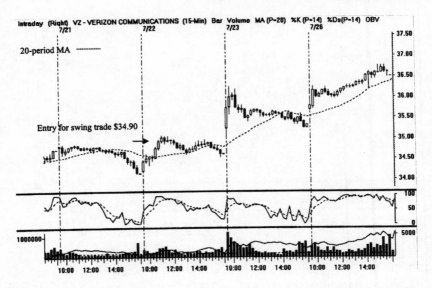

Figure 10–7. This 15-minute chart of Verizon Communications (VZ) displays our swing trade entry on July 22. This intraday chart shows how steady (if not ballistic) volume came into VZ early in the day, and—more important—rose up to the lunchtime doldrums. Day traders could have played the early bounce, or waited until VZ traded above the 20-period MA on increased volume.

Profit-taking Time

Monday, July 26, VZ gaps open again, up $0.38 to $35.70. The gaps indicate that short sellers are feeling pressure. (Awwww.) By midmorning, the protective stop is raised to $35.65, a few cents under the intraday low.

During the day, VZ moves steadily higher. At 2:00 p.m. EST, the telecom stock moves through our profit target of $36.60. I sell four hundred shares at $36.70, to pocket a $720 profit (not including commissions). I exit because the price met my profit target.

Plus, VZ gapped open two days in a row. Careful not to push my luck, I take profits when a stock I'm holding gaps open two days in a row.

> **Hot Tip:** Eighty-five percent of the time, gaps are filled on the day they occur.

Still, I've decided to keep a one hundred-share lot size to play with "the house's money." I haven't yet witnessed the panicky short covering I expected with a double bottom. A quick review of a daily chart check shows the next resistance at $38. VZ closes on rising volume at $36.50.

When the opening bell rings on July 27, I yell, "Got 'em!"

Figure 10–8 shows what happened.

On July 27, VZ gaps open to $37.50. When the stock hits $38, I sell my remaining one hundred shares. Profit: $150.

By now you're grabbing my sleeve. "Hey, Toni. After you sold, VZ kept going higher. You left big bucks on the table!"

Yes, sir-ree. I did. It's happened before. My crystal ball was in the shop, so I couldn't peer into the future. Rats! ☺

Crystal ball aside, I exited because VZ's next resistance lurked at $38, and round numbers will many times hold extra support or resistance power. Plus, VZ danced in overextended territory. I took profits while the gettin' was good.

Let's move to the next trade.

The Moving Average Leapfrog—Background

To enter this long swing trade, locate a stock moving in an existing uptrend on a daily chart.

The logic is universal and timeless in its approach. A stock (or other trading entity) has climbed out of its base and moves in the context of an uptrend.

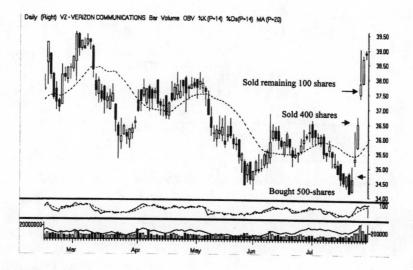

Figure 10–8. This daily chart of Verizon Communications displays how the "double got 'em" swing trade played out. If enough short sellers panic and cover their positions, it rockets the stock to new highs (got 'em!). Keep a tight stop "leash" on these trades and stick to your plan. Accept the fact that you may leave some extra profits on the table.

After a move up, the stock pulls back in an *orderly* retracement (no exaggerated down days, no huge gaps), on decreased volume. Message: investors and traders are holding—not folding. That's a good thing.

Now, here's the clinch. When the stock pulls back, or retraces, it finds support just above *both* the twenty-day MA and the fifty-day MA. These two moving averages create double support—kind of a doubly reinforced "bench" for the stock's price to "sit" on. If the twenty-day MA crosses above the fifty-day MA below the pullback price, so much the better.

> **Hot Tip:** Remember, the steeper the angle up, the steeper the pullback to the downside. For swing trade candidates, choose a stock that's risen in a methodical (not ballistic) uptrend, then retraced in a gentlemanly (not panicky) move down. We don't want to enter on the heels of chaos.

When upward momentum flows back into the stock, price hops up on healthy (average to increasing) volume. That's where we come in.

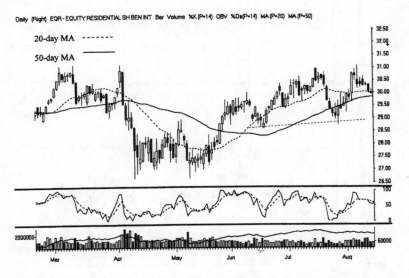

Figure 10–9. This daily chart of Equity Residential (EQR) shows the stock setting up in the "Moving Average Leapfrog" setup. It stepped through a double bottom in April and May, and now roils through the consolidation pattern that many times follows these types of reversal patterns. The consolidation's second pullback at the end of July ($27.84) did not break the previous pivot's low ($28.62). However, it sure came close! Now, the REIT has pulled back to its 20-day and 50-day moving averages, and ended "today" in a tiny spinning top. That candle indicates indecision. If EQR stays atop its MAs tomorrow morning and begins to reverse on healthy volume, we'll buy when EQR trades over today's high of $30.12.

Figure 10–9 shows a daily chart of Equity Residential (EQR), a popular REIT (real estate investment trust).

As you can see, EQR rolled through a double bottom in April and May. The residential REIT moved higher until it reached prior resistance at $31.

Once there, it hopscotched through a consolidation pattern typical of post–double bottom formations. The pattern resembles a sideways "handle" that usually corrects twice before price hops higher into an uptrend. The first pull-back in the "handle" may be relatively mild. The second pullback descends more deeply, sometimes 15 percent of the stock's price.

In this case, EQR's July dive did just that, correcting about 15 percent. That move usually scares the "weak hands" out of the stock. When it recovers, the "strong hands" take over, and if all goes well, the stock rises out of the consolidation pattern.

Now, please look at the hard right edge of the chart. On the most recent day, August 13, you'll see that EQR pulled back to the twenty-day and fifty-day MAs. More good news—the stock ended the day in a spinning top. Although you have to look hard for it—because it's partly obstructed by the twenty-day MA—it's there.

If it plays out, it presents an ideal setup for tomorrow. Any time you see a stock in an uptrend pull back to moving average support, then culminate the day in a spinning top or small range candle, get ready to boogie!

Moving Average Leapfrog—Setup and Strategy

Here are the criteria for the "Moving Average Leapfrog" trade. The setup is clear-cut and easy to spot.

- Stock (or ETF) moves in an uptrend on a daily chart. (EQR is in the midst of a consolidation pattern subsequent to a double bottom on a daily chart. Higher lows are in place.)

- After a move up, price pulls back, in an orderly fashion, to its 20-day and 50-day moving averages. (EQR's price pulled back to its 20-day and 50-day MAs.)

- Bonus: price culminates the day in a small range candle. (EQR ends "to-day" in a spinning top. Intraday price range: $0.17!)

- Check stochastics for buy signal and OBV for positive action. (EQR's stochastics reads in midrange and hooking up. OBV is neutral.)

- If tomorrow the stock opens in positive territory above its 20-day and 50-day moving averages, buy when it trades $0.05 to $0.10 over today's high. (EQR's intraday high = $30.12. Low: $29.95.)

- Alternative entry: Draw a mini-downtrend line over the tops of the pull-back candles. When price trades $0.05 to $0.10 above that trend line, buy.

- Once in, the initial protective stop will be established just under low price of entry day, or under strong support zone on sixty-minute chart.

- Initial profit target: prior high. (EQR's first resistance sits at $31 at consolidation highs—a point away. That's an all-time high for EQR. Once above $31, it's blue sky forever!)

- Risk-reward ratio should be 1:3.

> **Hot Tip: If it's still early in the trading day when your target stock signals an entry, consider buying one-half of your intended lot size. Buy the remaining shares before the closing bell. With that strategy, if the price doesn't close near the high of the day, or the market looks unstable, you can rethink your strategy without the pressure of a large lot size.**

Figure 10–10 shows the same setup on a sixty-minute chart. This chart reveals price action through the spinning top day, *only*. You're seeing the last four-

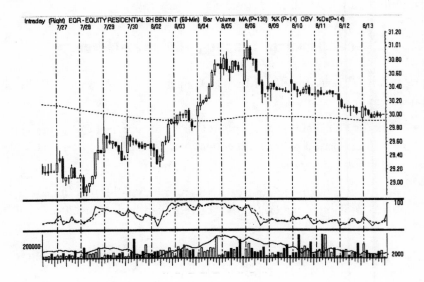

Figure 10–10. This 60-minute chart of Equity Residential (EQR) illustrates how the "Moving Average Leapfrog" setup appears on this intraday chart leading up to the entry day. The dotted line represents the 130-period moving average, which equals a 20-day MA on a daily chart. Notice how neatly EQR sits astride her moving average. Point of interest: check out the stochastic indicator at the end of this day. In oversold territory, it's signaling a bullish divergence and issuing a buy signal. This could forecast a positive open tomorrow morning.

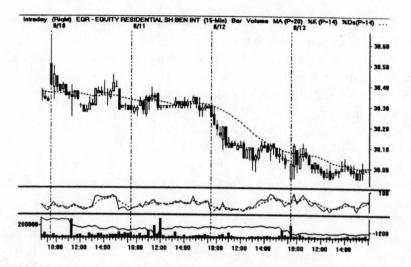

Figure 10–11. This 15-minute chart of Equity Residential (EQR) displays the most recent four days of the pullback we are monitoring. Now you can see the intraday action on August 13, and how the price dawdled down, then sideways, on light volume. Are the bears ambling off to greener pastures?

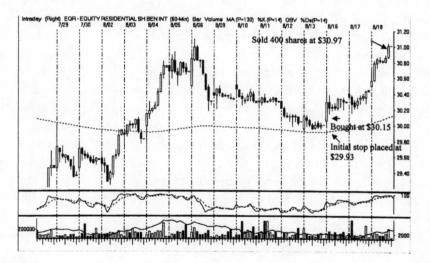

Figure 10–12. On Monday, August 16, this 60-minute chart shows Equity Residential (EQR) opening at $30.05. We buy 500 shares over the prior day's high ($30.13), as planned, at $30.15 Later in the entry day, the stop is raised to $30.10, almost break even.

By the third day of the trade, EQR touches $31. Since it rose in a steep angle and became overbought quickly, common sense plus former resistance indicate an exit. We sold 400 shares at $30.97. The remaining 100 shares wait to see if EQR can take out the day's high and soar to new historic highs at $31.11.

teen days of price action, up to, but not including, the entry day. Now you can observe the price action as it appears on the day *before* you enter the trade.

In the same light, Figure 10–11 zooms in for a fifteen-minute chart close-up of the past four days, up to, and including, August 13.

We have our plan in place if EQR starts up, tomorrow.

And . . . it does.

Figure 10–12 reverts back to an hourly chart. EQR gapped open $0.05 to $30.05. That's not a big enough gap to worry about, and it does signal in a gentle manner that demand for EQR is higher than supply. We give the stock a few minutes to trade, as well as for the market to work out any early-morning quirks.

Within minutes, EQR slides down to $29.97 to fill its short-lived gap. Reversing, it soon climbs above yesterday's high of $30.12. That's our buy signal. Since this is a relatively slow-moving stock, and since it has a modest price range, we'll buy our entire five-hundred-share position now, at $30.15.

We'll place our initial stop at $29.93, a few cents under the current intraday low ($29.97), with plans to move it higher, later in the day.

Please remember, when you establish a stop, everything's relative. Were I trading a rompin', stompin' semiconductor or biotech stock with a wide daily price range, I would not place an initial stop order merely $0.04 under the support zone.

Using common sense, of course, the wilder and more volatile the stock, the more room you give it to wiggle.

By midafternoon, I move my stop higher, to $30.10. That's $0.04 under the low of the second hour of trading. Now, the position is close to break-even. Why not go higher? Because we're reaching minor resistance, and I'm not interested in getting stopped out by a penny or two. EQR closes at $30.30.

The next day, our stock opens a few cents higher, at $30.40. It closes the gap in the second hour of trading, dipping down to touch $30.14, just $0.04 from our stop. (Wince.) Then it heads higher for the remainder of the day, closing at $30.45. Tomorrow, VZ may reach the $31 resistance area. We'll adjust the stop higher after the open.

On the following day, EQR opens at $30.50. The first hour of trading establishes a low of $30.48. I tighten the stop to $30.45.

The stock scoots higher on steady volume. By noon, it's printing $30.87. Sweet.

Check the chart again (Figure 10–12). Notice how overextended EQR appears on this intraday chart. Stochastics have bumped against their overbought ceiling most of the day.

A few minutes before the close, EQR touches $31. That's the initial profit target. Do I hold or fold?

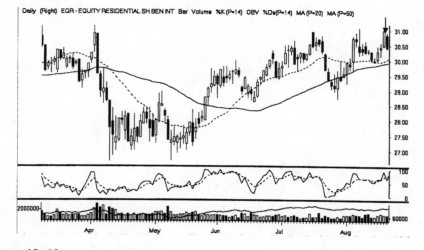

Figure 10–13. We're back to a daily chart of Equity Residential (EQR). You can see the long, black candle that opened down on the morning of August 19 at $30.87. The remaining 100 shares were sold immediately after the opening bell, at $30.84 for a profitable conclusion.

The S&P 500 looks lower tomorrow, and EQR certainly looks overbought, if only temporarily. That confirms my sell decision.

Still, EQR is going to close near a historical high, $31.11, on very strong volume.

I opt for safety and sell four hundred shares at $30.97. Profit (without commissions): $328.

Figure 10–13 shows the final price action for the trade. The next morning, August 19, the market gaps down at the opening bell. EQR opens at $30.87. I sell immediately at $30.84. Profit for this portion of the trade (without commissions): $69. Total profit (without commissions): $397.

I chose a well-mannered stock for this example, because the price pattern was clear. Also, know that slow-moving, orderly stocks can add to your bottom line faster than caffeinated stocks. Why? You can buy larger lot sizes with less trepidation. You don't get whipsawed as much.

Also your nerves aren't ragged, and your back doesn't hurt from crouching under your desk, yelling, "No, don't stop me out *again!*"

The Stealthy Sidewinder—Background

To enter this long swing trade, scan for a stock (or ETF) that's trading in an up-trend on a daily chart.

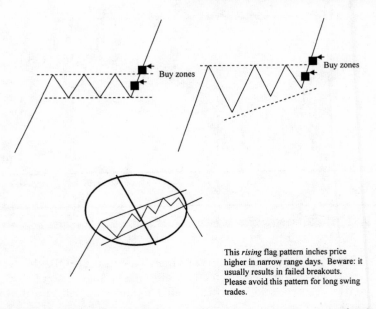

This *rising* flag pattern inches price higher in narrow range days. Beware: it usually results in failed breakouts. Please avoid this pattern for long swing trades.

Figure 10–14. Sideways consolidations form in continuation patterns that include ascending triangles and wedges. For this setup, look for tight, orderly pattern of price swings that form a wedge or triangle that angle horizontally.

Definitions:

- A wedge is a continuation pattern in which the price fluctuates within straight (or nearly straight) lines.
- A flag is a continuation pattern that forms in less than four weeks. The tight price range forms upper and lower boundaries that can be contained with parallel lines. For this setup, we're looking for bull flags (bull flags form in uptrends, bear flags form in downtrends) that "fly" in a perpendicular angle to prior leg (mast) up. Flags that angle up, or down, are not candidates for this trade's setup.
- The ascending triangles we are looking for develop into continuation patterns in an uptrend, with the highs developing in a horizontal line, and the lows slanting higher.

Avoid continuation patterns that slant to the upside, or develop with a series of lower lows (descending triangle).

Bottom line: Don't get stymied by the names and exact formations of these continuation patterns. The important traits to look for that provide the optimal upside potential are: 1) a tight, orderly sideways price range, 2) reasonably horizontal tops, and 3) lows that form either a horizontal, or a rising line.

Currently, you'll want the price etching a tight (contained price range) and orderly continuation pattern, such as a wedge or a triangle. If the setup plays out properly, price will use the pattern as a springboard to higher levels.

Here's an analogy: Stretch your garden hose across the back porch. (Aim it away from open windows. ☺) Turn on the water full-blast. Step on the hose a foot or so from the nozzle. See the hose strain with pent-up pressure? You can even feel the tension building under your foot.

Now, lift your foot. The released pressure causes the water to gush—explode—out of the nozzle.

Just so, players put pressure on price by supporting *and* resisting it at the same time. When the balance tips and the pressure is released, the price explodes. The trick is to anticipate the direction of the explosion. (Meaning, don't be the trader standing in the open window.)

Figure 10–14 illustrates the wedge, bull flag, and ascending triangle consolidation patterns we'll use for this setup.

You'll note I've combined the wedge and bull flag patterns into one graphic. Technically speaking, they are not identical, but for our purposes, you get the picture. You're looking for a continuation pattern that forms a sideways consolidation of prices.

> **Hot Tip:** You've identified a dandy continuation pattern, but you can't figure out where to draw the consolidation tops and bottoms. Start from the most recent low, then draw backwards (in time) to the previous low. Do the same thing with the highs.

You'll note two "buy zones" on each pattern. The zone within the consolidation represents an early, higher-risk entry. Why is it higher risk? It's elevated risk because price hasn't yet broken above the resistance tops of the consolidation pattern. Why would we enter there? Because an earlier entry translates into added profits. We contain risk by setting the initial protective stop a few cents beneath the consolidation threshold, or lows. If the price dives, we exit with a small loss.

The second buy zone occurs when the stock shoots above consolidation (wedge or triangle tops) resistance. That shows market players are willing to pay higher prices.

For those of you with "real" jobs, if you cannot hang out in front of your trading computer screen all day, waiting for the second entry to materialize, enter a buy stop order with your broker. Your buy price will be $0.05 to $0.10 over consolidation highs.

Figure 10–15 displays a daily chart of United States Steel Corporation (X). The basic materials conglomerate stock capitulated in a nosedive in May. It recovered nicely to carve out a hasty cup-with-handle. Now, it's shuffling in a wedge, or a sidewinder move. The bulls are pressuring it higher, while the bears hold it down. (Think "foot on garden hose.")

Figure 10–15. This daily chart of United States Steel Corp. (X) shows the iron and steel mill mining icon traveling in a tight and orderly sidewinder move that ranges between $33 and $35.50.

If X shows signs of a breakout to the upside, we'll jump in with an initial entry within the consolidation. We'll add to our position when (if) price breaks above the wedge resistance tops. Our stop will start under the ledge of the wedge (!) and move higher from there.

Let's see what happens.

The Stealthy Sidewinder—Setup and Strategy

I realize that many of you do not have access to intraday charts, or the time to look at them. For you, intraday techniques might even be confusing. To that end, we'll trade this setup using daily charts only.

Here are the criteria for this trade:

- Stock trades in an uptrend and currently consolidates sideways in a wedge, horizontal flag, or ascending triangle. (X is in an uptrend and consolidating in a wedge, or flag.)

- The price pattern trades just above the 20-day MA, and ideally, above the 50-day MA. (X's continuation pattern is moving into a rising 20-day MA—perfect! The fifty-day MA is under the price pattern.)

- Stochastics and OBV agree. (X shows stochastic readings below the over-bought zone and hooking up. OBV points higher.)

- Buy an initial position when stock begins to rise out of consolidation on healthy volume. Or buy after stock breaks through the upside horizontal resistance line, or both. (Since X trades 2 million shares a day and is an orderly stock, we'll plan to buy at both places. The last day in the consolidation, July 9, closed at $34.38, with a high of $34.52 and a low of $33.54. The buy window can stretch from $34.20 to $34.60, or the upper part of yesterday's range. This stock doesn't gap up much—or often—but that will give it a little "party" room.)

- Place an initial stop under the edge of the wedge. (X's lows of the most recent three days are at about $33.50. We can place an initial stop at $33.40, or higher, depending on our initial entry.)

- Set profit target that reflects initial risk-reward at 1:3 or better. (Once price moves through X's consolidation tops at $35.50, the next resistance appears at $37. Risk-reward will come out to 1:4 or better.

Figure 10–16 shows X opening at $34.40 the next day, July 12. Perfect! After the "opening smoke" clears, we buy three hundred shares at $34.51.

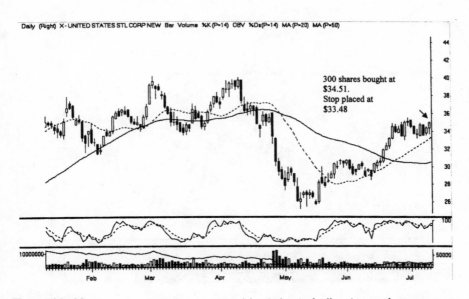

Figure 10–16. Our entry day for our "Stealthy Sidewinder" swing trade emerges on July 12, the most recent day on the chart. We buy 300 shares in our price window, shortly after the open, at $34.51. For now, the initial protective stop is placed under yesterday's low, at $33.48. The stock closes on its highs on healthy volume.

Figure 10–17. This daily chart of United States Steel Corp. (X) shows our trade moving up nicely. It looks poised to break above consolidation highs, tomorrow. The stop is raised to $34.60, break-even including commissions. The stock closed near its highs at $35.19.

Figure 10–18. Now we're truckin'. Our U.S. Steel (X) broke above resistance soon out of the gate. It opened at $35.48 and ran to a high of $36.86 on more than double daily average volume. We raise our stop and hang on.

The stop is set at $33.48. (Understand that we're using only daily charts for reference. That means early in the entry day, we have only yesterday's low to use for support—and thus the initial protective stop.) The stock closes near the high of the day on strong volume, at $34.95.

The next morning, July 13, opens even with yesterday's close, then closes at $35.44. Figure 10–17 adds that day's candle and price action.

X is poised to rise through consolidation resistance tomorrow, although there are no guarantees. We raise our stop to $34.60, so we'll break even, including commissions. Tomorrow, if the breakout occurs, we'll raise it again.

Tomorrow comes . . . and life is good. X breaks out with style, gapping open $0.04 to 35.48. It quickly skates down to fill the gap, to $35.30, then jumps higher and breaks consolidation resistance. We add two hundred additional shares at $35.58.

Figure 10–18 shows the July 14 bull party!

During the trading day, X more than doubled average volume, trading 4.7 million shares. The stock closed on its high at $36.86. It will probably reach the next resistance tomorrow at $37. Since it shot vertically today, plus it's rapidly become overextended, tomorrow may be the best time to capture profits.

Figure 10–19 shows the outcome to our "Stealthy Sidewinder" swing trade.

On July 17 (the last white candle), X opened even, at the prior day's close. It

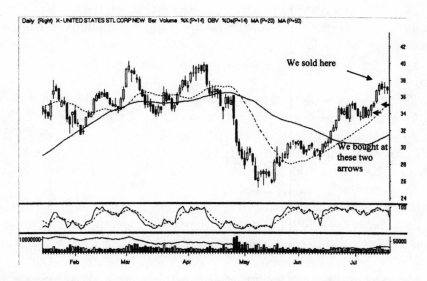

Figure 10–19. Our final daily chart of U.S. Steel (X) shows the final day of our four-day swing trade, as well as our two entry days. Our sell signals included prior resistance at $37, which gave us our profit target, a stochastic sell signal and an OBV rollover. All signs pointed to an exit. Good trade!

quickly zoomed to an intraday high of $37.61. Now the stock is overextended, for sure. And check out the stochastics oscillator.—It's hooking down in a bearish divergence. So is the OBV.

Right before the close, we sell all five hundred shares at $37.28. The stock closes at $37.40. Our total profit (without commissions): $1,171. Good trade!

Checking back to Figure 10–19, you can observe "the rest of the story." X gapped open slightly on July 18, then started down for the pullback.

We planned well, and executed the plan. Win or lose, that's what trading is all about. Now, we'll take a walk on the short side.

Selling Short—A Quick Tutorial

Before we plan this short trade, here's a quick overview of selling short.

When you sell short, you sell a stock you don't own, with the intent of buying it back later, at a lower price. Your profit is the difference between the price you sold it for, and the price you purchase it back.

What if you short a market and it rises higher? You take a loss, just as you do on the long side, when you purchase a stock and it falls in value.

Either way, when you buy the stock back, we say that you "covered" your short position.

Where do you find a stock to sell that isn't yours? You borrow it from your broker, who takes it out of another client's account and returns it when you close the position. That process is not your concern, however. When you place an order with your broker to sell short, if the stock is not available, he will inform you.

Two more short facts: 1) your account must be a margin account to sell short, 2) most brokers limit short sales to stocks with a minimum price of $5.

At present, the SEC (Securities and Exchange Commission) dictates that to sell a stock short, you must do so on an uptick. It's called "the uptick rule," and the definition varies with the exchange. (ETFs, stock index futures, and forex trades are not subject to the uptick rule).

On the NASDAQ, an uptick takes place when a bid is posted higher than the previous bid. On the NYSE and Amex, an uptick occurs when a stock prints, or trades, a tick higher than previous trades.

> **Hot Tip:** Avoid shorting illiquid (low-volume) stocks or other trading entities. Trade only stocks where you can cover your position where *you* want to—not at the whim of a market maker.

I keep my entries very simple when I short a stock. I enter a limit order a few cents ($0.02 to $0.04, depending on the stock's volatility) below the inside bid (best bid). If there's an uptick in the price window I've established as my shorting entry, fine.

In plays when the stock craters so fast that upticks are few and far between, the order is canceled and the price drops below the entry window, that's okay, too.

When a trade eludes you, learn to shrug it off and take your marbles to another game.

Moving Average Hot, Wet Blanket—Background

This swing trading setup to the short side represents a common and reliable pattern.

Start by scanning for a stock trading in the early stages of a downtrend and currently forming a continuation pattern. That way, the 50-day and 20-day

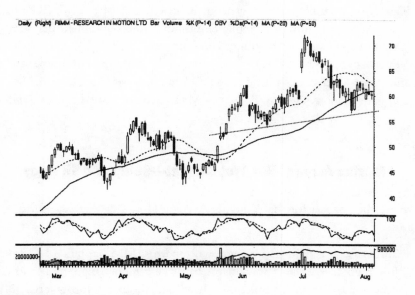

Figure 10–20. This daily chart of Research in Motion, Ltd. (RIMM) shows a tech stock in trouble! You can see a head-and-shoulders pattern forming; the right shoulder is in the last stages of completion (assuming price falls to $57, to the neckline). Also notice how our target short candidate has fallen below both the 20-day MA (dotted) and the 50-day MA (solid). The 20-day MA slants down over the price range, and the 50-day MA just flattened. The two most recent days on the chart (at the hard right edge) both closed under the 50-day MA, a sign of price weakness. The stochastic indicator reads in midrange, hooking down. The OBV is drifting down, as well.

moving averages are still close enough to act as nearby resistance and weigh the price down—just like a hot, wet blanket.

The continuation pattern that forms the setup for the "Moving Average Hot, Wet Blanket" can vary—either a rally or an orderly consolidation will do.

The clinch: both the 20- and 50-day MAs need to bear down over the tops of the price pattern. If the stock's in a downtrend, the twenty-day line will almost always slant down overhead.

In addition, this setup requires the 50-day MA to also slant *down* overhead. You'll run across many formations where the 20-day MA curls down, while the 50-day MA *rises* overhead. We don't want that combination. Look for stocks in downtrends, experiencing price patterns, where *both* moving averages point south. Exception: if the 50-day MA moves overhead in a horizontal direction, that's acceptable.

Why the big fuss over which direction the 50-day MA points? Logic tells me that when a stock in a downtrend rallies to a rising moving average, resistance holds little power. If, however, price slams up against a *falling* moving average—especially the 50-day line, which is watched by so many institutions—that line exerts more negative power to act as a "hot, wet blanket," and hold the price down.

Figure 10–20 displays a daily chart of Research in Motion, Ltd. (RIMM). As you can see, in early July, this mobile communications equipment manufacturer got ahead of itself on good earnings and guidance.

Now, though, the NASDAQ's screeching south on a summer bummer and taking most four-letter stocks with it. The DOT, the Internet index of which RIMM is a component, looks pig-ugly. Poor RIMM may have to "pay the piper," and *soon*.

Moving Average Hot, Wet Blanket—Setup and Strategy

Here are the criteria for the "Moving Average Hot, Wet Blanket" short swing trade.

- Target stock is falling in early downtrend. (RIMM has fallen $12 from its July high at $72.07. It was unable to make a higher high/higher low, and now appears to be completing a head-and-shoulders top reversal formation.)

- The stock is rallying or consolidating to resistance in a continuation pattern, but looks ready to slide south again. (RIMM tumbled to a low of $56.75 on July 26. Note the two back-to-back, black and white wide-range candles on Figure 10–20. It then rallied for three days, but was too feeble to rise through the 20-day MA.)

- Price is trading below the 20-day and 50-day MAs. The 20-day slants down overhead, and the 50-day MA either slants down or moves horizontally. (RIMM's lukewarm rally never rose above its 20-day MA. The 50-day MA rides horizontally, overhead. Plus, RIMM has closed two consecutive days below the 50-day MA—a negative sign.)

- Risk-reward calculates to 1:3, or better. (This trade works out to 1:4.)

Figure 10–21 displays a sixty-minute chart of RIMM. Shown are the last fourteen days of the daily chart (Figure 10–20). Both charts end with the doji day on August 4.

You'll see two moving averages on this sixty-minute chart. The dotted line is the 130-period MA on the hourly chart used on previous charts in this chapter. As you know, it falls in the same place on the price pattern as the twenty-day MA falls on the daily chart.

On Figure 10–21, I've also added the 325-period MA. It falls in approximately the same place as the fifty-day MA does on the daily chart. (6.5 hours in a trading day × 50 = 325.) Neat, huh?

As you can see by the weak price pattern and the moving averages, a bearish MA crossover has just occurred. This sixty-minute chart agrees with the daily

Figure 10–21. This 60-minute chart of Research in Motion, Ltd. (RIMM) offers a close-up of the last fourteen days displayed on RIMM's daily chart, Figure 10–20. Note how the tech stock white-knuckled it to lower successive highs. Now, it looks ready to drop further. If it does, we'll be ready. ☺

chart that it's time to establish a shorting plan for RIMM. (This setup also looks ripe for day-trading opportunities to the short side.)

Figure 10–22 displays a fifteen-minute chart of RIMM. A weak afternoon rally formed long, upward shadows on candles. These shadows tell us bears may be lurking above RIMM's price pattern at $60.50.

Now, to our plan. First, we assess August 4 *doji* prices: RIMM opened at $60.25. It rose to a high of 60.98, fell to a low of 59.46, and closed at $60.30.

Since this is a volatile stock, we'll give it some leeway. We'll sell it short tomorrow morning (August 5), if it opens between a price window $60.60 and $60.20. That gives it $0.30 to gap up and $0.10 to gap down.

Considering this is a short sale, why do we give it room to rise, or gap up?

Here's why: If RIMM gaps open higher to the moving average "blankets," and then starts to fall—that's a good sign. Plus, we enter at a higher price—and grab bigger profits. (Of course, if RIMM gaps up on high volume and continues to rise higher hand-in-hand with a strong NASDAQ, our trade is void.)

Depending on where it opens, we'll place an initial protective stop. The highest stop we'll tolerate will be at $61.05, just above yesterday's high and the round number of $61.

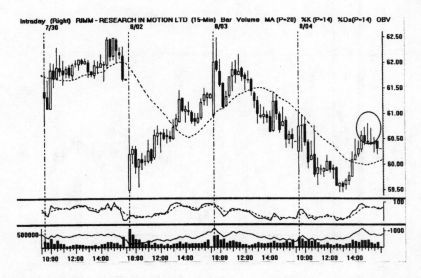

Figure 10–22. This 15-minute chart of Research in Motion Ltd. (RIMM), shows the four most recent days of the daily and hourly charts (Figures 10–20 and 10–21). The wireless communications stock closed within 5 cents of its open, showing indecision on the part of market players. A clue to their mindset appears in the afternoon candles. Note the long, upward shadows. These shadows infer that sellers, or bears, lurk in the area between 60.50 and 60.80.

> **Hot Tip:** Because stocks falling in downtrends act in such a volatile manner, exercise strict risk management and monitor stop-loss orders. When you ignore your stop in favor of the "hold and hope" attitude, you're asking for a big loss!

Assuming the stock goes our way tomorrow and drops through nearby support of $56.25, we'll look for RIMM to skid down to the next support zone at $53.50. That will represent our profit target.

It's the morning of August 5. The bell rings, and RIMM gaps open $0.25, to $65.55. Although that's within the entry window, we'll give it a few minutes to trade. (I do *not* jump into volatile NASDAQ stocks at the market open. During the first five to ten minutes of trading, the market makers are in control.)

Also, with a muscular tech stock like this, I'm going to watch NASDAQ 100 index futures. If the techs scream to the upside, RIMM will probably repair itself and jump on for the ride. That voids our trade.

To that end—and before you see the outcome of our RIMM trade—look at Figure 10–23. It displays a fifteen-minute chart of the NASDAQ 100 E-mini futures for the entry day of our swing short, August 5. As you can see, the NQs, as we call them, hopped slightly higher at the opening bell, then tanked for the rest of the day. Bet you know what RIMM did.

Figure 10–24 depicts a fifteen-minute chart of RIMM for the entry day, August 5, along with the following two days.

August 5: On the third candle of the fifteen-minute chart, RIMM starts to weaken, and so does the NASDAQ. We sell short two hundred shares of our intended lot size of four hundred shares at $60.21.

We place our initial stop at 60.90. It's an arbitrary stop determined by the simple fact that if RIMM manages to reverse here, and climb to that price, it can probably push higher. I'm not interested in losing more than $0.70 per share during the first few hours of the trade.

By lunchtime, RIMM tanks to $59. Ah, life is good. When it dives off the lunchtime support cliff at 1:30 p.m. EST, we add our intended two hundred shares at $58.20 and lower our protective stop to $59.

> **Hot Tip:** What if you hold a short swing position overnight, and it gaps *up* the next morning? This is every trader's worst nightmare—and it happens. As a general rule, exit a trade when it gaps against you 5 percent or more on high volume, and violates your stop on a daily chart.

Can you see how much more room I give a stormy tech stock—as opposed to the $0.04 leeway I gave to EQR? It makes sense—if we gave a stock like RIMM a $0.04 boundary, we wouldn't be in the trade for long!

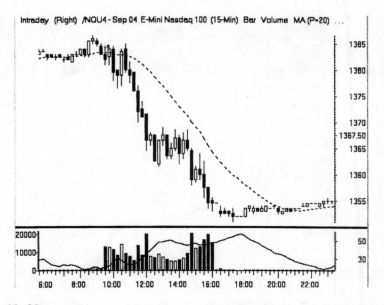

Figure 10–23. This 15-minute chart of the NASDAQ 100 E-mini stock index futures depicts a dandy downtrend.

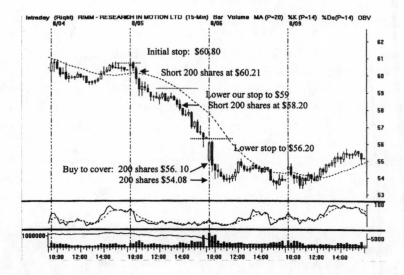

Figure 10–24. This 15-minute chart of Research in Motion, Ltd. (RIMM) shows how the swing trade progressed and the steps taken to enter, manage risk, and exit with a profit. If you match the chart to the NASDAQ 100 E-mini futures in Figure 10–23, and use the futures as a leading indicator, you can see how RIMM offered active traders one full day of obvious short opportunities (August 5) and one-half day of additional short ideas (August 6).

Figure 10–25. RIMM fell hard for our two-day swing trade (arrow). And we appreciate it. ☺ Then it regrouped and started back up. The point-plus gap down on the second day of the trade added nicely to our profits. It will be interesting to see if RIMM catapults back down into another summer slump, or whether it can defy gravity one more time!

RIMM closes out the day at its lows, $56.35.

It opens on August 6 at $55.01; $1.32 lower. I make a fast decision to cover one-half the trade. I pop in a buy-to-cover market order for two hundred shares (the market's moving too fast for a limit order). My fill: $55.10.

RIMM soon reverses to close the opening gap. I lower the protective stop on my remaining two hundred shares to just above the intraday high: $56.20. Wow—this is quite a ride, isn't it? And we're less than thirty minutes into the day.

By 10:30 a.m. RIMM falls to $54. I feel my trigger finger getting itchy.

I see volume coming into the stock. (Volume rule: increased volume after an extended move down can forecast a reversal.) Even though the candles are negative and unforgiving, RIMM's fallen quite a few points. Betcha my duck slippers, a few early bulls are grazing. More important, the prior resistance mentioned earlier at $53.50 arrives faster than I anticipated.

To avoid getting caught in a short squeeze, I cover the remaining two hundred shares at $54.10. Total profits (without commissions): $1,842.

Figure 10–25 shows a daily chart of RIMM, and "the rest of the story."

Please understand that all short trades do not cooperate as nicely as RIMM did. On days when the NASDAQ falls hard, though, most tech stocks will fall in sympathy.

> **Hot Tip:** Many professional traders prefer short plays to long ones. Why? When properly executed, short trades make more money, faster, than long trades.

Remember, even if you can't monitor your short swing trades on an intraday basis, stick to your trading plan and keep your protective stops in place where they make sense.

A Final *Aha!* Note

Here's a final note on these setups.

Remember when I said in chapter 3 that only four basic setups exist? They involve 1) a breakout to the upside from consolidation, 2) a breakout to the upside from a pullback, or retracement, 3) a breakdown from consolidation, or 4) a breakdown from a rally, or retracement.

The "Double Got 'Em" setup is 2), which is a breakout to the upside from a pullback—in this case, a retest of a prior low.

The "Moving Average Leapfrog" uses the same principle, a breakout from a pullback that moves an uptrend higher.

The "Stealthy Sidewinder" evolves from setup 1): a breakout to the upside from consolidation.

Finally, the "Moving Average Hot, Wet blanket" uses either 3) or 4) for its genesis.

When you connect basic principles with technical applications, it makes it easier to understand how and why the applications work. It also helps you to create your own variations on those themes.

In chapter 11, we'll delve into the world of exchange traded funds. They are fantastic tools for short-term trading and active investors. See you there!

Quiz

Questions

1. The average holding time for a swing trade is _____ days.

2. True or false: Swing trades work best in range-bound markets.

3. True or false: For optimum swing trading profits, you buy the upswings of an uptrending market and sell short the downswings of a downtrending market.

4. To take advantage of a double-bottom play, you allow at least _____ days to pass between the initial momentum low and the first reversal day of the retest low.

5. The market dynamic that may appear in the "Double Got 'Em" play is called a _____.

6. Why is it fortuitous when a stock in an uptrend pulls back to its major moving averages and forms a doji, spinning top, or other short-range day?

7. You spot a stock traveling in a strong uptrend. Now, it's consolidating sideways in a tidy consolidation pattern. If the stock starts higher, where would you place your initial protective stop?

8. When your long swing trade position gaps open two days in a row, do you 1) sell it during that trading day, 2) double your position and raise your stop, or 3) double your position and lower your stop so you don't get stopped out?

9. True or false: One tactic for executing a short sale is to place a limit order a few cents below the inside bid, or best bid.

10. Why do you want your short entries to show the 20-day and 50-day moving averages riding atop the price pattern?

Answers

1. The average holding time for a swing trade is two to five days.

2. False. Swing trades profit from the price swings exhibited by trending markets.

3. True.

4. To take advantage of a double-bottom play, you allow at least eight days to pass between the initial momentum low and the first reversal day of the retest low.

5. The market dynamic that may appear in the "Double Got 'Em" play is called a "short squeeze."

6. When a stock in an uptrend pulls back to its major moving averages and culminates in a doji, spinning top, or other short-range day, it means that market players are indecisive. The indecision often results in a reversal—in this case, to the upside.

7. When you enter a stock while it's still in consolidation mode, place your initial stop a few cents under the lows of the consolidation pattern.

8. When your long swing trade position gaps open two days in a row, sell it during that trading day.

9. True.

10. When you sell short, the 20- and 50-day MAs should act as resistance to price by exerting overhead pressure to the downside. A stock trading above these averages could be considered to be in at least an intermediate-term uptrend. Shorting a stock in an uptrend involves high risk.

CENTER POINT

Forgiveness—The Gift You Give Yourself

Without forgiveness, there's no future.
                                        —Desmond Tutu

Have you ever felt the sting of unfair treatment or betrayal?

Most of us have, at one time or another. And while human tendency is to cling to the resulting anger and pain, those who choose to forgive receive profound benefits—including better health.

Research shows that physical reactions to anger and grudges include back pain, low energy levels, and insomnia.

It makes sense. We humans are constructed to combat dangerous events with our inherent "fight or flight" survival system.

When someone treats us unjustly, or threatens our well-being, our bodies release the stress hormones adrenaline and cortisol. These hormones direct our heart rates to accelerate, our breath to quicken, and our minds to race.

This survival mode helps us get out of harm's way, but if that "switch" is left in the "on" position, the hormones meant to rescue us convert into toxins. Cortisol, especially, has a depressive effect on the immune system. The good news: the act of forgiveness slows or stops the flow of these hormones.

When you forgive, you don't need to condone wrongful actions. And you don't even need to forgive out loud (although it's more effective). Try looking at the event from a different angle. Probe for one good consequence, or lesson, that came from it. Or simply consider how much more enjoyable your life would be if you were free of the shackles of resentment.

When we make a conscious effort to forgive, we heal not only the person or situation involved, we heal ourselves, as well. Our bodies and our lives respond with a new lightness and energy that speed us on to new personal growth. Forgiveness is truly a gift we give to ourselves.

Exchange Traded Funds—A Flavor for Every Taste

A trader gets to play the game as the professional billiard player does—that is, he looks far ahead instead of considering the particular shot before him. It gets to be instinct to play for position.

> —Jesse Livermore, legendary trader, in
> *Reminiscences of a Stock Operator*
> by Edwin LeFevre

Want to trade a stock index, bond index, sector, or an entire country? Feel bullish on midcap stocks, corporate bonds, health care, or Malaysia? More than 150 ETFs await your trading and investing pleasure, and new issues arrive in the market frequently.

ETFs are collections or baskets of stocks bought and sold as a single stock. The Amex lists the majority of ETFs, with the remainder listed on the NYSE and CBOE.

Since the early 1990s, when they arrived on the market as "the new kids on the block," ETFs have flourished and skyrocketed in popularity.

In 1993, State Street Global Advisors, a large global money-manager, partnered with the Amex to launch the first ETF, the Standard & Poor's 500 Depository Receipt, or the SPYDR. Since the stock symbol for the SPYDR was SPY, traders nicknamed the stock "the Spiders."

The Spiders' success led to the creation and development of the "Middies," or the MDY, which tracks the mid-cap S&P 400 index. The Dow Diamonds (DIA), the Dow Jones Industrial Average tracking stock, and the proxy for the NASDAQ 100, the QQQQ, or the "Qs," as we call them, quickly followed.

In 1996, Barclay's Global Investors arrived on the scene, launching iShares. Now, nearly one hundred iShares offer ETFs representing indexes, sectors, and various countries.

Select Sector SPDRs emerged in 1998 and quickly became attractive to institutional traders. Each ETF corresponds to a sector within the S&P 500, and they have become popular trading tools for institutional, as well as private, traders.

As you can imagine, the popularity of these "flavor-for-every-taste" trading and investing tools spawned the birth of other index, sector, and country tracking issues.

Benefits of Trading ETFs

For a variety of reasons, ETFs appeal to both investors and short-term traders.

To investors, particularly, the use of ETFs reduces research time. Instead of wading through prospectuses (yawn) detailing the virtues of ten-thousand plus mutual funds, or choosing among stock components of an industry group, ETFs simplify the process.

Feel bullish on regional banks this month? Buy shares in the RKH (Regional Bank HOLDRS). *Click.* Done. You now own a variety of regional banks, all in one stock.

ETFs provide diversity within each share. When you buy shares of the Qs, for example, you own the top one hundred nonfinancial stocks in the NASDAQ Stock Exchange. If one of the component stocks wakes up to unsavory news— although it may jostle the index a bit—it won't gap the Qs, down to heaven-knows-where at the opening bell. Those owning the individual bad-news-bear stock, though, may be reaching for the Maalox bottle.

As compared to mutual fund fees, most index-tracking ETFs sustain lower expense ratios. Expenses such as accounting, marketing, and distribution are lower for ETFs, so fees are reduced.

Investors will also be glad to know that just like mutual funds, ETFs earn dividends paid by the underlying stocks. Plus, certain index funds can split; in early 2000, the Qs split two-for-one.

The tax structure of ETFs adds to their attractiveness. In a typical open-end mutual fund, a flood of redemptions may force the portfolio manager to sell shares in order to cover the obligations. That can trigger capital gains for fund shareholders, on which they have to pay taxes.

With ETFs, though, individual investors bypass the fund, buying and selling shares on an exchange. The portfolio manager doesn't have to sell shares or maintain enough cash to meet redemptions.

> **Hot Tip: As of this writing, the QQQQ is the most actively traded "stock" in the world.**

Unlike mutual funds, which are priced at the end of each trading day, ETFs undergo continuous pricing. We can enter or exit in a hurry.

Finally—and this is possibly one of the most alluring features for traders— the uptick rule for selling short doesn't apply to ETFs. You can sell short these products on a downtick.

Where to Find Them

At the moment, six main groups of ETFs provide the umbrella for these shares: HOLDRS, iShares, Select Sector SPDRs, StreetTRACKS, and Vanguard VIPERS. Although the components of these groups each come under the ETF heading, they represent diverse areas of the financial markets and may involve different characteristics.

The American Stock Exchange (*amex.com*) Web site has a great ETF corner. I particularly like the Quote Summary, which lists all the ETFs traded on the Amex, their symbols, current price, net change and percent change for the day, and volume.

In addition to the Web sites listed in the descriptions that follow, check these Web sites for additional information on ETFs:

- *etfconnect.com*

- *nasdaq.com/indexshares/about_funds.stm*

- *indexfunds.com*

Index Shares

The following table lists the most popular index shares and their symbols.

Dow Jones Diamonds	DIA
NASDAQ 100 Trust Unit	QQQQ
S&P 400 Midcap SPDR	MDY
S&P 500 SPDR	SPY

The price of one share of the DIA represents about 1 percent of the Dow Jones Industrial Average. So, if the Dow is trading at 10,000, one share of the DIA costs $100. The MDY trades at 20 percent of the S&P 400 Midcap index, the QQQQ trades at 2.5 percent of the NASDAQ 100 index, and the SPY trades at 10 percent of the index value. These percentages vary slightly from moment to moment during the trading day.

Within these ETFs, every stock has equal weighting. For example, a share of the QQQQs represents $\frac{1}{100}$ ownership in every stock in NASDAQ 100. A share of the MDY signifies equal ownership of each stock in the S&P 400, and so forth.

Merrill Lynch HOLDRS

Merrill Lynch created the HOLDRS (Holding Company Depository Receipts) (*holdrs.com*) ETFs. Each issue represents a sector or industry group, such as oil services, biotechs, regional banks, or telecom.

Keep in mind that you must buy or sell short HOLDRS in round lot sizes, and they trade with a hundred-share minimum.

Also know that many of these ETFs are too illiquid to trade on an intraday basis; they make better swing or position trading candidates.

At the moment, high-volume HOLDRS include the SMH (semiconductor HOLDR), BBH (biotech HOLDR), OIH (oil services HOLDR), and RTH (retail HOLDR). Please check current volume levels before you trade.

HOLDRS boast a unique feature: If you own shares in a HOLDR, for a small fee, you can "unbundle" the single trust (stock) and receive shares of the underlying stocks that construct it. That allows you to "fire" a single stock, or stocks, and still maintain sector integrity.

iShares

Barclays' Global Investors sponsors iShares (*ishares.com*), which include more than eighty ETFs. The comprehensive menu lists stock index funds, bond funds, sector funds, international index funds, and Morningstar and Russell index funds.

On the iShares Web site, you'll discover fund "flavors" that range from basic materials to real estate, from the NYSE Composite to emerging markets, and from the Russell 200 Value index shares, to the Morningstar Large Growth Index fund.

Currently, the most popular iShares are the Russell 2000 tracking stock (IWM) and the Japan iShares (EWJ).

> **Hot Tip: International iShares are based on Morgan Stanley Capital International (MSCI) indices. These indices track the performance of a country's stock market.**

Select SPDRs

As mentioned, State Street Global Advisors sponsors Select Sector SPDRs (*spdrindex.com*), which divide the equities in the S&P 500 index into nine categories, or sectors. These sectors include such ETFs as the XLK (Technology SPDR), XLF (Financial SPDR), and the XLV (Healthcare SPDR).

Some of these ETFs trade millions of shares per day. Others meander through an entire week, skating on thin volume. Again, please check liquidity before you target Sector SPDRs for short-term trades.

streetTRACKS

In addition to sponsoring the SPY and the Select SPDRs, State Street Global Advisors (*streettracks.com*) offers eight streetTRACKs funds ranging from the FEZ (EURO STOXX 50) the FFF (Fortune 500 Index Fund), to the MTK (Morgan Stanley Technology Index Fund).

As of this writing, StreetTRACKs average daily volume numbers remain thin.

Vanguard VIPERs

At this time, the Vanguard Group (*vanguard.com*), known for their mutual funds, carries sixteen ETFs, known as the VIPERs.

VIPERs index funds list the Total Stock Market Index, known as the Wilshire 5000. The Wilshire 5000 contains more than 6,500 issues, representing every actively traded stock in the U.S. financial markets. The corresponding VIPER trades as the VTI.

The Extended Market Index, or the Wilshire 5000 excluding the S&P 500 index stocks, trades as the VXF.

You can buy and sell growth and value indexes with Vanguard's Growth VIPERs (VUG) and Value VIPERs (VTV).

Additional VIPERs represent various sectors and include such issues as Consumer Discretionary VIPERs (VTI), the Information Technology VIPERs (VGT), and the Health Care VIPERs (VHT).

Hedging Tactics with ETFs

Because of their liquidity, accessibility, and varied representation, many traders, both private and institutional, use index and sector ETFs, such as the DIA, SPY, Qs, and SMH (semiconductor HOLDRS) as hedging vehicles to offset potential losses.

Say you're holding a group of tech stocks long, as position trades. Although the uptrend is still intact, the tech-heavy NASDAQ market begins to retrace.

To hedge your holdings, you'd sell short the NASDAQ 100 tracking stock, the QQQQ, in the same dollar amount as the value of your stocks. If you're holding $15,000 in total stock value, you'll sell short $15,000 worth of shares in the QQQQ.

In an alternative situation, imagine you were holding long a broader market index, such as the SPY. In an uncertain market, you could hedge your position by selling short an ETF that represents a weak sector, or industry group.

Or, if you're long the Internet HOLDR, the HHH, you could hedge it by selling short an equal dollar amount in the technology SPDR, the XLK.

Whatever your choice, please remember two points:

- Don't overhedge your account. If the market reverses, an overhedged account induces panicky, money-losing strategies.

- If you're holding an open position that's hit your stop-loss price, don't hedge as a substitute for exiting the position. That action can *really* land you in the soup line!

Trading ETFs

Let's look at a selection of ETFs, to see how they trade.

Before we get started, though, here's a quick note. When applied to index shares, OBV readings can be misleading because of hedging activity. On these charts, look at heightened volume as momentum signals and to measure the velocity of price moves.

> **Hot Tip: During bear markets, hedge-fund and institutional traders love to short the QQQQ. It's not uncommon for outstanding shares of the Qs being shorted to reach more than 50 percent.**

In the charts that follow, you'll see a fourteen-period ADX (Average Directional Movement indicator) over the volume spikes. It saves chart space to overlay the ADX over volume, and we'll use the ADX as a decision support tool for trend activity. (On your own charts, you may wish to plot other momentum indicators, such as the MACD for position trades, or stochastics for short-term trades.)

Along with the 20-day MA, 50-day MA, and 200-day MA, you'll also notice Fibonacci retracements plotted between selected highs and lows. Fibs lines can work especially well with moving averages to forecast potential support-and-resistance levels on index shares.

Figure 11–1 shows a daily chart of the Dow Diamonds (DIA).

Fibonacci retracements stretch from the March (six month) high to the Au-

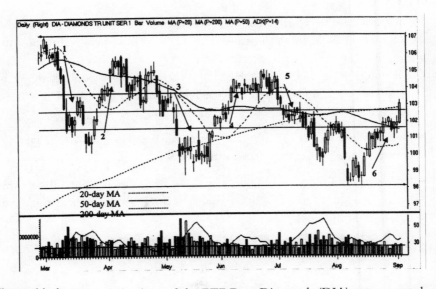

Figure 11–1. In this daily chart of the ETF Dow Diamonds (DIA), you can see how the index made a succession of lower highs from March through August, although rebounds were strong. Swing trading opportunities emerged from this seesaw action, even though the roller coaster caused investors—and many traders—headaches. Examples: 1) The cliff fall in the first week in March initiated by the bearish engulfing pattern dive below the 20-and 50-day MAs, plus a rising ADX, 2) a risky bottom-fishing long trade (DIA trades below 20-day MA), 3) another cliff-fall early in May (remember, you can short the DIA on a downtick, which gives you an easy entry), 4) a MA crossover in early June (20-day MA loops around the 200-day MA—an unusual pattern!), with the ADX stepping in a wobbly dance above the 30 signal line, 5) ADX flies higher as DIA struggles, then weakens, etching a lower high and finally succumbing to bears, and 6) after making a new, relative low, the DIA shoots higher in a rebound and penetrates the 200-day MA, to the upside, for the second time in six months. This setup is high-risk for a swing trade, especially until the DIA clears the 20-day MA. Still, those who jumped in prospered.

Note the Fibonacci retracement lines plotted from the DIA's March high of $107 to the August low of 98. During the August rally, the 38.2% line at $101.60 offered mild resistance. The DIA then shot through the 50 percent line at $102.70—a bullish sign.

gust (six month) low; they predicted support-and-resistance levels accurately. If you applied this study in mid-August, when the DIA bounced off its lows, you would have predicted the DIA's hesitation at the 38 percent retracement level and the fifty-day MA at about $101—and you'd have been right.

The next resistance level will be at the Fibonacci 62 percent level, just under $104, which the DIA is approaching.

Take a pencil and draw a down-sloping trend line over the highs of the overall pattern, connecting April and June highs. If you extend the trend line, you'll see that it coincides with the Fibs 62 percent line. Plus, the two-hundred-day MA is lumbering around that price zone. Those coinciding indicators tell you to use caution trading the DIA in this unpredictable price area.

> **Hot Tip:** While active index funds like the Qs and SPYs have the capacity to gap open both up and down at the market's open, most days price will fill the opening gap before the trading day concludes.

Figure 11–2 displays a daily chart of the NASDAQ Tracking Stock, the QQQQ.

This envoy of the NASDAQ 100 traded in a four-point range from March through July, then tanked to summer lows touched a year earlier (not shown). Keep in mind that historically, on a seasonal basis, the months from May to November represent the most negative months for tech stocks.

While we're on that subject, please look at the Qs price action in Figure 11–2, during the month of May.

Did you notice how I emphasize the word "orderly," when I talk about acceptable trading price action? The month of May on this chart is a perfect example of *disorderly* price action. Look at the lineup of sideways, up and down gaps, spinning top days, all bunched around the two-hundred-day MA. Talk about confusion! This is the sort of action swing traders should avoid. And I'd be surprised if intraday traders didn't get whipsawed by the helter-skelter motion, as well.

Other than that, the chart displays three of the best swing trading prospects, all with Moving Average Hot-Blanket setups, during April, July, and August. A few two-point runs to the upside took place; however, risk ran high due to price and moving average resistance.

The Fibonacci retracement levels extend from the June 30 pivot high to August lows (six-month high and low). This will give us potential support and resistance price levels for the post-August rally.

So far, the lines accurately predicted a price hesitation for the Qs at $34.60 and the 38 percent retracement levels. Look left on the chart, back to May and

Daily (Right) QQQ-NASDAQ 100 TR UNIT SER1 Bar Volume MA(P=20) MA(P=200) MA(P=50) ADX(P=14)

Figure 11–2. In this daily chart of the QQQQ, the NASDAQ 100 index tracking stock, you can see how the stock traded in a four-point range from March to mid-July. Like the comparable time period shown with the Dow (Figure 11-1), the NASDAQ's seesaw movement frustrated investors and many traders. In July, the Qs finally broke the mid-May lows. The event was precluded by two back-to-back wide-range days, July 20 and 21 (black arrow), which surely left some market players gasping for breath. Although high-risk swing traders would have found additional plays, three swing trade opportunities to the short side fit the criteria for the Moving Average Hot-Blanket setup:

1. The first appeared in April, when the Qs failed to make a higher high. The stock rolled over and quickly sliced through its 20-day, then falling 50-day MAs. Traders could have entered a short trade just under the 20-day MA, and covered the position as the ADX fell and volume came into the stock (potential early bulls) at the close of the third day down.

2. In early July, the Qs fell below all three MAs and their crossovers, on strong volume. The uncertain part of this trade lurked in the disorderly—but still potential—support that lurked from May and March. That warns traders to limit position size or even shrug off the trade.

3. On August 3 (long black candle), the exhausted Qs presented a final short swing opportunity. With the ADX still hovering over 30, and another price rally and failure at the 20-day MA, traders could have sold short as the stock rallied to the MA, then tumbled. When volume increased August 6, after a big gap down, it was time to cover the trade and take profits. Fibonacci retracement lines stretch from the June high of $38 to August lows at $32.35. Note how the August rally stopped in its tracks (about $34.50) at the 38.2 percent retracement. The QQQQ pulled back, formed a *doji* on the rising 50-day MA, followed by a bullish engulfing candle.

March lows, and you'll see that price resistance pressured the current move higher, as well.

The relative precision exhibited by Fibonacci retracement lines always amazes me. Even though we used the June high and August low as our boundaries for the Fibonacci retracements, the lines pointed to *previous* support-and-resistance levels with uncanny accuracy.

Next, let's look at an index ETF that's growing in popularity, the IWM, or the tracking stock for the iShares Russell 2000 Index. As you may know, the Russell 2000 represents the small-cap index. (For more information on Russell indexes, go to *russell.com.*

Figure 11–3 shows a daily chart of the IWM.

At the moment, the IWM trades at a relatively high price, $112 per share, and carries a two-point average daily range. The shares are expensive, but the wide range price action compensates.

You'll note that along with the QQQQ, the IWM also experienced a disor-

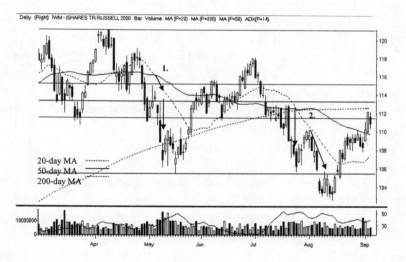

Figure 11–3. This daily chart of the iShares Russell 2000 index shows, the IWM, is trading in an overall downtrend. The pattern has a few similarities to the chart of the Qs, in Figure 11–2. As with the DIAs and the Qs, the best swing trading opportunities during this time period were to the short side. The Moving Average Hot-Blanket setup appeared on the IWMs twice in late April (1.), and twice again in mid-July (2.). "Wa-ait a minute!" you say. "The IWM made a moonshot the end of March, again at the end of May, and *again* in mid-August. What about swing trades to the long side?" My reply: the IWM certainly moved higher during those rallies, but I don't see strong setups that fit criteria for long swing trades. Can you go bottom-fishing for long swing trades? Yes, but trading the retest of a nearby low (Double Got 'Em setup) is safer than holding an ETF rally candidate overnight. Remember that rallies in a downtrend as strong as this one can be volatile ventures.

derly month of May. And, as with the Qs, the IWM's chaotic price jumps centered around the 200-day MA.

Since the 200-day MA is such an important watermark, price action in its vicinity, especially in the case of a prominent index, can be explosive. Intraday traders can profit in this environment. Swing and position traders will want to sit on their hands.

This time I used the April high and the May low as Fibonacci margins. You can see how the IWM's subsequent price action used these retracements for support and resistance and converged with other chart indicators to strengthen buy and sell signals.

After IWM hit its May 17 low, it clawed its way over the 200-day MA. Then it gained steam. On May 25, it shot higher in a three-point range, rocketing over the twenty-day MA and the 38 percent retracement line (long, white candle). On May 26, it closed on its high ($113.27).

Swing traders who hopped into long trades on May 25, when the stock cleared its twenty-day MA, would want to take profits at the May 26 close. The fifty-day MA, the 50 percent Fibs retracement, and prior price resistance from earlier in May—all converged to present the IWM with overhead pressure.

Sure enough, within a few days, the IWM reversed. For the next two weeks, it cavorted around the 50 percent Fibonacci line. Keep in mind, this 50 percent retracement level represents the halfway mark between the April high and the May low. Indecision breeds volatility, so wise swing traders sat on the sidelines. Most of trading profits in this fitful period belonged to intraday traders.

The next clear-cut swing setup appears on July 21, when the IWM gaps open slightly over its 50- and 200-day MAs, then falls like a rock tied to a brick (long, black day). With all the overhead resistance quickly established, the Moving Average Hot-Blanket setup emerges once again. Traders could sell short the stock once it confirmed its upside failure.

Three days later, on July 26, the Fibonacci line presented support, and the IWM fell right to the line! In anticipation, savvy shorts covered positions earlier in the day. Those who didn't cover by the day's close felt the pinch of a short squeeze the next day, July 27, when the IWM gapped higher at the open.

ETF Hit Parade

The following table lists the twenty-five most active ETFs at the present time. As you know, changes in the economic environment cause sectors to rotate in popularity. That means sector and industry group "parade leaders" will vary.

Also, additions to these products pop onto the market frequently. Check the Web sites mentioned to stay updated on the newest entries.

ETF Hit Parade

Name	Symbol
Dow Diamonds Trust Series	DIA
HOLDRS Internet	HHH
HOLDRS Oil Services	OIH
HOLDRS Retail	RTH
HOLDRS Software	SWH
HOLDRS Utility	UTH
HOLDRS Semiconductor	SMH
iShares Barra Value	IVE
iShares Emerging Markets	EEM
iShares Hong Kong	EWH
iShares Japan	EWJ
iShares Lehman 1–3 Year Treasury Bond	SHY
iShares Lehman 20+ Year Treasury Bond	TLT
iShares NASDAQ Biotech	IBB
iShares Russell 1000 Value	IWD
iShares Russell 2000	IWF
iShares South Korea	EWY
iShares U.S. Real Estate	IYR
NASDAQ 100 Trust Unit	QQQQ
SPDR Energy	XLE
SPDR Financial	XLF
SPDR Industrial	XLI
SPDR Materials	XLB
SPDR Midcaps	MDY
SPDR S&P 500	SPY

In the next chapter, we'll look at active trading techniques for stocks, including ETFs. We'll also look at tactics for trading the popular E-minis.

Before you turn the page, though, please read through the questions that follow. They'll test your understanding of basic hedging techniques and ask you to evaluate your own strategies.

Quiz

Questions

1. Define the financial trading and investment product known as the Exchange Traded Fund, or ETF.

2. What groups of financial instruments do ETFs reflect?

3. True or false: You can only trade the Merrill Lynch HOLDRS in round lots.

4. What's one similarity ETFs enjoy with mutual funds?

5. Are *all* ETFs safe to trade intraday?

6. Say you're holding long position trades in General Electric (GE), Citigroup (C), and Time Warner (TWX). The broader market is correcting. Assuming your stops for these positions are in place, give an example of how you could use an ETF to hedge, or protect your positions.

7. Imagine you are long five hundred shares of the QQQQ. You want to retain your shares, and execute a fast hedge to protect your profits. What could you do?

8. Once again, you are long five hundred shares of the QQQQ. Instead of hedging with an ETF, you want to short an individual stock to offset losses. What type of equity would be a logical choice?

9. Your neighbor, Fred, hedged a long-swing position with an ETF. The original position just hit Fred's stop-loss price. Fred's reaction: he shrugs, packs a cooler, and heads to the beach. Is Fred a smart or a foolish trader?

10. Why does the daily and weekly volume on index shares fluctuate with the economy?

Answers

1. ETFs are collections or baskets of stocks bought and sold as a single stock.

2. ETFs represent indexes, sectors, and international interests.

3. True.

4. Like mutual funds, the underlying stocks in ETFs earn dividends that are paid to investors.

5. No, they aren't! In fact, many ETFs trade with extremely low average daily volume, and fall far short of the one-million-share benchmark that gives you intraday trading safety. Please check volume on *any* trading product before you enter a position!

6. To guard against losses in positions such as General Electric (GE), Citigroup (C), and Time Warner (TWX), you could sell short an equal dollar amount in the SPY, or other index shares that represent the S&P 500. Alternately, you might sell short the DIA. If your account was weighted in technology stocks, you would short an equal dollar amount in the QQQQ.

7. To hedge against losses in your five hundred-share position of the QQQQ, you could quickly assess technology sectors to locate the weakest group, then short the correlating ETF in an equal dollar amount. Possible candidates include such ETFs as the SMH (Semiconductor HOLDRS), HHH (Internet HOLDRS), SWH (Software HOLDRS), and the Technology SPDR (XLK).

8. If you are long five hundred shares of the QQQQ and you want to short an individual stock to offset losses, choose a weak technology "general" to sell short. Check out such stocks as Microsoft (MSFT), Dell (DELL), Intel (INTC), Amazon.com (AMZN), or Cisco Systems (CSCO).

9. Foolish, foolish Fred!

10. Daily and weekly volume on index shares fluctuates with the economy, because they are used heavily for hedging. Also, sector ETFs receive alternating attention due to cyclical rotation.

CENTER POINT

The Power of Words

Knowledge and intention are forces. What you intend changes the field in your favor.

—Deepak Chopra

If thoughts are the most powerful forces on earth, the words spoken as a manifestation of those thoughts carry a mighty impact!

Consider the words "yes" and "no." For me, just thinking the word "no" brings on feelings of discomfort and heaviness. Expressing the word "yes," however, generates instant feelings of pleasure.

What if we take this process to a deeper level? The intentions behind the "yeses" and "nos" you've heard since childhood have created a major impact on the successes and challenges you experience today.

Words spoken to you by others—and yourself—stamp a mental imprint on your mind that lasts a lifetime. Most obstacles you mount easily today came from a parent or authority figure in your childhood, who said, "*Yes,* you can do it!"

Current hurdles that are difficult to overcome surely have a "No, you cannot do that" ("You're not smart enough . . . or strong enough," etc.) submerged in your past. The power of those words and their intentions, whether delivered consciously or casually, live on in your mind and manifest in your life today.

A collection of "nos" from my childhood still chase me around. Delivered by well-meaning adults, most were meant to curb my "hare-brained" aspirations. It's taken a lot of work to get over, around, and through those "nos."

Let's clean out all the "nos" we've dragged around since childhood. The next time you're confronted with a challenge and feel helpless or frustrated, before you declare, "No, I can't do that," stop and "map" the feeling you experience. Where did it come from? Trace it back in time. Do the reasons given then fit your present life? (They probably don't.) When you pinpoint it, mentally reverse it into a positive statement, or outcome.

Then return to the present, look the challenge squarely in the eye, and say, "*Yes,* I can do that."

Day Trading Stocks—Setups and Strategies

The true art of trading lies in the ability to juggle conflicting pieces of evidence and come up with a balanced judgment, superior on average to the collective judgment already rendered in the marketplace.

—William Gallacher

It's sort of like hearing your own obituary on the morning news channel. There you are, sipping your morning coffee and mulling over your trade sheets from the day before. Suddenly, a television announcer smirks smugly and says, "Since all the day traders went belly-up . . ."

Well, excu-uuuse me! As a card-carrying day trader, I can assure you, our bellies are in great shape, thank you very much! In fact, we are alive, happy, and profitable.

True, the face of intraday trading has changed since the price change from fractions to decimalization (April 2001). "Scalpers," who used to grab "teenies" (1⁄16 of a point) from their trades, discovered the change from fractions to penny spreads sliced their profits into smithereens.

And, oh, how we miss the twenty-point swings of the late nineties! Those of us who gleefully swiped ten-point profits from the riotous price antics of Yahoo! and eBay during the dot.com heydays now settle for more reasonable gains.

As you know by now, we define "day trading"—also known as "active" or "intraday" trading—as the process of opening and closing a trade within the space of one trading day. No overnight positions are held.

Main benefits to this style can be attributed to trends and to time. Swing and position traders need trending markets to provide for optimum setups and entries; as a result, they may spend quite a few days—or even weeks—waiting on the sidelines. Intraday traders, however, can trade in trendless markets on daily charts, although they still need to locate a trend, intraday.

When you trade in the short term, time converts into risk. The longer you hold a position, the more chance exists that outside factors can move prices against you. Intraday trades, by their nature, expose your money for abbreviated time periods, which lessens risk associated with time.

Remember Dr. Steenbarger's Three Dimensions (3D) Trader Personality Quiz in chapter 4? He said, "A risk-averse trader is one who cannot tolerate the possibility of large losses, and who would prefer smaller, more frequent wins with controlled losses, to larger wins with greater drawdowns."

Day trading has earned a reputation for high risk—*and rightly so*. To some traders, though, trading in a time frame confined to hours, provides more control and less risk than swing or position trading.

Is day trading for you? Only you can make that decision. Learn the techniques and tactics, then paper-trade until you decide whether it's a good fit for your personal trading style.

Tools of the Trade

When you trade on an intraday basis, remember you are up against the brightest minds in the world. Their goal is to take your money! Market makers and specialists see order flow that we, as individual traders, cannot. As well, they *want* you to buy too high and sell too low. That's how they make their profits.

How do you compete with market professionals and institutional traders? By gaining all the knowledge you can, trading with a disciplined plan, and sharpening your experience with each trade.

To this end, you'll want to consider day trading with direct access software provided by brokerages that cater to traders. A good trading platform equips you with intraday trading tools, including real-time intraday charts, Level II screens, news, market statistics, position minders, and internal market data, such as E-mini index futures, the NYSE and/or NASDAQ Stock Exchange TICK and TRIN, and the CBOE VIX and/or VXN.

At trade shows, people often ask me, "Can I day trade stocks successfully using only a traditional online broker and real-time charts from an Internet source? Do I *really* need Level II screens, futures quotes and charts, plus stuff like the NYSE and NASDAQ TICK and TRIN?"

My reply: Hey, I'm sure there are people out there who make big bucks trading their pet stock for days on end, using only their online broker's order screen, a delayed fifteen-minute chart, and a rusty bull-or-bear market compass. Bless them.

I can only tell you what works for me—what increases my bottom line. When I trade intraday, I need futures quotes, market internals, and real-time charts. To tackle the market with anything else would be like skating onto the ice in the middle of a raucous pro hockey game without a helmet or protective gear. Ouch!

Intraday Trading Guidelines

If you are new to day trading, you may want to review material in earlier chapters. First, turn back to chapter 2 and scan the intraday trading criteria. Then, go through the pre-market analysis routine. If you haven't already, you'll develop your own pre-market routine to prepare yourself for the trading day.

Next, turn to chapter 4, and study the section on intraday indicators, including the E-mini futures, TICK and TRIN, and the VIX and VXN. When you move through the setups in the next section, know that they work best when teamed with correlating index futures moving in the same direction as the trade. Plus, you'll want the TICK and TRIN (NYSE or NASDAQ, depending in which exchange your stock is listed), as well as the VIX (on an overall basis) or the VXN if you're strictly a NASDAQ trader, moving to compliment your trade direction.

> **Hot Tip: The stock market has its own internal clock.**
> **It will usually correct, or get choppy, from 9:50–10:10 a.m. EST, from**
> **11:30 a.m.–1:30 p.m. EST (lunchtime doldrums), then at 3:00 p.m.**
> **(bond market closes), then again from about 3:20 through to the close at**
> **4:00 p.m. EST. Keep in mind, these times are approximate.**

The most important thing to remember is this: Please develop a plan for every trade. Develop your strategy, then determine your entry window (you'll see examples in the setups section), initial protective stop, and your profit target *before* you enter a position. Nothing loses you money faster than diving headfirst into trades with no preplanned line of attack.

One way to develop this habit is to use the "trade sheet with a conscience," discussed in chapter 3. Although plugging in the numbers may take extra time at first, the process will train you to think through your trades and calculate risk-reward ratios before you plunk your hard-earned money on the line. You'll lower risk, maximize profits, and that's what it's all about!

Level II Screens—An Overview

In the late nineties, when stocks still traded in fractions and profits could be made in seconds, many Mach 2 scalpers made hundreds (or thousands!) of trades a day using only NASDAQ Level II order-entry screens. Reading the price action on the screen (reading the "blur" is more accurate—in those days, prices moved so fast they nearly jumped off the screen) became an art form for these techno tape-readers.

Now, though, most traders stick to charts for buy-and-sell decisions. We use Level II (also referred to as SuperMontage) screens for their primary purpose only, that of order entry. To be sure, when you enter your order on using these screens, your chances of obtaining the best entry price are optimal.

Three basic "levels" of quotes exist.

Level I quotes represent the best bid and offer prices. Those are the quotes you receive if you ask your traditional broker for a stock price. The offer, or ask, is the lowest purchase price at which you could buy "at the market." The bid is the highest price at which you could sell your stock "at the market."

Level II quotes are used by individual traders, and you see them in Figure 12–1, under the bid (left) and ask, or offer (right column) columns on the screens. The columns show a list of market participants who want to sell (bid) or buy (offer, or ask) a stock at a given moment, at different levels of prices.

Level III quotes show more information, including order flow. They're available only to market makers, specialists, and other market professionals.

EBAY		Last	88.69	Chg	-.69	Lst	100
C	89.38	↑Bid	88.67	Ask	88.69	Ratio	500x1600
O	89.57	High	90.45	Low	88.28	Vol	8757879

Name	Bid	Size	Name	Ask	Size
NAS	88.67	1	PRUS	88.69	1
SIZE	88.67	1	ASE	88.69	5
ASE	88.67	5	BRUTBK	88.69	8
ARCAX	88.66	1	BRUT	88.69	8
BRUTBK	88.66	26	NAS	88.69	9
BRUT	88.66	26	CIN	88.69	16
PSE	88.66	1	ISLAND	88.69	16
ISLAND	88.65	11	ARCAX	88.69	9
CIN	88.65	11	PSE	88.69	9
ARCAX	88.64	3	ARCAX	88.70	499S
ISLAND	88.64	3	ISLAND	88.70	6
BRUTBK	88.63	1	SIZE	88.70	1
UBSW	88.63	1	ISLAND	88.71	3
ISLAND	88.63	3	FBCO	88.72	1
ARCAX	88.63	1	ARCAX	88.72	2
BRUTBK	88.62	2	BRUTBK	88.72	2
ARCAX	88.62	1	ISLAND	88.72	1
ISLAND	88.62	2	ARCAX	88.73	7
ARCAX	88.61	2	ISLAND	88.73	8
ISLAND	88.61	40	LEHM	88.74	2
ADAM	88.60	1	BRUTBK	88.74	1
ARCAX	88.60	3	ARCAX	88.74	1499S
BRUTBK	88.60	2	AOXPS	88.75	7
BTRD	88.60	10	GVRC	88.75	10
ISLAND	88.60	1	WCHV	88.75	1
CIBC	88.59	1	UBSW	88.75	1
ARCAX	88.59	4	ARCAX	88.75	2
ISLAND	88.59	3	BRUTBK	88.75	4
BRUTBK	88.59	2	ISLAND	88.75	50

88.63	200
88.63	300
88.63	100
88.63	100
88.63	100
88.64	100
88.64	100
88.64	700
88.64	881
88.63	500
88.64	200
88.64	300
88.64	100
88.63	100
88.63	100
88.63	100
88.64	400
88.65	300
88.65	100
88.66	1000
88.67	300
88.67	100
88.67	100
88.68	300
88.68	500
88.66	3000
88.68	100
88.68	600
88.68	100
—15:13—	
88.69	199
88.67	1400
88.67	600
88.67	100
88.69	100

Figure 12–1 A. On this NASDAQ Level II screen, you can see the momentary price action and participants in eBay, Inc. (EBAY). The top portion of the screen shows Level I prices, or the inside bid and ask. It also displays other information, including the closing price from the day before, today's opening price, today's high and low prices established so far, share size of the last trade, and volume of shares traded. At the moment, EBAY is bid at $88.67 and offered at $88.69. Since more shares are offered out than are bid for, we have "depth of offer," which indicates selling, or more supply than demand. That may take prices lower, for now.

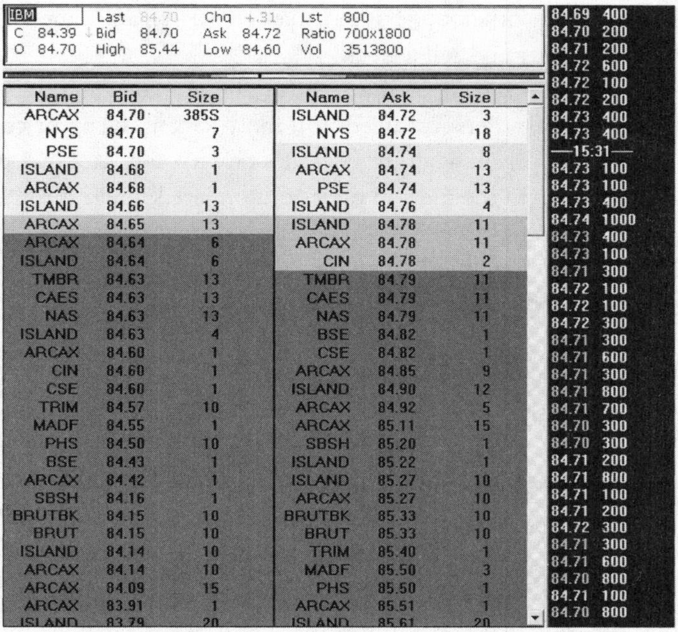

IBM	Last 84.70	Chg +.31	Lst	800		84.69	400
C 84.39	Bid 84.70	Ask 84.72	Ratio	700x1800		84.70	200
O 84.70	High 85.44	Low 84.60	Vol	3513800		84.71	200

						84.72	600
						84.72	100

Name	Bid	Size	Name	Ask	Size	84.72	200
ARCAX	84.70	385S	ISLAND	84.72	3	84.73	400
NYS	84.70	7	NYS	84.72	18	84.73	400
PSE	84.70	3	ISLAND	84.74	8	—15:31—	
ISLAND	84.68	1	ARCAX	84.74	13	84.73	100
ARCAX	84.68	1	PSE	84.74	13	84.73	100
ISLAND	84.66	13	ISLAND	84.76	4	84.73	400
ARCAX	84.65	13	ISLAND	84.78	11	84.74	1000
ARCAX	84.64	6	ARCAX	84.78	11	84.73	400
ISLAND	84.64	6	CIN	84.78	2	84.73	100
TMBR	84.63	13	TMBR	84.79	11	84.71	300
CAES	84.63	13	CAES	84.79	11	84.72	100
NAS	84.63	13	NAS	84.79	11	84.72	100
ISLAND	84.63	4	BSE	84.82	1	84.72	300
ARCAX	84.60	1	CSE	84.82	1	84.71	300
CIN	84.60	1	ARCAX	84.85	9	84.71	600
CSE	84.60	1	ISLAND	84.90	12	84.71	300
TRIM	84.57	10	ARCAX	84.92	5	84.71	800
MADF	84.55	1	ARCAX	85.11	15	84.71	700
PHS	84.50	10	SBSH	85.20	1	84.70	300
BSE	84.43	1	ISLAND	85.22	1	84.70	300
ARCAX	84.42	1	ISLAND	85.27	10	84.71	200
SBSH	84.16	1	ARCAX	85.27	10	84.71	800
BRUTBK	84.15	10	BRUTBK	85.33	10	84.71	100
BRUT	84.15	10	BRUT	85.33	10	84.71	200
ISLAND	84.14	10	TRIM	85.40	1	84.72	300
ARCAX	84.14	10	MADF	85.50	3	84.71	300
ARCAX	84.09	15	PHS	85.50	1	84.71	600
ARCAX	83.91	1	ARCAX	85.51	1	84.70	800
ISLAND	83.79	20	ISLAND	85.61	20	84.70	800

Figure 12–1 B. This Level II screen shows intraday price action for International Business Machines (IBM). At the inside bid, you can see Archipelago's order (AR-CAX) (that might be your order if you trade through that ECN), as well as orders from the New York Stock Exchange (NYS), and the Pacific Stock Exchange (PSE). At the inside offer, the ECN, Island, shows first in line; the New York Stock Exchange is second. If you were to buy IBM at this moment with a market order, assuming you were filled quickly, you would pay $84.72 for your shares. Were you to sell the stock right now, you could sell it for $84.70. Of course, you could issue a limit order to "split the bid and ask," and attempt to either buy, or sell, IBM at $84.71. You could also enter a limit order to buy at the bid price, or sell at the offer price. Whether or not your order is filled is determined by the number of shares at those price levels, and the price action itself.

Figures 12–1 A and B display two Level II screens. The first screen shows eBay, Inc. (EBAY), which is listed on the NASDAQ Stock Exchange. The second screen illustrates price action for International Business Machines (IBM), listed on the NYSE.

Market players you see listed on Level II screens represent market markers, national and regional stock exchanges, and ECNs. ECNs are electronic communications networks, such as Island and Archipelago; these networks match buy and sell orders, electronically.

The advantage to trading with a Level II screen, as opposed to trading with only Level I quotes, is that the Level II screen offers transparency. We can see limit orders placed by other traders and market participants, and the price at which they want to buy and sell a stock.

The Time and Sales screen, to the right of the bid and offer, lists the time, price, and share size of orders just filled. On most screens, when price trades up one tick, it appears in green; when price trades down a tick, it shows up red.

The topmost prices in the bid and offer columns are known as the NBBO, or the National Best Bid and Offer. We also call these two prices the "inside bid" and "inside offer," or "high bid," "low offer." Bids and offers shown at different prices from the NBBO are referred to as "away from" or "out of market" prices.

Level II screens show momentary demand-and-supply levels. When more than three to five participants line up at the inside bid price, we say the market has "depth." That means market players are lining up to purchase the stock, and thus support it. If the market shows depth at the inside offer, it indicates weakness, or mounting supply.

Finally, when you watch prices change between the two columns, you'll see that prices moving in a counterclockwise direction (offer to bid) indicate momentary bullishness. When prices rotate in a clockwise direction (bid to offer), it signals bearishness.

> **Hot Tip: When you use direct-access order entry software,**
> **you bypass the broker and place your order directly with the exchange "floor."**
> **That gives you an advantage over traders and investors who order**
> **stocks through more traditional methods.**

If price level flip back and forth between the bid and offer, the market is undecided.

Those of you who use direct-access software can place your orders directly from Level II screens. This gives you the ability to place your order with precision and control. Direct-access brokers add more bells and whistles to their order entry screens by the minutes, making them fast, competitive, and robust. For the best entry and exit prices, stay updated on the order entry options provided by your direct-access broker.

Now, let's move on to day-trading setups for stocks.

Intraday Setups for Stocks

As mentioned previously, I use swing-trading setups to locate optimum day-trading opportunities. My reasoning: I'm looking for price action that points to high-momentum days, to the upside or downside.

Those days are great for swing-trading entries, as well as intraday trades. That's why those setups are "two-fers," as we used to say in the South. (For you Northerners and Westerners, that means "two-items-for-the-price-of-one.")

> **Hot Tip:** When you trade stocks intraday, if you access the E-mini futures quotes, is it a *must* to also watch the TICK, TRIN, VIX, or VXN? Nope, it isn't. Still, the TICK, TRIN, VIX, and VXN provide heads-up information that some traders find helpful.

For the day-trading setups that follow, we're going to use the swing-trading setups discussed in chapter 10.

Double Got 'Em—The Day Trade

As you remember, the dynamic behind the "double got 'em" setup is the bounce of the retest of a momentum low.

By way of a quick review: On a daily chart, we're looking for a stock that experienced a downtrend, fell to a low, and rebounded. Now, eight or more days later, price is retesting that low.

In Figure 12–2, May Department Stores (MAY) displays that setup. (As of this writing, MAY trades in an average daily range of one-point plus. Average daily volume equals 1.75 million shares.) You'll also see the retest price action developing with two spinning tops, both of which show relatively long lower shadows. That means early bulls may be grazing at support prices.

Tomorrow, if the retail stock doesn't gap open more than $0.40 or so, *and if* it holds its lows and shows signs of positive price action, *and if* market internals agree, we'll plan to enter a day trade, or trades, to the long side. A gap down, and/or negative market internals will invalidate the trade.

Trade plan: Enter between $24.30 and $24.80. (Today's price range: high $24.48, low $24.06, open $24.40, close $24.36.) I don't want to enter the stock if it gaps down more than minimally from the prior day's closing price, so I established the first entry price at $24.30. I also will not enter the stock if it gaps open higher more than $0.40—thus the high of the entry window of $24.80.

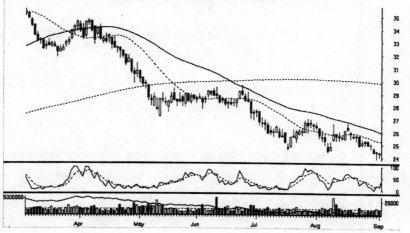

Figure 12–2. On this daily chart of May Department Stores Co. (MAY), you can see how this component of the RLX, the S&P retail index, skated south in an orderly downtrend for the last six months. (I see some great, stress-free, short swing-trading opportunities on this chart!) Now, MAY slows her descent, and retests prior August 6 lows of $24.45. On the chart's most recent day, the retailer touched a low of $24.06, finishing in the second spinning top in a row. Both spinning tops closed with lower shadows. That indicates buyers may be coming into the stock. The stochastics indicator drilled into its oversold zone; now, it's hooked higher in a dramatic bullish divergence. Tomorrow could incite a short squeeze and a dandy day-trading setup to the long side.

Once in, the initial protective stop will be established no lower than $23.95. Next resistance on daily chart lurks at $26. That gives us a small risk to the downside, and plenty of room for a point, or two, profit on the upside.

Figure 12–3 shows our trade on a five-minute chart, and how it progressed until 11:45 EST.

Please note: On the intraday charts in this chapter, the chart indicators include a twenty-period moving average. You'll also see the ADX plotted over the volume spikes, with the Plus Directional Indicator (+DI) and the Minus Directional Indicator (–DI) on the middle panel. The Plus Directional Indicator is the dotted line.

Note how MAY opened on our entry day, September 2, at $24.31, $0.05 under yesterday's close ($24.36). Since I typically don't enter during the first five minutes of the trading day, and since MAY's first five minutes evolved with less-than-enthusiastic volume, I'll give her a few minutes to warm up. (I know this is a female stock, because the ticker symbol is a woman's name, and it stands for a department store!)

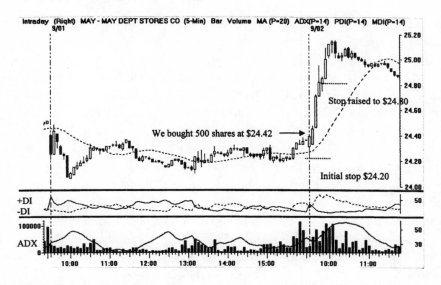

Figure 12–3. On this 5-minute chart of May Department Stores Co. (MAY), you can see how, on our entry day (9 September), the stock opened a few cents under the prior day's (September 1) closing price. We gave MAY a few minutes to warm up. Market internals (futures, TICK, and TRIN) were positive, as was the S&P retail index, the RLX. MAY jumped higher on the second 5-minute bar, trading just above the 20-period MA on increased volume, with the +DI hooking higher, accompanied by the ADX. All signals point to an entry, so we buy 600 shares at $24.42. For the next half-hour, the stock goes vertical, no doubt fueled by a gaggle of scared-spitless shorts, who got caught in the squeeze! When the first negative candle closes at 10:10 a.m., we sell 300 shares at $25.05. To protect remaining shares, we raise the stop to $24.80.

> **Hot Tip: The 20-period moving average serves as a great indicator on intraday charts, particularly the 5-minute chart. Some traders live by a simple rule: when a stock trades over the 20-period moving average on a 5 minute chart, they day trade to the long side. When the stock slices through the 20-period moving average, they sell, or sell short.**

Also know that at the open, the ES, or S&P 500 E-mini futures traded steadily higher, the NYSE TICK moved higher, and the NYSE TRIN held steady below 1.0, a bullish reading.

At 10:35, the ADX moved over 30, and the +DI broke above the −DI, indicating a positive trend. Volume increased. Could the shorts be getting jittery? Awwww!

We entered MAY for a long intraday trade during the second five-minute bar, buying six hundred shares at $24.42. The protective stop will slip in nicely at $24.20, just under the first five-minute low at $24.23. We'll move the stop up in a few minutes.

MAY goes ballistic, surely propelled in part by some hysterical short covering. (Remember—this stock is "legally" in a downtrend, and probably has a lot of short interest.) When it reaches overbought status in just a half-hour, we sell half our position at $25.05. We protect the remainder of shares by raising the protective stop to $24.80.

Figure 12–4 displays the remainder of the trading day. At 1:30 p.m., MAY trades above her prior intraday high of $25.15. The S&P E-mini futures are continuing their uptrend, and other market internals look strong. MAY's +DI is climbing, and her ADX rockets to the upside on increased volume.

We buy three hundred shares at $25.17. Then we raise the stop to $24.95. Even if we get stopped out, we'll make a profit.

At 2:30 p.m., MAY reaches $25.48. We raise our protective stop to $25.25.

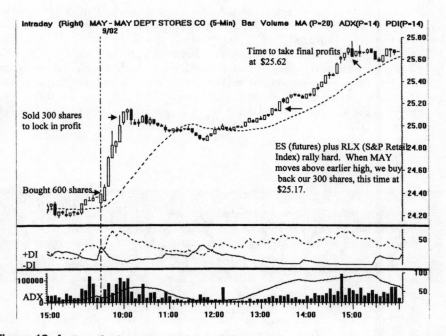

Figure 12–4. Our final 5-minute chart of the May Department Stores Co. (MAY) shows how the afternoon progressed. When the volume dropped off fast, by 10:10 a.m. EST, logic tells us price will wane as well. To seal in profits, we sell half the position. By 1:30 p.m., though, the retail stock climbed out of the midday blues period, and regained momentum. Since the market looks good, as the chart notes, we bought back 300 shares. By 2:45 p.m., MAY gets tuckered out. We watch it closely as it consolidates into the 20-period MA. At the 3:20 p.m., weakness sets in. We sell our entire position (600 shares) at $25.62. Good trade!

By 3:00 p.m., MAY saunters up to $25.75. (Keep in mind the $26 resistance on the daily chart.) Then she sidesteps for a few minutes. My trigger finger itches. When she starts to tire at $25.65, I sell all six hundred shares and close the trade at $25.62. Total profit: $684, without commissions.

Keep in mind that you could have executed different strategies, with different results. I used conservative, low-risk methods. You may want to review the chart and strategize different techniques you would have chosen.

> **Hot Tip: Remember that when you trade actively, you'll want to target a stock that trades an average of 800,000 to a million shares per day or more, and has a one point, or higher, average price range.**

Moving Average Leapfrog—The Day Trade

The "moving average leapfrog" setup for a swing trade can produce some dandy day-trading opportunities.

By way of review: Scan for a stock moving in an uptrend on a daily chart. After a move up, price pulls back, in an orderly fashion, to its twenty-day and fifty-day moving averages (which reside under the price pattern). Momentum indicator, such as stochastics, shows a bullish divergence, or is heading up; so is OBV. Bonus: price culminates the day in a small range candle.

Figure 12–5 shows a daily chart of Research in Motion (RIMM). The telecommunications equipment manufacturer has danced in a hot-blooded uptrend since its October 2002 lows of $4.18(!). Now, as extended uptrends have a way of doing, RIMM is showing an even rowdier side, but so far, shows no signs of slowing.

On the chart, you can see where RIMM shot higher starting mid-August. Once to resistance, it consolidated for a few days, and then moved down on August 30 and 31 (first two of the three most recent days on the chart's hard right edge). On September 1, it stopped on the twenty-day MA and closed in a spinning top.

Note that the 50-day MA runs horizontally, just above RIMM's September 1 high. Although the "moving average leapfrog" setup calls for the 50-day MA to run below the price pattern, in this case, it's perched only $0.75 above the close. Plus, the 50-day MA is traveling horizontally, which renders it less potent than a rising or falling MA. Stochastics are hooking higher in a bullish divergence, and the OBV is positive.

If RIMM starts higher tomorrow, and market action and internals agree, we'll enter a long day-trade. September 1 stats: RIMM opened at $59.90, then made a high of $61.53, a low of $59.60, and closed at $60.70.

Figure 12–5. This daily chart of Research in Motion, Ltd. (RIMM) shows the stock in a capricious uptrend. You may see the head-and-shoulders formation that formed between mid-May and August. In this case, the pattern did not play out as a top-reversal pattern, and RIMM never broke its 200-day MA (lower dotted line). At the end of the summer, RIMM moved up from its August lows to break through its 20-day, then 50-day MAs. During the most recent week, in an orderly retracement, it's pulled back to its 20-day MA. The latest day on the chart's hard right edge, September 1, closed in a spinning top. If RIMM bounces tomorrow, day-trading opportunities to the long side may crop up.

We'll plan an entry window ranging from $60.30 to $61.00. It's a volatile stock, and if it doesn't open in the upper portion of September 1 trading range, we won't take the trade.

Once in, we'll set our initial stop at no lower than $0.40 below our entry. Price resistance lies at about $64.40, so we have a lot of leeway to the upside.

Figure 12–6 shows a five-minute chart of RIMM, and how the trade played out.

On September 2, RIMM gapped open $0.15. We waited until the five-minute bar and bought four hundred shares at $60.92. For added information, the NASDAQ 100 E-mini futures ripped out of the 9:30 a.m. gate and rocketed higher. Other market internals looked positive.

Once in, we used the previous day's long consolidation "ledge" as support for the stop, and for the moment, placed our initial protective stop just under it, at $60.45. You can see the logic. If RIMM were to drop through that elongated support level . . . it would surely fall fast and hard.

RIMM neatly blew through the first reversal time period from 9:50 to 10:10

Figure 12–6. This 5-minute chart of Research in Motion, Ltd. (RIMM) shows the day before our entry, and the first half of our entry day. You can see how the stock consolidated all afternoon on September 1. On September 2, our entry day, the wireless technology provider gapped open to $60.85, a $0.15 gap. No problem. We wait for the market to settle down and for RIMM to fill its gap. It does so quickly. We enter on the second 5-minute candle, buying 400 shares at $60.92. Since this is a volatile stock, we'll limit share size, at least for now. Our initial stop-loss logically slips under yesterday's consolidation, at $60.45. RIMM climbed higher, fast. We raised the stop to $61.15, creating a sure profit if the stock weakens. RIMM shoots higher, reaching a high of $61.91 only 35 minutes after the market's open. The fast profit and an overextended stock convince us to take gains while the gettin's good. We do, and sell all 400 shares at $61.69.

a.m. EST. So, by the way, did the NQs. And, as is usually the case when the market ignores this "resting" period, it got tuckered out early.

At 9:55 a.m., we raised our stop to $61.15, locking in gains.

By only 10:05, RIMM flew over the prior day's high and soared to $61.91. Now price was highly overextended on an intraday basis. This is one of those times you look up to heaven, murmur a quick "thank you," and punch the sell button—fast. We jumped out at $61.78 on the long, white candle (10:05 a.m.). Profit: $344.00, without commissions.

Those who didn't take their profits and run had ample warning—a high-volume spike on the 10:05 a.m. completed candle, signaling the probable end of the move. A hammer formed next, followed by dark cloud cover. Finally, the ADX reversed and the +DI headed south. All of those signals predict a correction.

RIMM tapered off into the midday doldrums. At 1 p.m., though, fresh from its "nap," the stock edged higher. At 1:20 p.m., RIMM broke above its intraday high of $61.91 on strengthening volume. As the NASDAQ futures broke higher, we bought five hundred shares of RIMM at $62.04. We placed a stop at $61.65, under the prior consolidation, and plan to raise it, soon.

> **Hot Tip:** If you're buying the breakout over the intraday high, wait until price trades 5 cents above it. Otherwise, the stock may succumb to a double-top pattern, then head lower, fast.

Figure 12–7 shows the rest of the trading day. It turned into quite a party!

The chart text details the trade. RIMM climbed higher with enthusiasm, and we raised our stop to guarantee a profit. By 3:00 p.m., towering volume spikes told us the uptrend party was nearly over. We sold our five hundred shares for $63.40. Profit: $680, without commissions.

> **Hot Tip:** Remember, ETFs that trade a million shares per day, or more, make great intraday trading targets. Plus, you may want to day trade an index or sector ETF to hedge against losses in a longer-term position.

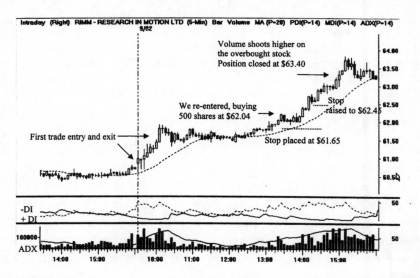

Figure 12–7. This final 5-minute chart of Research in Motion, Ltd. (RIMM) shows the tech stock riding an afternoon uptrend. We entered our second play of the day when the stock broke its earlier intraday high of $61.91. Our stop rests under consolidation lows. We soon raised it to $62.45, under another brief "rest stop." Note the rising volume spikes as the stock approached 3:00 p.m. While rising volume in a breakout is bullish, huge volume spikes on an overbought, overextended stock signals an upcoming price reversal. To stay on the safe side, I closed the position at 3:05, at $63.40. RIMM partied hearty, continuing to a high of $63.82, then drifted down into the market's close.

The Stealthy Sidewinder—The Day Trade

Remember the analogy for the "Stealthy Sidewinder" swing-trading setup, when you stepped on the garden hose? The compression of prices and the subsequent release and "explosion" give this trade its profit-making opportunities.

Again, you'll look for a stock trading in uptrend on a daily chart, and consolidating in a tight wedge, horizontal flag, or ascending triangle. The price pattern rides just above the twenty-day MA, and ideally, above the 50-day MA. Stochastics (or momentum indicator of your choice) and OBV should read positive.

Figure 12–8 shows a daily chart of Sepracor, Inc. (SEPR). The price action shows SEPR trading in a range for the past six months, from $40 to $53. Currently, the research-based pharmaceutical company is consolidating from an August upswing.

At the moment, the price trades above its 20-day and 50-day MAs, with the twenty-day MA rising higher below the consolidation. Volume rose on SEPR's August push higher, and settled down through the consolidation. Stochastics are rising in a bullish divergence; the OBV is popping higher.

Figure 12–8. This chart of Sepracor, Inc. (SEPR) shows the stock (right edge) sidestepping in a tight, horizontal flag formation. Just like a garden hose with the water turned on full force and our foot pressing down on top, the bull-bear battle on this pattern suggests that it will explode soon—either up or down. Here's a clue that the explosion may be to the upside: Look at the drug maker's volume during the last week of August. Extremely strong volume pushed the stock higher. Price met with prior price resistance, and consolidated to where it is now. Increasing volume tells us a day-trading opportunity may present itself soon.

Any day now, we can look for a move in this stock. The broader market and the NASDAQ are just waking up from their summer slump, and futures look higher. Both the DRG (Amex Pharmaceutical Index) and the BTK (Amex Biotech Index) trade in positive patterns. I've checked both, as Sepracor's business model fits into both industry groups.

The last day on the chart's hard right edge, Friday, September 10, shows SEPR's open at $50.26. It made a high of $50.92, low of $49.86, and closed at $50.72. We'll enter a long day-trade "tomorrow," if the stock and market internals agree with our plan.

Entry window on Monday, September 13: between $50.40 and $50.90. That gives us a range of a few cents below the prior day's opening price, to a fraction of a point over the closing price.

> **Hot Tip: You may want to utilize the support-and-resistance areas from a 10-minute, 15-minute, or even 60-minute chart to pinpoint your day-trading entry window.**

We'll assign a temporary stop at $49.80, just under the recent day's low. After (if) the stock breaks out of its consolidation, the next major price resistance on the daily chart waits at $53.50. Those numbers tell us it's a fairly low-risk trade. We'll see what the intraday patterns present.

Figure 12–9. On this 15-minute chart of Sepracor, Inc. (SEPR), you can see how to use the prior day's support-and-resistance levels to target your entry window. If SEPR opened higher or lower than our entry window, it would have taken a direction we didn't expect—and so violated our entry.

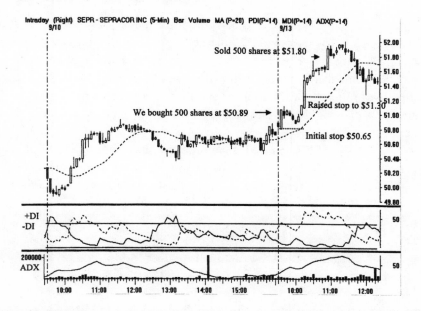

Intraday (Right) SEPR - SEPRACOR INC (5-Min) Bar Volume MA (P=20) PDI(P=14) MDI(P=14) ADX(P=14)

Figure 12–10. This 5-minute chart of Sepracor, Inc. (SEPR) shows our entry. After closing the small gap open during the first 5-minute bar, the stock started higher, along with the market. Note also how its ADX rose higher, along with the +DI (dotted line). Once in, we immediately placed a stop order at $50.65. SEPR pulled back in an orderly fashion for the first reversal period (9:50–10:10 a.m.). Then, the biotech/drug manufacturer went ballistic. We went along for the ride, yanking our stop higher.

Now, look at Figure 12–9. I think you'll find it helpful to see a fifteen-minute chart of Sepracor, Inc. (SEPR) that defines the entry window. As you can see, the window coincides with support-and-resistance levels developed the day before our entry day. It also defines a logical price progression into our trade day.

Now we'll zoom in for a close-up of the trade.

Figure 12–10 displays a five-minute chart of SEPR of our entry day, September 13, up to 12:30 p.m., where we jumped in. The price "exploded," as we predicted, but it held off long enough for us to enter early on.

Right out of the gate, the NQs, the NASDAQ-100 E-mini futures, sped higher. The ES, or S&P 500 E-mini futures, got a slower start, but within minutes, they also soared. For those who watch the VIX and VXN, they slid down right out of the open—a bullish sign for contrarian indicators.

The DRG faltered, but soon found its legs and sailed up. The BTK (the Biotech Index) moved up with the NASDAQ futures. (Much of the time, the BTK will follow the NASDAQ futures.)

SEPR opened at $50.88, $0.16 higher than Friday's close, and within our entry window. (Remember, $0.40 or higher gap open negates the current strategy.)

During the first five-minute candle, the stock quickly dips down to fill the gap. Good. Got that over with! As market internals move higher, and SEPR joins in, we buy five hundred shares on the second five-minute candle, at $50.89. We immediately place our initial protective stop at $50.65, $0.10 under the first five-minute low. If SEPR reverses and dives below the low of the day established so far, we don't want it. We'll raise the stop as (if) the stock trends higher.

As you can see, SEPR retraced, in an orderly fashion, through the first reversal period. Then, at 10:05, the drug maker shot vertical (long, white candle) to $51.54. We raised our stop to $51.30, targeting the midpoint of the candle.

> **Hot Tip:** Frequently, the midpoint of long, extended candles act as support or resistance, depending upon which side of it price is trading.

Now the stock is overextended on an intraday basis, and we know it has to come in, or retrace, soon. By 11:15 a.m. EST, it struggles to $51.97.

Consider: Round numbers act as resistance, and SEPR is pushing $52. Timewise, we're moving into the midday doldrums. By 11:20 a.m., the ADX rolls over and the +DI does, as well.

Taking the "sell when you *want to*, not when you *have to*" tack, we sold at

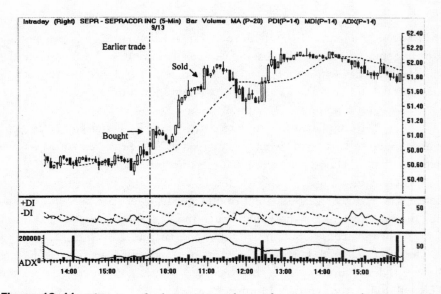

Figure 12–11. This is a final 5-minute chart of our target stock Sepracor, Inc. (SEPR). The stock rose in a quick, unexpected midday rally (no trade taken), then drifted sideways into the close.

11:25 a.m. at $51.80. If SEPR's uptrend resumes after lunch, maybe we'll enter another trade. For now, though, we're satisfied with the $455 profit (without commissions).

Figure 12–11 displays SEPR's price action for the remainder of the day.

The stock moved higher in a surprise midday rally. Since I rarely open trades during the midday doldrums, and since the futures "slept" through the move, I didn't play it. SEPR drifted sideways to down for the remainder of the day, offering no more setups.

The Moving Average Hot Blanket—The Day Trade

For the final day trade setup, we'll move to the short swing trade setup, the "Moving Average Hot, Wet Blanket." This shorting setup offers great prospects for day trades.

> **Hot Tip:** Although this point seems obvious, in the heat of battle, many traders ignore it: buy as your target stock bounces off support, *not* after the stock has soared into the stratosphere. Sell short when your stock "hits its head" on a resistance ceiling and begins to fall, *not* after the stock has tumbled in a cliff fall.

To locate this setup in chapter 10, we looked for a stock in a downtrend, with the fifty-day and twenty-day MAs (the 50-day will ride above the 20-day MA) creating pressure from above the price pattern. Optimally, look for a stock that's consolidated into—or rallied into—moving average, trend line, or price resistance. You want to enter intraday trade(s) when the stock crumbles under the resistance and starts to tumble.

Figure 12–12 shows a daily chart of Fifth Third Bancorp (FITB). The stock has scowled, slouched, and generally slogged south for the past six months.

The most recent week of price action shows it trying to get up one more time, like a jelly-kneed prize fighter struggling to his feet. "C'mon," he mumbles, "hit me again."

We won't refuse the invitation. ☺

FITB recently sprung off its August lows, only to smack up against the fifty-day MA (August 27), which held it down. It tried again to climb above the moving average on the chart's most recent day, September 7, without success. That signals more possible downside for the bank stock.

September 7 price action: FITB opened at $49.53, made a high of $53.10, a low of $49.22, and closed at $49.33.

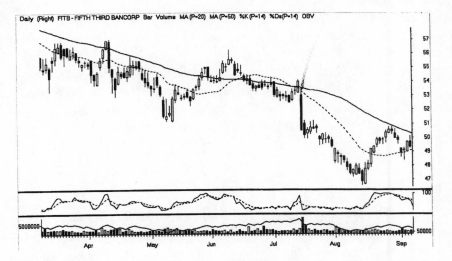

Figure 12–12. This daily chart of Fifth Third Bancorp (FITB) shows the bank stock slipping in a months-long downtrend. The fresh gap to the downside in late August suggests more weakness. Plus, poor FITB can't seem to rally over its 50-day MA. The most recent day, September 7, closed with an upper shadow, which tells us sellers bullied the stock down. The stochastics indicator hooks down, as does the OBV. On September 8, if FITB drops below its 20-day MA, and if market internals agree, we may discover an intraday short opportunity.

> **Hot Tip: Calculate your entry window to range between $0.40 and $0.70, depending on the price and volatility of your stock. Naturally, a $10 stock would have a narrower window than an $80 stock. A stock with an average daily range of a point will probably open with less fanfare than a volatile, stock that trades in a 3-point daily range.**

Tomorrow, September 8, our objective is for FITB to slice below its twenty-day MA, which sits at $49.09.

Our entry window: we'll sell short between $49.40 and $48.95. (Just below the September 7 open). Once in, we'll set our initial protective stop no higher than $49.65. The next minor support area on the daily chart lies at $48.30, then $46.50. For a day trade, we have room to boogie.

Figure 12–13 displays a fifteen-minute chart of FITB, with the entry window and subsequent price action.

Figure 12–14 shows a five-minute chart of FITB. It gives the details of our trade, our entry, shares addition and motivating logic, and the exit. Know that the BKX, the bank index, also trended down on the day, as did the ES. (Even though FITB is listed on the NASDAQ Stock Exchange, banks generally follow the direction of the S&P 500 futures.)

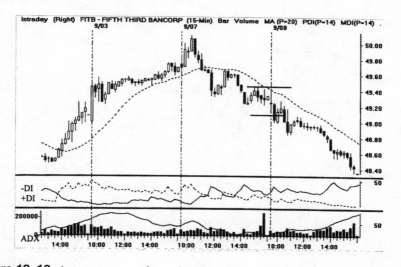

Figure 12–13. As you can see from this 25-minute chart of our target stock, Fifth Third Bancorp (FITB), our entry window—between $49.40 and $48.95—defined the price parameters in which we want the beleaguered bank stock to open on our entry day, September 8. FITB did, in fact, open within our boundaries and provided us with a nice entry and subsequent trade. If the stock opened higher or lower, though, we would have looked elsewhere.

The bank stock progressed in a clear downtrend, making our trading decisions fairly easy. Our profit on this trade: $437, without commissions.

> **Hot Tip: Watching a Level II screen of your open position can cause a syndrome known as "Level II Fakeout." If the stock makes a sudden move on the screen, even though it doesn't hit your stop, it can produce enough panicky feelings to make you exit your trade—often unnecessarily!**

Again, the trades shown in this chapter play out in profitable fashion. As you know, that doesn't happen 100 percent, or even 80 percent of the time.

The trick to making consistent profit: Limit your losses and exit quickly when a trade goes against you. If the trade plays out to your advantage, raise (longs) or lower (shorts) your stop-loss to just under advancing support areas (longs), or just above progressing resistance areas (shorts). Well-thought-out stops help your trade escape market "noise," while keeping your strategy low-risk. They help you relax, so you don't jump out with every intraday "hiccup."

I also used conservative share size with these trades. Many of you will play with bigger lots—just make sure your lot sizes correlate with your experience level and account equity.

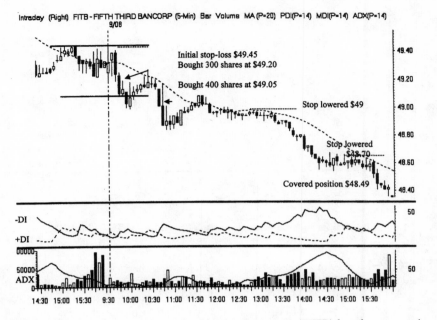

Intraday (Right) FITB - FIFTH THIRD BANCORP (5-Min) Bar Volume MA (P=20) PDI(P=14) MDI(P=14) ADX(P=14)

Figure 12–14. This 5-minute chart of Fifth Third Bancorp (FITB) has the entry window still intact. It also displays the trading day's entire progression. FITB stock opened at $49.25, then pushed higher to $49.41. Still, that's not higher than the previous day's consolidation into the close, so we'll keep watching. The second 5-minute candle treaded water. The third candle developed into a complete reversal bar (long black candle). That's better. Now, an entry looks promising. As the fourth candle drops below the reversal bar, we sell short 300 shares of FITB at $49.20. We'll add to the position when (if) it drops below its 20-day MA on the daily chart, at $49.09. Until then, we're still cautious. We place an initial stop-loss order at $49.45, just above the reversal candle's high. FITB rallies, and halts under resistance. When it falls again, this time cutting through the $49.09 watch-point (20-day MA), at 14:40 p.m., we add 400 shares to our position at $49.05. The stop-loss is lowered to $49.27. FITB continues to fall, and we let the trade unfold throughout the day. Twice we lower the stop to just above consolidation highs, to $49, and again to $48.70. We covered our position one-half hour before the market's close, at $48.49.

In chapter 13, we'll explore the worlds of E-mini futures and the cash forex market. Most aspects of technical analysis discussed already apply nicely to these markets, so their application will be easy to understand.

Before you move on to that chapter, though, read through the questions and answers that follow. It will help you organize the material in this text and give you added information.

Quiz

Questions

1. When you trade in the short-term, time equals _____.

2. Name market internals that point to intraday market direction, and so can keep you on the profitable side of your day trades.

3. Your neighbor Fred, the "trader," says it's okay to grab a cup of coffee, dive head first into your desk chair, flip on your computer and trading platform, then assess a stock chart and enter a trade. After all, speed is a hallmark of trading. Is Fred right?

4. Define Level I, Level II, and Level III quotes.

5. Why do swing-trading setups offer profitable day-trading opportunities?

6. The "Double Got 'Em" setup can produce explosive price action because _____.

7. Name one criterion for the "Moving Average Leapfrog" setup.

8. When you enter an intraday trade, in order not to get caught in a thinly traded stock, what guideline do you use for average daily volume?

9. True or false?: Your entry window should be calculated to follow the natural price progression.

10. The "Stealthy Sidewinder" takes advantage of a possible price explosion to the upside resulting from a horizontal _____ pattern.

11. Give one criterion for the "Moving Average Hot, Wet blanket" setup.

Answers

1. When you trade in the short term, time equals risk.

2. Intraday market internals include: E-mini S&P 500 (ES) and NASDAQ 100 (NQ) stock index futures, the NYSE and/or NASDAQ Stock Exchange TICK and TRIN, and the CBOE VIX and/or VXN. You may also want to watch the industry group or sector index that corresponds to your stock.

3. Fred has gone bonkers!

4. Level I quotes represent the best bid and offer *at that moment*. Level II quotes are shown on NASDAQ Level II screens, and display not only the best bid and offer (or ask) at the moment, but also a list of market participants who want to sell (bid) or buy (offer, or ask) a stock at a given moment, at different levels of prices. Level III quotes are available only to market makers, specialists, and other market professionals. These quotes relay comprehensive price information, including order flow.

5. Swing-trading setups offer profitable day-trading opportunities because they pinpoint where breakouts and breakdowns may occur, which can result in powerful momentum and price swings.

6. The "Double Got 'Em" setup can produce explosive price action because if price traveling in a downtrend retests a prior low, and holds the low, it can result in a short squeeze. That makes price shoot higher—fast!

7. "Moving Average Leapfrog" criterion: After a move up, price pulls back, in an orderly fashion, to its 20-day and 50-day moving averages.

8. When you enter an intraday trade, look for stocks that trade an average daily volume of 800,000 to 1 million shares, or more.

9. True. Your entry window should be calculated to follow the natural price progression. You can figure that by using the previous day's support-and-resistance levels.

10. The "Stealthy Sidewinder" takes advantage of a possible price explosion to the upside resulting from a horizontal *consolidation* pattern.

11. One criterion for the "Moving Average Hot, Wet Blanket" setup: It forms in a downtrend, with the 50-day and 20-day MAs slanting down from above the price pattern.

CENTER POINT

Commit to Success!

The secret of making something work in your life, is first of all, the deep desire to make it work; then the faith to make it work; then to hold a clear, definite vision in your consciousness and see it working out step-by-step, without one thought of doubt or disbelief.

—Eileen Caddy

When you commit to an idea, goal, or plan, you create a picture of it in your mind and thus form the event before it happens. Then, if you hold that picture as a reality, and *commit* to achieving your goal, your automatic response locks in that image and creates it, no matter what obstacles lie in your path.

First form a mental image of the goal, or change you want to create in your life. Be sure to formulate a precise picture. Cloudy images create cloudy futures. You can even design a physical picture of your desired state or object, such as a drawing or photograph of the house you've dreamed of owning, or image of the personal goal you wish to achieve.

Make sure your goal or desired change is reality-based and achievable. And make sure it will enrich your life, as well as the lives of those around you.

Once you establish a concise vision, lock in the image by holding it in the forefront of your mind and your actions.

Now—here's the important part—commit to your objective with all your energy, and all your heart. Believe it will happen, *know it will happen,* fervently and with passion. Commit to the process and to the outcome.

When you commit, you will be surprised at the people, situations, and opportunities that appear in your path.

To me, these unexpected arrivals are "the fun part" of tackling a target. When my commitment to a project runs deep and strong, I'm *always* amazed at the "gift" situations that arrive on my doorstep. It's as though my mental picture and applied energy act as magnets to draw people and circumstances I need into my life.

Remember, commitment is the necessary ingredient for creating success. It's the driving force behind your energy and the secret that fuels victory!

Introduction to E-mini Stock Index Futures
and
Cash Forex Markets

To learn that a man can make foolish plays for no reason whatever was a
valuable lesson to me.

—Jessie Livermore.

Are you pooped from keeping track of a gaggle of unruly stocks? Would you enjoy a change of pace from equities trading?

In this chapter, we'll talk about two alternative trading products rapidly gaining popularity in the new stock market: E-mini stock index futures and the cash forex markets.

Mini versions of the stock index futures popped onto the trading scene in 1997, and have since skyrocketed in popularity.

Spot (cash) currency trading has been around for many years. Until recently, however, FX or forex (foreign exchange) trading remained the domain of banks, hedge funds, and institutional traders. Now retail forex brokers are providing individual traders, like you and me, easy access to the currency markets.

First, let's head into the futures markets.

Futures Markets—What They Are, When They Emerged

A futures contract is a binding agreement that takes place today, with the legal obligation to fulfill the contract by a later, specified date. Most contracts are offset, or exited, before the actual settlement date.

Unlike stocks, which can be traded through a number of market sources, futures are traded only on the exchange that offers the product. Exchanges are both pit and electronic.

For example, the Chicago Mercantile Exchange (CME), located at 30 Wacker Street in Chicago, houses actual "pits." In these circular arenas, traders use the open outcry method (think "live auction with hand signals and shouting") to trade CME futures products. Top contracts traded include meats and livestock, interest rates, and stock indices, such as the standard, or full-size, S&P 500 futures contract and the standard NASDAQ 100 futures contract.

The CME also offers around-the-clock electronic trading through its GLOBEX platform. Products traded include E-mini futures and currency futures.

> **Hot Tip:** With equities, a set number of shares for each company are offered to trade. With futures, there is no limit as to the numbers of contracts that exist.

Futures Markets—A Quick Time Line and Who's Who

Futures markets actually emerged thousands of years ago, when rice traders in Japan bought and sold coupons for silos of rice. (In an earlier chapter, we mentioned one of those traders, the legendary So-kyu Honma. His trading techniques led to candlestick charting technology.)

Later, in the Middle Ages, traders at fairs bartered with forward agreements for wool and wheat.

1848. The Chicago Board of Trade (CBOT) opened to fill the needs of U.S. grain farmers and their fluctuating wheat crops. The exchange offered forward contracts for the wheat and grain markets.

1898. The Chicago Butter and Egg Board was founded. In 1919, the board became the Chicago Mercantile Exchange, with trading focused on a variety of agricultural products.

1972. The CME launched the first financial futures in foreign currencies. This innovation provided the financial community with exciting tools for risk management—virtually the same tools used for decades by agricultural businesses.

> **Hot Tip:** Less than 1 percent of all futures trades result in the delivery of a physical commodity.

1974. The Commodities Futures Trading Commission Act established the Commodities Futures Trading Commission (CFTC) to regulate the exchanges. The agency ensured open and effective operation of the futures markets.

1982. The CME presented the first successful stock index futures contract, using the Standard & Poor's 500 as the underlying index.

1997. In September, the CME launched the first "E-mini" contract, the S&P 500 futures. And for good reason. By that time, the notional value (underlying, or face value) of the "big" or standard S&P 500 futures contract had soared to $400,000. A 1 percent move in the contract equaled $4,000! That's a mammoth move in comparison to commodities futures, such as soybeans, live cattle, or crude oil futures contracts. Institutional investors, who took on large lot sizes, found it hard to dispose of the cumbersome product. Plus, the standard contract's margin requirements (we'll discuss margin requirements in a moment) made it inaccessible to individual traders. The new E-mini version became an instant hit.

1999. In June, the CME released the E-mini version of the standard NAS-DAQ 100 futures contract.

2002. In April, the CBOT introduced the mini-sized Dow futures, using the standard Dow Jones of futures contract as the underlying instrument.

At the present time, futures contracts are separated into broad categories: agricultural, food and fiber, metals, energy, and financial. "New kids on the block" include insurance and weather futures.

The following table shows major U.S. futures exchanges, Web sites, and primary products traded.

U.S. Futures Exchanges and Products

Chicago Mercantile Exchange (CME)	*cme.com*	Stock indices, currencies, interest rates, meats/livestock
Chicago Board of Trade (CBOT)	*cbot.com*	Interest rates, stock indices, grains
New York Mercantile Exchange (NYMEX)	*nymex.com*	Energy and metals
New York Board of Trade (NYBOT)	*nybot.com*	Food, currencies, stock indices, and interest rates
Kansas City Board of Trade (KCBOT)	*kcbt.com*	Grains, stock indices
Minneapolis Grain Exchange (MGEX)	*mgex.com*	Grains
One Chicago (joint venture of CBOE, CBOT, and CME)	*onechicago.com*	Single-stock futures

What Purpose Do Futures Markets Serve?

We know that the futures exchanges and their forward products originally cropped up to serve farmers. Beyond that, though, futures markets serve two crucial roles necessary to the survival of global commerce.

First, the futures markets provide the vital function known as "price discovery." The exchanges represent central market forums, or "auctions," where buyers and sellers congregate to identify, or "discover," prices for that exchange's designated products. The prices discovered are then quoted and used in business transactions around the globe.

Second, the futures markets serve as a conduit for the reassignment of risk. Exchanges offer traders the opportunity to offset positions (read: risk) to parties who are willing to accept them in order to seek future reward.

E-minis—What They Are, How Their Symbols Work

E-minis ("E" means electronic.) are small versions of standard index futures contracts. When you trade these products, you trade the future trend, or direction, of their underlying equity indexes.

You've probably noticed that stock index futures trade at a discount, or premium, to their underlying cash indexes. The difference in points is called "basis" points.

The cash price—futures price = basis. Basis is determined by "cost of carry." "Cost of carry" refers to three cost applications:

- The cost of purchasing the commodity now

- The cost of financing, or the interest rate you pay, on the purchase

- The cost of storing it until the contract matures

As each contract month approaches, the basis points will narrow. When the contract expires, the basis closes at the cash index price.

In this chapter, we'll talk about three mini stock index futures: the mini-sized Dow, the E-mini S&P 500, and the E-mini NASDAQ 100. Additional mini contracts to explore: the E-mini Russell 2000 and the E-mini S&P MidCap 400, both traded on the CME.

Just as with stocks, we use symbols to designate the contracts. As mentioned in previous chapters, mini-sized Dow root symbol is YM. The E-mini S&P 500 root symbol is ES. The NASDAQ 100 root symbol is NQ.

While the root symbol always remains the same, stock index futures change the final part of their symbol according to contract expiration dates and year.

Contract months for the E-minis are March, June, September, and December. Corresponding symbols are:

- March—H

- June—M

- September—U
- December—Z

If you trade the mini-sized Dow in November 2005, the root symbol is YM. The contract month is December 2005. (December is the front month for the second half of September, October, November, and the weeks leading up to contract expiration in December.)

	Root Symbol	Contract or Front Month	Year
That forms the symbol:	YM	Z	05 or 5
Or: YMZ(0)5			

If you trade the E-mini S&P 500 in January 2006, the root symbol is ES. The contract month is March 2006.

	Root Symbol	Contract or Front Month	Year
That forms the symbol:	ES	H	06 or 6
Or: ESH(0)6			

If you target the E-mini NASDAQ 100 in July 2006, use the root symbol NQ. The contract month is September 2006.

	Root Symbol	Contract or Front Month	Year
That forms the symbol:	NQ	U	06 or 6
Or: NQU(0)6			

Your trading software may require additional keystrokes to access futures contract quotes. Contact your broker for the exact symbols needed.

E-mini Trading Objectives

As individual traders, we use financial futures for two main objectives—speculation and hedging. We speculate when we buy and sell E-minis to profit from the market's rise and fall. We hedge by trading mini stock index futures to protect open equity positions from loss.

Here are three hedging examples:

- Say you are long equities that correlate to the S&P 500 index. Or maybe you hold an open long position in the SPY. Now, you expect the broader market to pull back during the next trading session. If your portfolio value is $50,000, you sell short one E-mini S&P 500 futures contract to hedge your account. (As of current market prices, the contract size of one E-mini S&P contract is $55,000.)

> **Hot Tip: Since E-minis are highly leveraged products, many traders don't hold them overnight.**

- Are you holding shares short in a high-tech stock, or are you short the QQQQ? Imagine you are, and the position totals $25,000. You expect the NASDAQ to rally briefly on good news, perhaps an economic number or positive earnings report. You day-trade long one NASDAQ 100 E-mini contract to protect your holdings from loss. (As of current market prices, the contract size of one E-mini S&P contract is $28,000.)

- Finally, perhaps you're holding positions in value stocks that reside on the Dow Jones Industrial Index, such as General Electric (GE), Johnson & Johnson (JNJ), or Minnesota Mining & Manufacturing (MMM). Or maybe you're holding long a position in the DIA. Let's also agree the account worth totals $48,000. If you believe value stocks will endure a correction, you can hedge your account by selling short one mini-sized Dow futures contract. (At current market prices, the value of one mini-sized Dow contract equals about $50,000.)

When you hedge with E-minis, remember to correlate the index futures with the type of equities you seek to protect. Then, match the value of the index futures contract to the total value of your portfolio.

Benefits and Bummers of Trading Stock Index Futures

E-mini stock index futures have become trendy trading vehicles. The following lists the benefits of trading these whizzy contracts.

Leverage. When you trade futures, you control a sizeable amount of a market with a small amount of money. Far from the 50 percent required with a standard equities margin account (25 percent for pattern day traders), futures exchanges require you to put up a performance bond that represents a small percentage—usually less than 10 percent—of the contract's actual value. (We'll discuss performance bonds shortly.)

Single Source of Liquidity. Each mini stock index futures contract is traded *only* on the exchange that sponsors it. That means all orders pool in a central exchange. Everybody's in line on an equal basis, so you have equal footing with the institutions.

Flexibility. Say the stock market is heading higher (or sliding lower), and you haven't the time to research stocks. E-mini contracts have the same advantage as ETFs, meaning you can buy or sell an entire index in one quick trade. An added advantage to trading stock index futures: you can buy or sell an index with E-minis for far less money than it takes to buy an index ETF.

Around-the-Clock Trading. Most stock index futures trade from Sunday afternoon through Friday afternoon, with the exception of brief, scheduled maintenance breaks.

No Uptick Rule. The uptick rule doesn't exist in futures trading. Assuming you're trading a highly liquid contract, you buy or sell short with equal ease.

Tax Advantages. When you day-, swing-, or position-trade equities, you pay short-term capital gains taxes on all profits. When you trade stock index futures, you pay long-term capital gains taxes on 60 percent of your profits, and short-term capital gains taxes on 40 percent of your profits.

That's the good news. But before you hock your watch to buy E-minis, let's look at the challenges to trading stock index futures.

Big Leverage, Big Losses. The leverage that produces large percentage gains in futures trading can also create large losses. This means if your position moves against you when you are trading on minimum margin (margin requirements explanation follows), you can find yourself with *a loss greater than the equity in your account.* And yes, your unhappy broker *can* chase you down for the difference in funds.

Low Liquidity. Another consideration: As with stocks and ETFs, liquidity can be an issue when trading E-minis. While the most popular E-minis offer high liquidity that contributes to ease of execution, less trendy contracts many trade with low volume that results in wider spreads and more frequent slippage.

> **Hot Tip:** When you see time of day of day stated in conjunction with stock index futures trading, it's usually in Central Standard Time, or CST. That's because the primary financial futures exchanges, such as the CME and CBOT, are located in Chicago.

Rollovers. When you invest in equities, you can shovel them into an account and leave them there until your kids badger you for the money—no maintenance required. When you hold open futures contracts, they expire. It's your job to "roll" your open positions forward to the next contract month by closing them, then reopening them in the new contract month.

Finally, some folks insist that trading futures "forces" people to become good traders. They mean a trading plan is imperative for each trade, and "live" stops are a way of life. While I agree that plans and stops form the backbone of any profitable trade, I *don't* agree that trading E-minis "forces" good trading habits.

At the risk of sounding like your mom: please paper-trade index futures *before* you jump in. Some of the contracts move *very* fast.

Finally, when trading mini index futures, you must be focused, disciplined, and willing to switch sides fast. If those traits seem alien to you, or cause your nose to wrinkle, you'll be happier trading slower-moving vehicles.

Your Futures Trading Account

To open an account to trades futures, you'll locate a Series 3 licensed commodities brokerage firm.

When it comes to trading services, I prefer a word-of-mouth recommendation from good trading friends. If you can't find leads for a first-class broker, go to the National Futures Association's Web *site: nfa.futures.org.* The CME also lists brokers at *www.cme.com*, under "Find a Broker."

The brokerage firm you choose will ask you to sign a long list of forms. Included will be a risk-disclosure statement that confirms you understand the high-risk exposure of trading futures. You'll also sign a performance bond agreement that states you'll cover any losses incurred while trading.

Of course, you'll also fund the account with cash or securities. Part of your deposit will be assigned to an initial performance bond. This acts as an initial margin requirement, and you must deposit a set amount for each contract you intend to trade.

The amount required varies with the type of contract traded, and with the current volatility of the market. The more volatile the markets, the more margin is required to trade futures contracts.

Once you begin trading, if you hold a contract overnight, you'll have to sustain your account equity to meet maintenance margin requirements for that contract.

The futures exchanges designate minimum margin levels that must be met. Keep in mind that your broker's requirements may be higher than those of the exchanges.

Here's an example of how margin works: Say you have $10,000 equity in your account. At present, the *initial margin* requirement for one E-mini S&P contract is $4,000. If you wanted to trade the E-mini, you could buy or sell two contracts. (Margin requirement of $4,000 × 2 contracts = $8,000.)

The margin *maintenance* requirement is $3,200. That means, if you held those two contracts overnight, and they each lost more than $800 ($4,000 minus $3,200) the next morning you would have to deposit $1,600 (2 contracts × $800) into your account to bring your balance back to initial requirement levels.

When you open a futures trading account—as with *any* trading account—please fund it with money you can afford to lose. As well, please provide yourself with an adequate cushion, to weather losses. I suggest you maintain at least twice the margin requirement needed for every contract.

After all, it makes no sense to plunk $8,000 into a futures account . . . max it out on two ES contracts . . . hold them for a loss . . . and then answer the phone to hear, "Ahem, this is your broker. You have a margin call. Wire more funds NOW!"

Bottom line: If you have $10,000 with which to fund a futures account, keep your trading to one ES contract until you gain more experience. (Presently, the mini-sized Dow and NQ require smaller margin minimums than the ES, although that may change.)

Spotlight on the Mini-sized Dow

The mini-sized Dow futures contract—we call it the "d-mini"—trades on the Chicago Board of Trade (CBOT). The underlying index is the Dow Jones Industrial Average.

The following table lists the contract's specifications:

Mini-sized Dow Futures Contract Specifications

Ticker symbol	YM
Multiplier	$5
Minimum tick	One index point, which equals $5 per contract
Trading hours (Central Time)	Sunday afternoon through Friday afternoon, 7:15 a.m.–4:00 p.m. CST

Contract months with symbol	March (H), June (M), September (U), December (Z)
Last day of trading each contract month	Third Friday of contract month

Here's an explanation of items in the table not previously discussed:

The *multiplier* is the dollar amount by which you multiply the index futures level to determine the contract size, or value.

For example, let's say the standard Dow futures contract is trading at 10,000. To arrive at the mini-sized Dow contract size, multiply 10,000 by $5. That equals $50,000, or the actual value of a single contract.

To trade one contract, the minimum margin requirement (performance bond) can total less than 10 percent of the contract size—or less than $5,000. That means you control $50,000 with $5,000. Makes your palms damp, doesn't it? ☺

The *minimum tick* relates to the contract's minimum price fluctuation. The minimum tick in the mini-sized Dow equals one point. So, if you own one contract in the "d-mini," and the contract moves up from 10,000 to 10,001, you've profited $5.

While that doesn't sound like much, keep in mind that the Dow often experiences a daily trading range of a hundred points, or more.

Day-trading the Mini-sized Dow Futures (YM)

When trading the YM on an intraday basis, you'll first conduct your pre-market analysis, then develop a directional bias (up or down) for the day. Even if you move away from your original bias during the trading session, you'll start with an initial plan.

> **Hot Tip: If you start the day with a positive directional bias, it means your research indicated the index you are trading will move higher. That doesn't stop you from fading the gap, or shorting the opening gap to the upside (with appropriate signals). Still, your positive bias compels you to cover your short position as, or before, the gap fills.**

When you're trading the YMs, it's a good idea to keep a market minder of the Dow equities on your screen. Because of the number of component stocks in each index, it's obviously easiest to do with the thirty Dow stocks, as opposed to the five hundred component stocks that comprise the ES, or the one hundred component stocks that form the NQ.

You may want to watch the NYSE TICK and TRIN for market direction and overbought/oversold signals. You may also keep an eye on an intraday chart of the VIX for the same indications. (Chapter 4 explains these indicators.)

At the moment, the YM makes a good tool for fading, or trading against, opening gaps.

Fading the gap of single stocks can produce a high-risk trade. Some traders insist that all gaps close. And, while that may be true, an individual equity can take days, months, or even longer to fill a price gap.

The YM, however, with its thirty "moving parts," offers good odds that an opening gap will fill in short order. Why? Because only some—not all—of the equities in the index will agree with an opening move several levels higher or lower.

Again, compare the YM's focused collection of stocks to the E-mail S&P 500's hefty list of stocks, and the E-mini NASDAQ 100's cumbersome group of techs. With the YM's limited components, its gaps are many times cleaner and more precise. This is especially true when gaps to the upside relate to frothy economic news.

There's a trick to fading gaps: A "professional opening," in which the market opens significantly higher in a breakaway gap, can continue its momentum in the direction of the gap for huge point spreads. Please do *not* fade those moves.

How do you know whether the opening gap is ripe for fading? One technique: Assess the pre-market volume of the YM and price/volume activity of the generals. If pre-market volume for leaders like INTC, KLAC, NVLS, and XLNX is comparatively strong, then demand is strong, and a gap up may have the momentum to continue. If the generals show weak pre-market volume, then a gap to the upside can form a bull trap, which can deliver tasty profits.

Caveat: *A stock or stock index can gap down on weak volume and keep on falling.* Just because a stock gaps down on lukewarm volume, please don't fade (buy) it. You'll need to use other market internals aside from volume to guide a fading strategy.

Figure 13–1 shows a daily chart of the mini-sized Dow. The index has soared in a steep, short-term uptrend since its August lows. Recent price activity shows the index retracting a portion of its prior move up, and moving nicely to price and moving average support. (Think " 'Moving Average Leapfrog' setup.")

The second-to-last trading day formed an "inside day," with the high and low contained in the previous day's range (long, black candle.) Since inside days ultimately cause pressure (foot on garden hose) to build, we'll look for the next day, September 17, to trade in an expanded range. Keep in mind that, as traders, we're constantly looking for volume and volatility.

September 17 did, in fact, gain momentum from the inside day. The YM shot up and moved down in an eighty-three-point range.

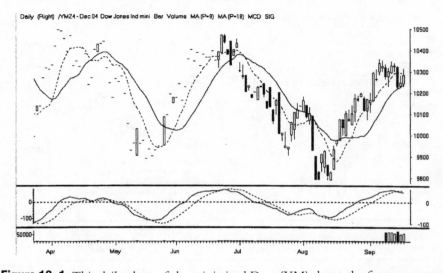

Daily (Right) /YMZ4 - Dec 04 Dow Jones Ind mini Bar Volume MA (P=9) MA (P=18) MCD SIG

Figure 13–1. This daily chart of the mini-sized Dow (YM) shows the futures contract rising from its August lows of 9,790 and forming a short-term uptrend. (The candles are more distinctive on the chart's most recent weeks, as the contract symbol just rolled from September to December, making December the front, or contract, month). The 9-day MA and 18-day MA work well with stock index futures, and you'll see them on this chart; the dotted line forms the 9-day MA, and the solid line forms the 18-day MA. The MACD is plotted on the middle scale. As you can see, a moving average crossover during the third week of August coincided with the MACD's move over the zero line. With the market in an uptrend, you'll see more positive days since the crossover than negative ones. Now, look at the second most recent day of the chart, September 16. It's an "inside day." That means the high and low of the day were contained in the prior wider range candle (long black candle.) Of course, the inside day is also a spinning top. After an inside day, the YMs can gather momentum and so create a wider range day that creates profitable trading opportunities.

Figure 13–2 shows a five-minute chart of September 17, which we'll use for our trading day example.

An opening twenty-four-point gap to the upside gave us a low-risk, quick-profit fading vehicle. Once the gap filled, the index reversed, then offered a profitable long opportunity by soaring more than sixty points.

Although the d-mini screeched south after the spike up, most of the move took place during noon–2 p.m. We followed our discipline: no trading during the "chop period," or lunchtime doldrums.

During the afternoon session, the YM meandered sideways. We stayed on the sidelines and protected earlier gains.

> **Hot Tip:** If the gap open does not equal at least ten Dow points, avoid a fade trade. Momentum is not clear-cut enough to warrant the risk.

Intraday (Right) /YMZ4 - Dec 04 Dow Jones Ind mini (5-Min) Bar Volume MA (P-18) PDI(P-14) MDI(P-14) ADX(P-14) ...

Prior day's high of 10,281
Use as technical stop for
opening gap fade play. Toward
the end of our trading day's
session, the YM clings to that
prior high as support.

The 24-point gap up on lukewarm volume
fills quickly. Play: short YM soon after open.
Cover just before index fills gap at
approximately 10:20 a.m. (Arrows show
entry/exit.) As price fills the gap, side-by-side
hammers predict a reversal to the upside!

+DI (dotted),
-DI

2000 ADX

Figure 13–2. This 5-minute chart of the mini-sized Dow futures (YM) plots the 9-period MA and 18-period MA, with the +DI (dotted line) and −DI in the middle panel, and the ADX over the volume spikes. As September 16 was an inside day, we expected a possible wider range day from September 17—and we got it. The YM gapped higher. You could have faded this 24-point gap, shorting the YM after it smacked up and into resistance from the previous day's high of 10,281 (4th candle from the gap open). Your stop is just above the high, providing a good risk-reward ratio. The gap quickly filled for a quick profit. Note the three candles with long lower shadows at the pivot point, and right on the rising 18-period MA. That tells you to exit if you haven't already. Once the gap is filled, the +DI dips below the −DI for a few minutes, then breaks above the −DI. The ADX rises. You could buy at this point, then wait for the break above 10,281 to add to your position. At 10:55 a.m., the YMs become highly overextended, euphoric volume soars to climactic levels, and +DI hooks down. Sell now, if you haven't already.

Take a minute to look once again at the daily chart of the YM, Figure 13–1. Please understand that if our pre-market analysis and market internals showed the contract falling to the downside at the open, with the appropriate signals, we would sell it short. (The YM did, in fact, reverse right after our positive day, and subsequently fell to retrace a portion of its move up from August lows. If you noticed the MACD starting to roll over on Figure 13–1, it makes sense the index would correct.)

Spotlight on the E-mini S&P 500 Contract (ES)

The E-mini S&P 500 futures contract trades on the Chicago Mercantile Exchange. Its underlying index is the S&P 500 Index.

The following table lists the contract's specifications.

E-mini S&P 500 Contract Specifications

Ticker symbol	ES
Multiplier	$50
Minimum tick	0.25 index point, or $12.50 per contract
Trading hours (Central Time)	Sunday afternoon through Friday afternoon. Weekdays, 3:30 to 3:15 p.m. CST (5 p.m. open on Sunday)
Contract months with symbol	March (H), June (M), September (U), December (Z)
Last day of trading each contract month	Third Friday of contract month

As you can see, the multiplier for the ES is $50. Let's imagine the S&P 500 Index futures level is 1,200. To calculate the contract size, multiply 1,200 by $50; the contract value is $60,000.

The minimum tick for the ES is 0.25 index point. If you are long one ES contract, each time the index advances one-quarter of a point, or one tick, you earn $12.50. When the contract advances an entire point, you profit $50 (4 × $12.50). Of course, if you are short a contract, and the ES dives for a point, you would also profit $50.

> **Hot Tip:** Remember, during most trading sessions, the market only spends a few minutes trading at its highs and at its lows. Who gets caught buying the highs and selling the lows? The "dumb money" does.

Note: You've probably noticed that I've not mentioned performance bond or minimum margin requirements for the ES or the NQ. That's because dollar amounts for mini index futures (including the YM) change with market volatility. Check with your broker for initial and maintenance margin requirements.

Day-trading the E-mini S&P 500 (ES)

When you trade the ES, conduct your pre-market analysis and establish your directional bias.

Stay updated on economic reports about to be issued that influence the futures. The reports usually come out at 8:30 a.m. or 10:00 a.m. EST. Also remember—don't trade the news. Trade the market's *reaction* to the news!

> **Hot Tip:** When you trade the futures, you are trading *the* leading indicator. That means you have to find other sources to predict future price movement. Using fundamental analysis, you'll assess geopolitical events, economic reports, and earnings announcements. Applying technical analysis, you'll use such chart tools as Directional Indicators, traditional pivot-point analysis, and Fibonacci retracements.

As with the YM, you'll want to watch the NYSE TICK and TRIN, and perhaps the NASDAQ TICK and TRIN. You may also want to keep track of the VIX, and keep an eye on the put/call ratio. Remember that the higher the TRIN(s), the VIX, and the p/c ratio spike, the more volatility is coming into the markets.

Figure 13–3 shows a daily chart of the ES. The index pattern is similar to that of the YM, shown on Figure 13–1. It makes sense—most of the time the Dow Jones industrial index and the S&P 500 indices trend in comparable patterns.

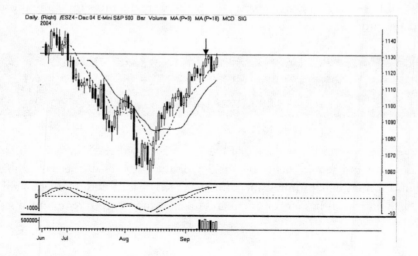

Figure 13–3. On this daily chart of the E-mini S&P 500 futures (ES), we see the contract in a short-term uptrend, similar to that of the YM. (The 9-day and 18-day MAs are plotted, along with the MACD.) Notice the fourth and fifth most recent days, September 13 and 14, (arrow); the ES runs into overhead price resistance from June. The next day, September 15, pre-market analysis indicates the contract will retrace. And it does (long, black candle), offering good intraday shorting opportunities.

This time, however, market conditions told us to establish a negative directional bias. The ES cooperated by gaping down on negative news, and continuing to fall.

Flash Lesson: Traditional Pivot-point Analysis

On the five-minute chart of the ES in Figure 13–4, you'll notice that I plotted pivot lines to indicate intraday support and resistance levels. Pivot analysis is a simple process. If your trading software includes this feature, it will do a lot of the work for you.

When you plot pivot lines, you project future price levels that can act as decision support tools for entry, risk management, and exit points.

The daily pivot line is drawn from the average of the high, low, and closing prices of the prior bar, or candle. Then you add to, or subtract from, that candle's reference points to come up with support and resistance levels for intraday trading.

Here's the formula:

- Daily pivot point (P) = High (H) + Low (L) + Close (C) divided by 3

- First resistance level (R1) = (P $\star$ 2) − L

- Second resistance level (R2) = P + (H − L)

- First support level (S1) = (P $\star$ 2) − H

- Second support level (S2) = P − (H − L)

Basic pivot point trading strategy:

- If price is falling and you are short, cover your position when price approaches and finds support at either of the two support levels, S1 or S2. Combine price action at support levels with other signals to consider opening a long position.

- If price is rising and you are long, sell your position when the index reaches finds resistance at R1 or R2. Combine with other signals for possible short position.

- Conversely, if the rising price is approaching R1 or R2, don't buy when price is just below these resistance levels. Wait for it to close above the lines.

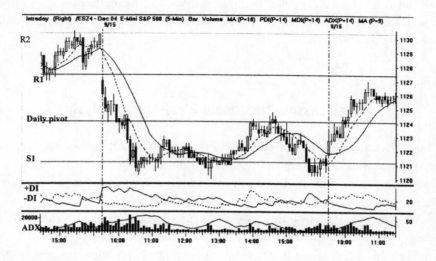

Figure 13–4. This 5-minute chart of the E-mini S&P 500 (ES) shows the contract gapping down 2.5 points from the prior day's (September 14) open, then continuing to fall. Moral of the story: don't fade an opening gap without checking the daily chart, and completing your pre-market analysis and directional bias. On this day, the ES showed a very negative open that was likely to continue—a great short opportunity. In addition to the 9- and 18-period MA, I've plotted daily pivot lines provided by Real Tick® software. (Pivots may be available on other chart services). They are the horizontal lines you see that act as decision support tools at intraday support-and-resistance levels. Trading software typically colors the lines for easy identification (red for the pivot line, green for S1, blue for R1, etc.). Because you cannot see colors, however, I've labeled the levels shown on this chart. The daily pivot represents the midpoint and is the strongest support/resistance line, depending on which side of it (higher or lower) price is trading. Note how the ES gapped down at the open to just under R1. It fell, then used the daily pivot line as support for three candles. Once the ES broke support under the daily line, traders shorted the ES, while keeping an eye on S1 (support level one). S1 is the first support level under the daily pivot. You can see how accurately it provided support for the ES, and warned shorts to cover intraday positions. (S2 doesn't show on this chart.) Most traders find pivot lines combined with moving averages and directional indicators work very well on 5-minute E-mini charts.

- When a falling price is sliding toward S1 or S2, don't sell short—the contract may bounce. Wait for it to fall (if it does) and close below the support lines.

As you can see, pivot point calculations represent resistance and support levels above and below the most recent closing price.

You can keep it simple and only use the five pivot lines (R2, R1, P, S1, S2) as intraday trading tools. You may want to add Fibonacci levels to the pivot lines. When Fibonacci lines and pivot lines appear in close proximity, it strengthens resistance/support zones. You can also add weekly and monthly pivot lines to the daily lines, and look for a confluence of signals at particular price zones.

This is a basic introduction to pivot point analysis. Please investigate the technique further before you use it to trade.

Now let's look at the NQ, or the E-mini NASDAQ 100 contract.

Spotlight on the E-Mini NASDAQ 100 Contract (NQ)

The E-mini NASDAQ 100 futures contract trades on the Chicago Mercantile Exchange. The NASDAQ 100 Index is its underlying index.

The following table lists the contract's specifications.

E-mini NASDAQ 100 Contract Specifications

Ticker symbol	NQ
Multiplier	$20
Minimum tick	.50 index points, which equals $10 per contract
Trading hours (Central Time)	Sunday afternoon (opens at 5 p.m. CST) through Friday afternoon, with 15-minute break between 3:15–3:30 p.m. CT
Contract months with symbol	March (H), June (M), September (U), December (Z)
Last day of trading each contract month	Third Friday of each month

The multiplier for the contract is $20. To calculate the contract size, multiply the NASDAQ 100 Index futures by $20. If the futures are trading at 1,400, multiply that by $20 to arrive at $28,000.

The minimum tick is 0.50, or one-half index point. Each tick is worth $10. That means if you're long the NQ at 1,400 and it moves to 1,400.50, you've earned $10 per contract. If it moves up a full point, to 1,401, you've gained $20 per contract.

Day-trading the E-mini NASDAQ 100

Now, let's look at a sample trading day. Figure 13–5 shows a daily chart of the NQ.

The NQ rose from its August lows of 1,308 to recent highs of 1,442.50 and 1,446.50. Our sample trading day is September 22, the long black candle and most recent day on the chart.

Figure 13–5. On this daily chart of the E-mini NASDAQ 100 (NQ), our sample trading day is the most recent day on the chart, the long black candle of September 22. (The 9-day and 18-day MAs are plotted, along with the MACD.) Note that the week before our trading day, the NQ ran up to a high of 1,442.50 (arrow). The contract pulled back, then made another run at the high, barely taking it out with a high of 1,446.50, on the day before our sample day. Note the MACD hinting at a rollover and the subsequent pullback.

Figure 13–6 displays a five-minute chart of September 22.

Here's another example of how fading the gap automatically, without thinking it through and watching additional market internals, could have resulted in a long trade stopped out quickly.

Trading mini stock index futures is an exciting occupation. Before you start trading them with real money, however, please consider attending a course or seminar on E-mini trading, offered by a reputable school.

Both the CME (*cme.com*) and the CBOT (*cbot.com*) Web sites have valuable information on the minis. You'll also want to paper-trade them for a few weeks, while you research different strategies.

Remember to set live stops with your broker as soon as you enter a trade. Keep an eye on market internals and listen to a financial news network. Avoid trading on tight margin.

Now, let's take a quick look at the popular cash currency markets.

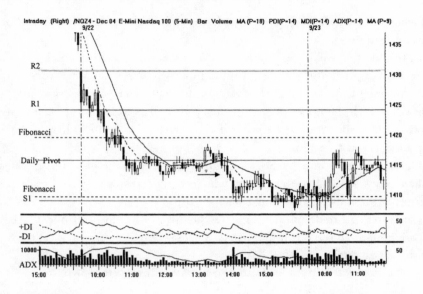

Figure 13–6. On this 5-minute chart of the E-mini NASDAQ 100 (NQ) and our sample trading day, September 22, you'll again see daily pivot lines, 9- and 18-period MAs. Note how the NQ fell at the stock market's open, to gap down exactly below R2. Once again, it's important to know when *not* to fade an opening gap—and this is one of those times. Traders shorted the NQ at the open, trading in the direction of the gap. The NQ hesitated at R1, and scalpers covered positions. Soon, the contract fell below R1 and slid to 1,419. The NQ consolidated for five candles, then dove to its daily pivot line. Short should cover, as the daily line contains potential strong support. The contract darted around the daily pivot through lunch, then, about 1:45 p.m., lost strength, creating an MA crossover to the downside. As volume came into play, scalpers could short the NQ (arrow), keeping an open eye on the support area at the 1,410 zone where S1 sat waiting with impending support. At 2 p.m., a volume spike plus a bounce off S1 signaled shorts to cover.

Introduction to Forex Markets

The stock market crash of 2000 sent equity traders scampering to find new trading products. That's one reason global currency markets, also known as the forex (foreign exchange) or FX, has enjoyed a newfound popularity among traders.

Just as online discount brokers mushroomed in the stock market's 1990s bull market, forex brokers now pepper the financial landscape and offer easy access to the former domain of banks, hedge funds, large commodity trading advisers (CTAs), and institutional traders.

You and I can now trade the Japanese yen, Australian dollar, British pound, or euro cash markets with the same ease and access as we buy one hundred shares of General Electric. We can participate in the cash forex market, futures, and options on futures.

In this section, we'll talk mainly about cash currency, or forex markets.

When you trade forex, the concept compares to a conventional stock trade. You exchange U.S. dollars in your account for a product—in this case, another currency—with the hopes of reacquiring your dollars in the future and profiting from the trade. You earn a profit if the exchange rate moves in your favor. If it doesn't, you take a loss.

Currencies trade in pairs. So, for example, if you buy the U.S. dollar, you simultaneously sell its base currency, which is the currency you're trading it "against." (We'll discuss base currencies shortly.)

Forex markets trade uniquely, in that there is no central exchange. Currencies are bought and sold through banks. That's why you hear Forex called "the interbank market."

To check out a Web site dedicated to forex trading, go to *dailyfx.com*.

Benefits to Trading Cash Forex

Trading currencies represents an asset class that's an entirely different animal from equity and stock index trading. Since factors that drive forex valuations vary from those that propel equities and equity indices, individual traders use forex less for hedging and more for speculation or portfolio diversification.

Here's a list of benefits you can expect from trading forex markets:

Diversification. As just mentioned, currencies "march to the beat of their own drummer." Trading forex markets diversifies a portfolio that contains stocks, commodities, and fixed-income instruments.

Liquidity. Forex is the world's most liquid market. When you trade currencies, you trade shoulder-to-shoulder with banks, investment funds, corporations, and other individual traders from around the globe. As well as offering depth of market, the bid/ask spreads are typically tighter than those of equities.

Low or No Commissions. Many cash forex brokers forgo commissions. Instead, they make their money on the bid/ask spread. That's why, in place of low commissions, you see forex broker-dealers advertising their low spreads.

> **Hot Tip: Global equities trading presently averages more than $25 billion per day, while forex markets total $1.5 trillion per day.**

Round-the-Clock Trading. The forex market trades seamlessly, twenty-four hours a day except for weekends. Trading begins at 2:00 p.m. EST each Sunday and follows the sun around the globe. The markets open for the week in Wellington, New Zealand (it's Monday, there). Sydney opens next, followed by Singapore. At 7:00 p.m. EST, the Tokyo market opens. London, the largest forex market, opens at 2:00 a.m., followed by New York (second largest), at 8:00 a.m. EST. Since market openings overlap, you can arrange a flexible trading schedule that suits your "night owl" or "early bird" lifestyle.

Leverage. If you can "shop 'til you drop" with leverage offered to you by e-mail margin requirements—wait until you see the leverage offered by cash forex brokers. You can easily find a broker who will give you 50:1, and many brokers offer 100:1. Yes, you read that correctly. That means for every $1,000 you trade, you could control from $50,000 to $100,000!

Before you sell your car to fund a forex account, know that it is extremely difficult to trade this market with only a few thousand dollars. If you don't have an extra cushion, a run of bad trades can wipe out your account.

And, just as with the hootin' an' hollerin' leverage offered by E-minis, there's the good news and bad news. Yes, you can enjoy big percentage gains with a small investment. If the markets turn against you, however, and your discipline slips, you can also suffer gut-wrenching losses.

Opening Your Account

Most forex brokerages require minimum opening deposits. Some offer "mini account" minimums of under a thousand dollars. That way, if you're new to the forex markets, you can sample forex trading and develop a disciplined approach, without losing great gobs of money.

Some brokerage firms also establish position limits relative to account equity. If you stray beyond your limits, you'll receive an automatic margin call. Plus the trading software provided by your broker will close out your positions.

Before you open an account, please check out your broker's registration and qualifications thoroughly. Forex brokers flew under the regulatory radar for years. Up until the early 2000s, dishonest brokers and "bucket shops" perpetrated the industry's reputation of the "Wild, Wild West."

The Commodity Futures Trading Commission (CFTC) and National Futures Association (FTA) cracked down on several fraudulent retail forex "bucket shops" that promised 10 percent or more ROI (return on investment) per month, then pocketed customer cash and disappeared. In addition, the

CFTC and FTA increased registration requirements and added substantial regulations.

Under existing rules, brokerage houses that deal in forex trading must be approved as a Futures Commission Merchant (FCM). That's also helped eliminate many fraudulent firms.

> **Hot Tip: The U.S. dollar and gold have an inverse relationship.**

How to Read Currency Quotes

Currencies trade in pairs. So when you see a currency denomination listed, you'll always see two symbols, each representing a different currency.

Here's a sample currency pair: USD/JPY. Translation: U.S. dollar/Japanese yen.

The first currency symbol—we'll call it "currency one"—is the *base currency*. It will always have a value of one. In the above example, the U.S. dollar represents the base currency.

The second currency symbol, or "currency two," is the *quote currency*, or the *counter currency*. This is the exchange rate of that currency, as compared to the base unit of one.

For example, if we take the currency pair USD/CAD, the rate between the Canadian dollar (CAD) and the U.S. dollar (USD) currently stands at 1.2726. That means it takes 1.2726 Canadian dollars to equal the value of one U.S. dollar.

The USD is the base currency against which the CAD is quoted. If the quote moves higher, such as 1.2735, then the exchange rate has moved higher, and the USD appreciated in value against the CAD. It now costs more Canadian dollars to buy the same amount of U.S. dollars. The CAD depreciated against the USD.

Further, if you charted the USD/CAD, and the CAD fell in value, the pattern would actually trend higher as the dollar strengthened.

> **Hot Tip: The exchange rate between the U.S. dollar and the British pound is called the "cable."**

Cross-currency rates refer to currency pairs that don't include the U.S. dollar. Examples include the EUR/GBP (British pound vs. euro currency), the

AUD/JPY (Japanese yen vs. Australian dollar), or EUR/NZD (New Zealand dollar vs. euro currency).

> **Hot Tip: Remember, when you trade forex, you speculate on the appreciation or depreciation of the currency exchange rate between your target currency and its base currency.**

As of this writing, the most active currency pairs are: EUR/USD, GBP/USD, USD/JPY, and USD/CHF (Swiss franc).

Fundamental and Technical Analysis

Just as with equities trading, two camps of analysis—fundamental and technical—represent the two methods of arriving at buy/sell decisions.

Due to long-term macroeconomic conditions that drive exchange rates, such as interest-rate cycles or global-trade imbalances, currencies have a tendency to run in trends—trends that we can plot on monthly, weekly, and daily charts.

Microeconomic news, such as economic reports and earnings news, steers day-to-day international capital flow in and out of currencies. That flow creates short-term trends we can trade on intraday charts. (If we're awake and trading at 11 p.m., should we call them "intranight" charts? ☺)

The Fundamental Approach

As you know, fundamental analysis targets key economic, political, social, and even weather forces and the impact they have on supply and demand.

Within the realm of those forces, interest rates, unemployment rates and world events drive currency moves.

Overnight interest rates issued from a country's central bank play a key role in the exchange rate of its currency. When interest rates sink to low levels, currencies also tend to drop in value. People move their money to a place where they earn more money on their investment.

Unemployment rates reflect a country's economic health. When the unemployment is high, it signals an unstable economy. That can result in a weaker currency. If the unemployment rate falls, it tells us the economy is strengthening—which, in turn, bolsters the currency.

Across the board, financial markets react to global events and news. Of course, events and data releases that affect a country's economy can have a profound impact on its exchange rates.

If you trade currencies, stay updated on upcoming reports, including:

- Changes in interest rates

- Inflation news

- Unemployment numbers

- Money supply

- Trade imbalances

- GDP (gross domestic product)

> **Hot Tip:** The U.S. dollar is involved in 90 percent of all currency transactions.

Just as it's dangerous to chase stocks, it's ultra-dangerous to chase currencies. Please know that you cannot wander in a half-hour after an interest-rate change, and expect to party with the forex pros.

Forex reacts to news immediately. According to research, exchange rates adjust to new data with lightning speed—from under one minute, and often in less than ten seconds!

> **Hot Tip:** A "pip" stands for "Point in Percentage." It is the smallest movement in which (think "tick") an exchange rate can move, usually .0001

While it's imperative to stay abreast of reports coming out and either trade the market's reaction quickly, or not at all, you'll also need to know *which* reports the market regards with importance, and which it shrugs off. As with stocks, the market views different economic data, with different levels of importance, at different times. Data that moved markets months ago may not hold the same significance today.

Fundamental Strategies

The following list contains four examples of logic you might use to open currency trades.

- USD/JPY (The U.S. dollar is the base currency.) You believe the U.S. dollar is undervalued against the Japanese yen. Since you think the USD will appreciate against the JPY (USD/JPY), you buy the pair. Conversely, if you think the Japanese community is forsaking the U.S. financial markets, then the yen will appreciate against the dollar, so you'll sell the pair.

- GPB/USD (The British pound is the base currency.) You've studied the current role of Great Britain in the European economy, and you've determined it to be an economic leader. Anticipating strength in the pound, and resulting weakness in the dollar, you'd buy the pair. If you thought Britain's economy was faltering and would continue to spiral downward, you'd sell the pair.

- AUD/USD (The Australian dollar is the base currency.) Australian exports are rising, which should benefit that country's economy. You buy the pair, anticipating the U.S. dollar to weaken against the Australian dollar. Or, perhaps Australia is immersed in deep economic woes. You sell the pair, expecting the U.S. dollar to rise in value against the Aussie dollar.

- USD/EUR (The U.S. dollar is the base currency.) Low U.S. interest rates, coupled with the current administration's acceptance of a dollar decline to support manufacturers, causes investors to shy away from owning U.S. dollars. You sell the pair, expecting the dollar to decline in value against the euro. Or, the U.S. economy perks up and Federal Reserve Board begins a series of rate hikes. You buy the pair, anticipating the euro's exchange rate to rise against the dollar.

> **Hot Tip: When you trade currency pairs, quote conventions are fixed. Sorry, but you can't rearrange currencies in the pairs to suit yourself.** ☺

The Technical Approach

On charts, you'll find that currency pairs move in price patterns similar to equities. In fact, frequently, currencies etch clearer, more well-defined patterns than stocks do.

Traditional chart indicators work well with cash forex charts. On the charts shown, however, I kept indicators to a minimum, so you could see how the patterns progress.

Keep in mind that in spot currency markets, volume is absent on charts.

And, although your broker will furnish you with bid and ask prices, you won't have the luxury of evaluating a Level II quote screen. Nor will you see any Time & Sales data.

The fact is, you'll rely less on market dynamics and more on pure price and trend action. Now, *that's* a chartist's dream!

Figure 13–7 shows a weekly chart of the USD/JPY, or the Japanese yen against the U.S. dollar.

You can see how the JPY appreciated in value against the USD for more than two years. Anyone who shorted the U.S. dollar for that period of time made a dandy profit on the trade.

Figure 13–8 displays a five-day, sixty-minute chart of the USD/JPY. (Chart contains twenty-four hours in each trading session, marked in Eastern Standard Time.)

Note the sharp intraday uptrends that appeared three out of five days. Clear trend patterns such as these have contributed to the growing popularity of the forex markets.

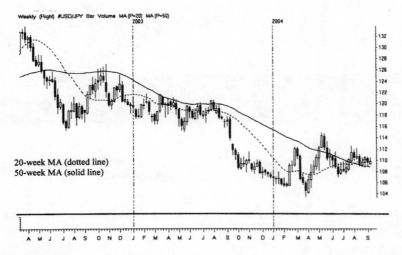

Figure 13–7. This weekly chart represents the USD/JPY, or the Japanese yen (JPY) vs. the U.S. dollar (USD). The USD is the base currency against which the JPY is quoted. This chart shows how the USD fell against the JPY for more than two years. If you were to exchange yen for a dollar in September 2004, you would need less yen to equal the value of a dollar than you would have during 2002–2003.

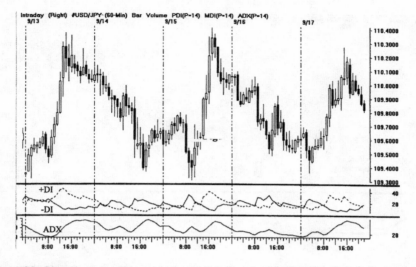

Figure 13–8. This 60-minute chart of the Japanese yen (JPY) against the U.S. dollar (USD) shows 5 days of range-bound movement. Still, the clearly etched trends and signals from Directional Indicators guided traders to profits. With this denomination, an uptrend indicates the USD is stronger; a downtrend shows the USD becoming weaker. Although the currency pair trades around the clock, keep in mind that New York currency markets open at 8 a.m. EST. During three days out of five, September 13, 15, and 17 the yen fell hard against the dollar at, or just after, the New York open.

Figure 13-9 shows a sixty-minute chart of the GBP/USD.

The British pound is the base currency, and the USD is the quote currency. Depending on short-term trend reversals, continuation patterns, indicator signals, and pure price action, you could have traded the pair for tidy profits.

Before this section concludes, here's a special note to Forex newcomers: I realize that references on charts that refer to uptrends caused by depreciating currency values, or downtrends relative to appreciating values appear contradictory. Plus, the concept of buying and selling simultaneously boggles the brain. If currency trading appeals to you, please take a course from a recommended source. The explanations in this text are brief descriptions of a very large playing field.

Just as when you trade any financial product, strategize by referring to multiple time frames. Immediately upon entering a trade, please establish a stop-loss order. Also consider setting a limit order at your profit point. That way, if you're trading in the wee hours and snooze off in your chair, you won't miss out on your profits. ☺

Finally, to trade Forex markets successfully, you must develop iron-clad discipline and well-thought out strategies. And, as with any trading tool, the instrument and the way it trades has to agree with *your* trading style, and *your* personality.

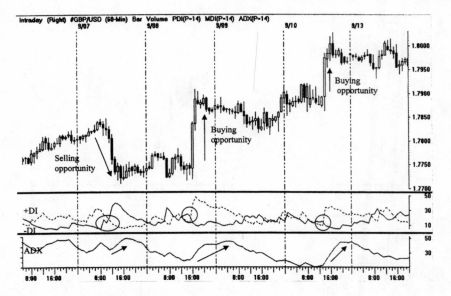

Figure 13–9. This 6-day, 60-minute chart of the U.S. dollar against the British pound (GBP/USD) shows the clear trends etched by the currency pair. The GBP is the base currency, with the USD acting as the quote currency. Definitive moves in the pair took place on September 7, when the USD appreciated against the GBP (arrow down). The next day, the USD depreciated against the pound (arrow up). It fell again two days later (arrow up). In each case, you see signals from crossovers from the directional indicators and an ADX rising over 30.

In chapter 14, we'll talk about an exciting subject—you! Perhaps the most important chapter of all, it explores facets of trading psychology, and how you can train yourself to win.

Quiz

Questions

1. What is a futures contract?

2. True or false: Even if the CME creates and launches a certain futures contract, you can still trade it on other futures exchanges.

3. The underlying cash index for the NQ is the _____.

4. You plan to trade the E-mini S&P 500 in February 2007. What will the complete symbol be?

5. What are the main objectives for trading futures?

6. Briefly describe one hedging tactic using the mini-sized Dow futures (YM).

7. Your neighbor Fred said he found a broker who lets him day-trade the E-minis like a wild man. The broker even encourages Fred to trade on a smaller margin than minimum maintenance required by the futures exchanges. Is Fred telling the truth about the broker?

8. The multiplier for the YM is _____. The multiplier for the ES is _____. The multiplier for the NQ is _____.

9. True or false: When an E-mini contract gaps open, the cool thing to do is to fade the gap, no matter what.

10. What are the minimum tick amount and the dollar value for the ES?

11. When you trade currencies, you speculate on the _____ _____ between two currencies.

12. When you read a currency quote, which comes first, the base currency or the quote currency?

13. The base currency always has a value of _____.

14. Define cross-currency rates.

Answers

1. A futures contract is a binding agreement that takes place today, with the legal obligation to fulfill the contract by a specified date.

2. False. Futures products, be they agricultural, energy, metals, financial, or weather, are each traded *only* on the exchange where they originate.

3. The underlying cash index for the NQ is the *NASDAQ 100 Index*.

4. If you trade the E-mini S&P 500 in February 2007, the symbol will be ESH7, or ESH07. (The stock index root symbol is ES. The contract, or front, month is March, which has the symbol H. Then we tag on the year by adding 07 or 7, depending on your software platform).

5. We use financial futures for two main objectives—speculation and hedging.

6. If you were Dow components long in an account, and the Dow Jones Industrial Index looked poised for a pullback, you could sell a dollar amount of the YM equal to that of your portfolio, and hedge, or protect your long-term account against a short-term loss.

7. Sadly, Fred could be telling the truth. Just hope Fred doesn't beg you for a loan after he wipes out his account! Yes, a handful of futures brokers advertise that you can open an account and *day trade* E-minis on reduced margin. You cannot, however, hold positions overnight that exceed minimum maintenance requirements, without receiving a margin call.

8. The multiplier for the YM is *$5*. The multiplier for the ES is *$50*. The multiplier for the NQ is *$20*.

9. While gaps to the upside or downside usually fill, all opening gaps do not fill immediately, or even during the trading session in which they occur. Betcha my duck slippers, traders who fade gaps without forethought get stopped out more than they need to.

10. The minimum tick for the ES is 0.25 index point. The dollar value is $12.50, or $50 per point, per contract.

11. When you trade currencies, you speculate on the *exchange rates* between two currencies.

12. When you read a currency quote, the base currency is stated first and the quote currency second.

13. The base currency always has a value of *1*.

14. Cross-currency rates refer to currency pairs that don't include the U.S. dollar.

CENTER POINT

Live with Excellence!

It is unlimited power to change your perceptions, to change your actions, and to change the results you are creating. It's your unlimited power to care and to love that can make the biggest difference in the quality of your life."

—Anthony Robbins in
Unlimited Power

In the last twelve Center Points, we've focused upon concepts that deal with effectiveness and productivity. We've talked about living proactively, leaving the past behind, enjoying true prosperity, and conquering the sort of perfectionism that slows personal growth. We've examined our thoughts for positive or negative "charges," and learned that forgiveness is a gift we bestow upon ourselves. We've dwelt on the incredible impact words have on our lives. And we've explored one of the most potent forces on earth—commitment.

Now let's look at a quality that we can weave through each of the concepts above, a quality that instantly strengthens and empowers our thoughts, communications, and actions. That quality is *excellence.*

To evaluate the levels of excellence in your life, begin by asking yourself questions . . .

First, review your thought processes. Have you banished the old, disempowering belief systems that clogged your personal "operating system"? If not, start now. Replace negative, limiting beliefs with the truth: You are a talented being capable of incredible success!

Second, review your actions. Do you project excellence in your outward expressions? Do you sit and stand tall, and move with confidence? Do you communicate with precision? Do you base your decisions on principles of excellence, such as compassion, honor, and integrity?

Finally, how do you inject excellence into your personal relationships? When you spend time with your family, do you give them 100 percent of your attention? Do you focus on forwarding their lives (which automatically forwards your own)?

Examine your circle of friends and business associates. Who supports your quest for personal growth—and whom do you support? Do you surround yourself with winners, with those who consciously pursue excellence in their own lives?

Choose to live with excellence. Make a conscious effort to instill it into each area of your life. When you do, you will raise the quality of your life instantaneously and produce exciting changes that last a lifetime!

Your Journey Through Inner Space

If you don't know who you are, the stock market is an expensive place to find out.

—George Goodman (aka Adam Smith)

We've come a long way together, you and I.

We've looked at how the markets work as a whole. We've poked our heads into a success-oriented trading program. We've decided whether day, swing, or position trading best supports our lifestyle. We've evaluated chart patterns and indicators by the bucketload. We've studied risk-reward ratios, stop-loss tactics, and what to do if the sky falls on your trade. We've ripped through stocks, ETFs, E-mini futures, and global forex markets.

Everything you've absorbed from this book, and other trading books, is important. Every bit of high-quality information you've divined from trading courses or conferences you've attended improves your odds of executing profitable trades. Every hour you've spent in front of your screen soaking up market action adds to your knowledge store and boosts your level of expertise.

The one aspect of trading, though, that outweighs all others in significance, is *you*. The *core* you. When you click "buy" or "sell," the decision that signals your hands to act emerges from within you. You—the totality of thoughts, feelings, and actions previously experienced—processes your flow of information and filters it through your personal operating system.

Just like you, I've waded through every step of trading. I've not forgotten what it feels like to be a raw beginner. I've not forgotten my first, frustrating days (months?) spent in a trading room, where the guy sitting next to me routinely amassed thousands for the day while I stared numbly at my losses.

I also remember moments early on when I puffed up my chest and said, "Yes, sirree. I've *got it*. I understand this stuff. I'll never make another losing trade." Mother Market laughed out loud. Then she smacked me down to size. Again. And again.

When I finally crawled out of the more-losses-than-wins ditch, and hoisted myself onto the more-wins-than-losses ramp, I realized that the 80–20 rule applies. Successful trading results from 80 percent mindset, and 20 percent evaluation of external forces.

If you stay in this business long enough, you'll surely agree. After you read enough books, attend enough courses, listen to enough good speakers, and make enough trades, a light glimmers. You come to realize that the level of success you attain depends solely on you. *You* tap the keystrokes. *You* click the mouse. And the genesis of those actions comes from the *you* inside the actual physical, mental, and emotional process.

You've taken a journey through "outer space." You've examined the market's machinations. You recognize the external devices and processes you need to perform as a market participant.

What about "inner space"? What about *your* machinations? When did *you* last explore the inner devices of your mind and body that compel you to action?

From experience, I can promise you this: No matter how many monitors you buy, how many seminars you attend, or how much knowledge you can spout, at the end of the day, your triumphs as a trader ultimately relate to the health of your mental, physical, and emotional state.

Here's a true-life example. I know a trader who is a fantastic guy. He's considerate, generous, and a great family man. He knows more about technical analysis and market workings than most market professionals. He's written a book on trading. He's published articles and taught classes. A few years ago, his personal trading account totaled seven figures. I've seen him execute trades so fast, his keyboard sounded like a Lamborghini.

At the moment, he's broke.

Why? How can an expert—someone who knows so much, who's amassed so much experience, who teaches others—blow up his own account?

And think about it . . . he didn't blow out his capital with *one* trade. It took hundreds, maybe thousands of trades to destroy his bottom line.

Somewhere inside this talented, intelligent man, there's a glitch. Somewhere in his thought processes, a belief system stops him from reaching fulfillment as a trader.

This chapter's quote, from highly respected PBS television journalist and financial author George Goodman (aka "Adam Smith"), sums up the theme of this chapter: "If you don't know who you are, the stock market is an expensive place to find out."

The remainder of this chapter focuses on practical mindsets and processes, as well as thought-provoking methods of self-discovery. Each is important. Each supports the other. And each is devoted to minimizing the tuition you'll pay to the stock market.

Your Trading Day—Plan to Win

While it's vitally important to prepare and complete your pre-market analysis before you execute your first trade for the day, you'll also find it valuable to plan an overall methodology. The following guidelines target intraday thought processes geared to that process.

Start Fifteen Minutes Early. What if you arrived at your desk fifteen minutes earlier each morning? What are the odds that the value added to your day would gradually build into a big chunk of benefits? Preparation improves skill levels. Plus, an extra fifteen minutes per trading day equals an hour and a half worth of extra knowledge you'll acquire each week. That knowledge could easily raise your statistical edge of winning trades.

Consistency represents the key element in a successful trading career. That applies to risk-averse traders who keep tight stops and accept limited profits, as well as risk-tolerant traders who give their trades more leeway in both directions. (Dr. Steenbarger discussed risk-averse and risk-tolerant traders in chapter 4.) Even if your percentage of winning trades is less than your percentage of losing trades—for example, 45 percent winning to 55 percent losing—you can still show a green bottom line at the end of the month as long as your winners *consistently* make more money than your losers lose. Remember, if you lose 50 percent of your account, you have to earn back 100 percent to return to even. Make sure you plan risk-reward levels on a consistent basis and adhere to them without fail.

Know when to stop trading. My personal rule: If I'm day-trading, and the first two trades of the day go against me, I stop and reassess my view of the market. If I lose more than 2 percent of my account equity, I stop trading for the day. If I hit a losing streak, I stop trading, or I "get small." To get small means that I cut my share size down and take profits faster until I regain equilibrium.

Heroism doesn't exist in the stock market. If you feel out of sync with the market, stop trading. It takes courage to fold 'em and walk away. A break that lasts from minutes to weeks can give you the respite you need to clear your head. It can also help you see which direction represents a better course of action. When you decide to reenter the market, do so slowly and stay in tune with your personal comfort levels.

Your Physiology—A Powerful Mind in a Powerful Body

Your physical, mental, and emotional states are inextricably tied to one another. Your emotions don't park in a chair across the room while your brain hovers over your monitor and your body takes a nap on the couch. ☺

That's why it's important to acknowledge that your physical and emotional health play a vital role in the success of your trading career.

Who do you think makes the most winning trades? The guy or gal who slouches in his or her chair, chest sunken, staring at the screen with eyes puffed and bleary? Or the trader who sits straight, clear-eyed, alert and pumped for action?

It's a fact: When you trade in a strong, fit body, you think more clearly, develop faster reactions, and operate with heightened accuracy levels.

In Dr. Brett's 3D Trader Personality Quiz (chapter 4), Dr. Steenbarger talked about neuroticism—the tendency to experience negative emotions—and the detrimental effect it can have on trading.

Studies show that undernourished, unfit, or exhausted bodies generate negative emotions. Negative emotions "put the brakes on" your trading perspective.

On the other hand, when you arrive at the stock market fresh from a workout or invigorating walk—strong and fit with increased circulation and fresh oxygen to your brain—you make better, cleaner decisions. Your ability to process new decisions and turn on a mental dime accelerates. You maneuver at the peak of your potential, ready for whatever action the market throws your way.

Here's a checklist of fitness tips that help keep your trading edge sharp:

- Do weight training, go on a fast, thirty-minute walk, or take up some type of physical exercise at least five days a week. Don't negotiate with yourself. Don't whine. Don't think about it. Just *do* it! The paybacks are awesome.

- Drink plenty of water when you trade. Dehydration causes "traders' trance," which means you disconnect from reality.

- Eat protein and fresh fruit and vegetables for breakfast and lunch. Carbs and sugar slow the mind. Cold pizza or a doughnut for breakfast do not support a strong trading mentality. Low-fat, high-protein meals do.

- Remember to take your vitamins. (*Yes, mom* . . . ☺) Also remember that stress burns the B-vitamins in your system. I tend to take on too many projects at once, so stress is a frequent companion. During those times, I increase B-vitamin intake to offset the stress syndrome and enhance energy. (Ask your doctor for advice.)

- A good night's sleep contributes mightily to your trading success. A brain fogged from lack of sleep spawns foggy trading plans.

- If you're angry, flu-ridden, or hungover, keep your mittens off your mouse! Maladies like these distort your perception of the market with a "gray film." Play only when you're on top of your game.

Your Self-worth—Define It, Nourish It, Protect It

You are not your trades. To those of you new to the trading world, this might come as a great relief.

In my early trading years, I somehow developed the unconscious belief system that my losing trades made me an unworthy person. I berated myself constantly. Which threw a negative impact on my next trades. Which created more self-depreciation. Then I lost more money. Talk about trading with the brakes on . . .

When I finally realized what I was doing, I had a talk with myself. *Hey, I'm a good person, with strong core values, who happens to be learning how to trade. My trades are not* me, *or a reflection of my self-worth.*

This assertion produced a delicious feeling of liberation.

Check your self-worth vs. losing trades circuit. Do you feel depressed if you lose money? Do you yell at yourself?

"What a dope you are! You're not the brightest bulb on Broadway, are you? That was the dumbest trade I've ever seen. Did you just fall out of the turnip truck?"

Seriously, would you talk to a good friend the way you talk to yourself? Of course not. You'd support a friend. So please support yourself. Realize that you are not your trades.

The Top Two Emotional Enemies You Can Divide and Conquer

Fear, in all of its disguises, lurks as the trader's most constant companion. We've all felt it at one time or another. Any trader who says he hasn't felt his gut twist while trading will soon grow a gigantic Pinocchio nose.

We fear losing money. We fear being wrong—not being *right.* And we fear missing out by letting the "big one" get away. All of these fears serve as emotions detrimental to accumulating wealth.

To help diminish your fears and promote confidence levels, consider the following techniques . . .

Check your analysis process and methodology for planning trades. If you need to, find an expert, or mentor. Make sure your processes, including identifying setups, risk-reward assessment, and money management strategies, are valid and will deliver a high percentage of positive results. Once you become secure in your overall course of action, fears attached to losing money should dissipate.

Second, shed your fear of being wrong by ditching your need to be right. It makes you hold on to losing trades.

Accept that controlled losses are part of the game. Trade your plan, not your emotions. You're not "right" or "wrong." You develop a plan of action and implement it to the best of your ability. The only time you're wrong is when you ignore your plan and expose your capital to unnecessary risk.

Finally, realize that the fear of missing out is truly one bad dude. It's the devilish fear that goads people to buy high and sell low. If a high-flying green candle or racing Level II screen tempts you to click and join the other folks in Euphoria-ville . . . *stop*. Push back your chair, stand up, and walk away. Do that until you gain enough discipline to shrug off the sight of running stocks.

After fear, *perfectionism* is fast becoming universally recognized as the trader enemy #2. (Personally, it drives me bonkers!)

While "doing things right" during trading hours is a great idea, carrying it to perfectionistic levels ensures performance anxiety.

Performance anxiety results from turning an intense focus on yourself. You scrutinize your own actions in such a way that you block your ability to perform.

An interesting article by Dr. Steenbarger, titled "Behavioral Patterns that Sabotage Traders—Part Two" (downloadable from *brettsteenbarger.com*), lists actions you can take to reduce perfectionism and its resulting performance anxiety. Let's briefly discuss three of those steps:

Focus on process goals rather than profits and losses. Traders are achievement-oriented. We tend to hold ourselves to high standards. When we apply strict standards to monetary goals (*I have to make a thousand dollars today*) the pressure we create usually sabotages the goal. Instead, focus on process-oriented goals, such as sticking to certain risk-reward ratios, or executing your trading plan four times out of five.

Tackle risk incrementally. When you heighten your risk by increasing share size, you'll focus on your performance like a cat watching a gopher hole. If you're used to trading two hundred shares per trade, and you decide to raise it to a thousand shares, your anxiety level will surely skyrocket. You'll pressure yourself to take such quick losses, or profits, that the tactic actually goes against you. If you choose to raise your share size, and with it your risk, please do so in small increments.

Add balance to your life. When an occupation becomes all-important, we frequently ramp up performance pressure exponentially. If you trade for a living, you probably eat, sleep, and breathe the financial markets. That creates unbalance in your life which can, in turn, destroy self-confidence.

Dr. Brett says, "If trading is your whole world, and trading isn't working, it's going to feel like your world is collapsing."

Whether you're a part-time or a full-time trader, remember to direct attention to other parts of your life, such as family, friends, and health and fitness, to diversify your self-esteem portfolio. When you hit a losing streak or negative period, it won't deliver such a powerful wallop that keeps you down for the count.

Hardwire Yourself for Success

Dr. Steenbarger has counseled many professional traders. He states that guided imagery is perhaps "the single most effective technique I have found for reducing and eliminating performance fears."

He goes on to say that by using guided imagery to face threatening situations (think "volatile market" "losing trade"), and mentally rehearsing the way you want to respond, you can eliminate much of the stress when those situations actually occur.

I agree with Dr. Steenbarger. Guided imagery is a terrific tool that you can use to not only reduce anxiety levels, but also to improve trading performance. It's used by Olympic athletes and professionals in all walks of life who want to improve performance quickly. Many traders, myself included, do it each morning as part of the preparation process. It's free, fast, and effective.

Here's a basic guided imagery process: Go to a quiet place where you won't be disturbed. Turn off the television and unplug the telephone.

Sit in a chair (or lay down) with your back straight, your legs unfolded. Place your hands palms-up on your thighs. Close your eyes and take a deep breath. Continuing to take deep, soothing breaths, consciously relax each area of your body . . . your feet . . . your legs . . . your hips . . . internal organs, chest, shoulders, arms, neck, and facial muscles.

Now, imagine yourself at your trading desk. A setup you've waited for develops on your screen. You check your analysis and trading plan, then buy a position at the appropriate price.

Suddenly, you see the stock reverse. The price dives, and a long red candle (or bar) shoots the price down—*fast*. Quickly but calmly, you glance at your trading plan. Your stop-loss point is a few cents away. The price continues to fall, then touches your stop-loss point.

Without flinching, second-guessing, or justifying, you bring up your order entry screen. Calmly you place your order and sell the stock. The market dives lower. A sense of satisfaction courses through your body. By following your plan, you've taken another step to becoming a successful trader.

When you feel ready to end the session, take more deep breaths and count out loud from one to five. As you reach the number five, open your eyes and declare yourself wide awake and full of positive energy.

If you want to repeat the scenario over again, do so, reliving in detail the calm, confident, and focused way you reacted to the trade turning against you. Imagine different situations that challenge you, such as chasing stocks, overtrading, trading with the need to be right.

Next, picture winning trades, where you raise your stop, and manage your trade to plan. Always see yourself act with calm confidence, in complete control.

What you are actually doing is mentally rehearsing, or practicing. You're not only practicing positive actions, you're rehearsing and imbedding positive emotions that will accompany them. Just as when you *consciously* practice a skill, if you repeat the action enough times, it will become second nature.

Now, when the market turns against you in a real-time trading situation, your body and mind will react with, "No problem. I've handled this event before."

And, when your trades surge into winners, you'll manage them and take profits with competence and precision.

Know that guided imagery itself takes practice. A trader's mind is always busy, and sometimes it's difficult to filter out stray thoughts that encroach on your session. When that happens, gently tell those thoughts to leave and come back later. Then refocus on your image. Within a few sessions, you'll be able to concentrate effectively.

Try it. It works!

Where Do You Want to Go?

Now that you've finished this book, I hope you have a clearer image of yourself, and where you fit in the financial markets.

Here's my question to you: In the world of trading, where do you want to go?

Evaluate your strengths as a trader, as well as your challenges. What can you polish? Where can you raise the bar? What actual steps will you take to accomplish these changes?

I commend you for reading this book from start to finish!

Thank you for your commitment to learning, and your dedication to the process.

Thank you, also, for allowing me to share with you the concepts, facts, and principles I've learned during the past decade-plus. I sincerely hope the knowledge you've gained in these pages will help you grow in your trading career and advance confidently with each step you take.

I also hope you reach all of your goals, financial and otherwise. May you support the lives of others in the trading field, and find enrichment from their support, in return. May your obstacles and losses remain small, and your victories and profits large.

I wish all good things for you and your family, now and always.

God bless!

CENTER POINT

The Good Life

Live well, laugh often, love much.

—Anonymous

When I travel, I collect decorative porcelain tiles. Small and flat, they fit easily into my suitcase.

I found my favorite tile in a gift shop on Catalina, a tiny island just off the California coast. Inscribed on the tile in script, it says, "Live well, laugh often, love much."

In our hectic world of 24/7, overnight deliveries, and Internet time, it's easy to immerse ourselves in the prevailing "I need that yesterday" mentality. It's easy to forget that true success comes from a nourished soul, a life *well lived*. Indeed, the inscription on my Catalina tile delivers the simple, yet profound, formula.

Live well. To me, living well has nothing to do with who's accumulated the most toys. Living well is a choice we make to live life to the fullest. Live with gusto, enthusiasm, passion. Make fun a priority. Take delight in small victories—a room well painted, a batch of killer cookies, a birdie on the eighteenth hole.

Laugh often. Giggle, chuckle, chortle, laugh out loud! What's more fun than laughing? What's more enjoyable than sitting with family or friends, laughing until your sides hurt?

The act of laughter heals bodies and situations. Laughter lowers blood pressure, raises circulation, and boosts immune defenses. A burst of laughter can stop an argument in its tracks and mend a relationship in a heartbeat.

Smile, grin, laugh more often. It's fun, free, and raises your happiness quotient exponentially.

Love much. Start with yourself. You can't give what you don't own. Start each day by looking in the mirror and giving yourself a dose of healthy self-love. Say it out loud, "You're a darn good person. I'm glad you're *you*."

When you go out into the world and give your love to other people, you initiate a circle of giving and receiving that contains life's greatest gift. Remember that a smile, a hug, and a "hey, good job" can change someone else's day from ho-hum to terrific.

Finally, love life! Love what you do, where you live, whom you live with. Love your goals, your visions, your dreams. When we weave love into the fabric of our lives, we experience the best life has to offer.

RECOMMENDED READING LIST

Beyond Candlesticks: More Japanese Charting Techniques Revealed, Steve Nison (John Wiley & Sons, 1994)

Big Trends in Trading, Price Headley (John Wiley & Sons, 2002)

Exchange Traded Funds and E-mini Stock Index Futures, David Lerman (John Wiley & Sons, 2001)

If It's Raining in Brazil, Buy Starbucks, Dr. Peter Navarro (McGraw-Hill, 2002)

Japanese Candlestick Charting Techniques, Steve Nison (New York Institute of Finance, 2001; second edition)

Martin Pring on Market Momentum, Martin Pring (McGraw-Hill, Trade, 1997; reprint edition)

Market Evaluation and Analysis for Swing Trading, David Nassar and William S. Lupien (McGraw-Hill, 2004)

Mastering Futures Trading, Bo Yoder (McGraw-Hill, 2004)

New Thinking in Technical Analysis, Rick Bensignor, Editor (Bloomberg Press, 2000)

Reminiscences of a Stock Operator, Edwin Lefevre, (John Wiley & Sons, 1994)

Secrets for Profiting in Bull and Bear Markets, Stan Weinstein (McGraw-Hill, 1988)

Stock Traders Almanac, Yale and Jeffrey Hirsch

Technical Analysis from A to Z (second edition), Steven B. Achelis

The Candlestick Course, Steve Nison (John Wiley & Sons, 2003)

The Psychology of Trading, Brett Steenbarger Ph.D.

The Richest Man in Babylon, George S. Clayson (New American Library, reissue August 1997)

Trading in the Zone, Mark Douglas (Prentice-Hall Press, January 2001)

INDEX

Italicized page numbers refer to charts and other figures and the accompanying captions.